DEFIANT DICTATORSHIPS

Also by Paul Brooker

THE FACES OF FRATERNALISM: Nazi Germany, Fascist Italy and Imperial Japan

TWENTIETH-CENTURY DICTATORSHIPS: The Ideological One-Party States

Defiant Dictatorships

Communist and Middle-Eastern Dictatorships in a Democratic Age

Paul Brooker
Victoria University
Wellington

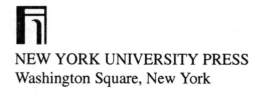

NEW YORK UNIVERSITY PRESS
Washington Square, New York

© Paul Brooker 1997

First published in the U.S.A. in 1997 by
NEW YORK UNIVERSITY PRESS
Washington Square
New York, N.Y. 10003

This book is printed on paper suitable for recycling and
made from fully managed and sustained forest sources.

Library of Congress Cataloging-in-Publication Data
Brooker, Paul.
Defiant dictatorships : communist and Middle-Eastern dictatorships
in a democratic age / Paul Brooker.
p. cm.
Includes bibliographical references and index.
ISBN 0-8147-1311-4
1. History, Modern—1945–   2. Dictatorship.   I. Title.
D445.B765 1997b
909.82—dc21   97–15332
                                                    CIP

Printed in Great Britain

Contents

Introduction

The wave of democratisation that swept through the Communist world and Third World in the 1980s and early 1990s did not eliminate all the dictatorships – some survived the onset of a democratic age.[1] (By 'dictatorship' is meant a regime that is not a democracy nor a monarchy, and by 'democratic' is meant freely competitive, regular elections for public office.) Among the most prominent examples of dictatorships which survived into the mid-1990s were the four remaining Communist regimes of any significance, namely China, Vietnam, North Korea, and Cuba, and also four well-known Middle Eastern regimes: Baathist Syria and Iraq, Qadhafi's Libya, and Khomeinist Iran. These eight dictatorships had avoided even the façade of democratisation involved in setting up semi-competitive multi-party elections to reconfirm the regime party and/or leader in power.[2] Nor had their defiant refusal to democratise forced them to *reshape* their dictatorship. There had been no parallel to Communist Poland in 1981 and socialist Burma in 1988, when resistance to popular pressure for some democratisation had led to not just a change in the regime's leadership but also a shift to open militarisation and rule by a military junta, respectively the Military Council of National Salvation and the State Law and Order Restoration Council.

The defiant 'stability under pressure' of these dictatorships had been so great that in most cases the same personal ruler, senior leader or collective leadership who had headed the regime in 1980 was still in power in the middle of the 1990s. Where this was not the case, either a) the ruler had died of natural causes and been replaced by his designated successor or deputies, as in North Korea and Iran, or b) a collective leadership had replaced itself with a new generation of leaders, as in Vietnam. These regimes' defiance of the trend towards replacing dictatorship with democracy was therefore only part of their overall stability and their broader defiance of the political turmoil occurring in the rest of the Communist world and Third World.

Therefore any answer to the obvious question of *why* these eight Communist and Middle Eastern dictatorships have proved so stable must go beyond providing an explanation for the lack of democratisation and instead consider the wider question of their overall stability. Unfortunately, the various explanations that have been put forward to account for these regimes' lack of democratisation are not

1

easily transformed into wider explanations of overall stability. For example, the 'exceptionalism' of the still predominantly non-democratic Arab world in this democratic age has commonly been accounted for by pointing to Islam as a purportedly anti-democratic influence upon Arab societies.[3] In fact the argument has been applied on occasion to the whole Islamic world from West Africa to Indonesia.[4] But any explanations based upon religious, cultural or other long-standing factors cannot explain the overall stability of the four Islamic defiant dictatorships because such long-standing factors were clearly unable to prevent the relative *in*stability shown by these Middle Eastern countries in the decades *before* the onset of a democratic age.

When their political history in the fifteen-year period 1965–79 is compared with the stability shown by these countries in 1980–94, there is a marked difference that can hardly be explained by such long-standing factors as religion or culture. Iran had just completed a revolution in 1979 that had overthrown the Shah's regime and established an Islamic Republic under Khomeini's rule. Iraq had seen in 1979 (with Saddam Hussein's succession to the Presidency) the completion of the shift in power from the military to the civilian wing of the Baathist regime which had originated in a 1968 coup. Syria had seen in 1970 the coup which brought Defence Minister Asad's faction to power after years of internal factional conflict within the Baathist regime, including a 1966 coup by leftist Neo-Baathists. Libya had seen the monarchy overthrown by a Qadhafi-led coup in 1969 and then in the later 1970s the complete restructuring of the military regime into a purportedly direct democracy guided by the Leader of the Revolution.

Explanations based upon religious or cultural factors also have problems in accounting for the stability of the four remaining Communist regimes. It is true that all four experienced a similar degree of political stability in the 1960s–70s as they have in the 1980s–90s. These Communist regimes' stability is highlighted only by the standard contrast with the number of fellow-Communist regimes, including the superpower Soviet Union, that collapsed in the 1980s–90s. Nevertheless, any attempt to use a cultural explanation for this contrast, such as the influence of 'Confucian' or 'Asian' values, faces the problem of how to account for the survival of the Cuban Communist regime in Latin America. Furthermore, the only one of the three Asian Communist regimes, the Chinese example, which did not follow on from a long period of foreign, colonial rule was preceded by a half-century of political instability. By 1950 China had seen the overthrow of the monarchy, the descent into warlordism, the establishment of the Kuomintang party-state regime, its transformation into a military-party regime under Chiang Kai-shek's rule, and then finally the replacement of the Kuomintang by a Communist party-state regime. If Chinese culture was apparently quite unable to exert a stabilising influence upon the country's political development *before* the Communists took power, it is hard to understand how a cultural factor could be so influential during the Communist era.

Explanations of stability that are based upon the nature of the regimes' *origins* are also difficult to sustain. It is often pointed out that the few surviving Communist regimes were established through local revolutionary and armed struggle rather than being imposed (as most of the East European Communist regimes were) by the occupying forces of the Soviet Union in the aftermath of the Second World War. However, this argument overlooks two awkward facts. First, the North Korean Communist regime imposed by Soviet postwar occupying forces is still defiantly stable and second, the locally established Yugoslavian and Albanian Communist regimes are now defunct – and so is the Soviet Union itself.

As for the Middle Eastern examples of dictatorship, all have been established by local forces, not by an external power, but so, too, had been all the African dictatorships that collapsed in the 1980s–90s. What is more, some of these African dictatorships had originated in a popular struggle against colonial rule – a prestigious heritage which none of the four Middle Eastern dictatorships can claim. Only the Iranian regime can rightly claim, thanks to the 1978–9 revolution, to have originated through *any* form of popular movement. The other three regimes claim a revolutionary heritage but in reality were the product of military coups, and in the Libyan case developed a revolutionary programme only several years after the coup. The Baathist military coups in Syria and Iraq were at least carried out by officers belonging to or sympathising with the Baathist political movement. But their seizures of power still lacked the popular support and mobilisation seen in Iran or in such African anti-colonial movements as the Guinean PDG, whose party-state regime was overthrown in 1984. Therefore if the origins of the Middle Eastern dictatorships are to provide some explanation for their stability, it could only be through the very implausible argument that a dictatorship is more likely to maintain stability if it originated not as an anti-colonial movement but as a military coup lacking organised popular support. As in the case of the Communist regimes, such origins-based explanations lack any *prima facie* plausibility as explanations of why a small minority of dictatorships was able to show such remarkable stability in the new democratic age.

However, three other possible and more plausible explanations for the defiant dictatorships' stability will be considered in this book. (It will not extend its coverage past the end of 1994, but the key points and arguments are usually valid for as late as the end of 1996.) The explanations will be based on the regime's 1) external relations, 2) structure and ideology, and 3) economic policies. The first possible explanation will be presented in the next chapter as a *prima facie* case that the regimes' defiant stability was in turn protected by their defiance of military or political foes of their country. All eight regimes were able to enjoy the domestic regime-stabilising benefits – the 'defiance effect' – which normally flow from defiance of the country's external foes.

The other two possible explanations, the structural/ideological and the economic, will be investigated as alternative or supplementary explanations to this 'defiance effect'. Being more wide-ranging and complex, they will be covered in a more extensive fashion, with the regime-by-regime investigation devoting a separate chapter to each regime and covering both explanations in the same chapter. The structural/ideological alternative or supplementary explanation recognises that all the regimes (even the four Communist regimes) varied markedly in structure and ideology but suspects that these defiant dictatorships may have instituted similar *changes* in their structure or ideology in the 1980s and early 1990s. For example, they may have placed a greater emphasis upon nationalism in their ideology or upon the role of an individual leader figure in their structure. (The regime-by-regime chapters will point out the pre-1980 distinctiveness of each regime's structure and ideology as well as investigating the 1980–94 changes, and a sketch of the orthodox Communist and Baathist models of political structure, economy and ideology has been provided in Appendices I and II.) The economic-policy alternative or supplementary explanation is based upon the suspicion that the defiant dictatorships were able to defy the trend towards democracy because they *accepted* the accompanying international trend towards *economic* liberalisation. The shift to more liberal economic policies – marketising, privatising and internationalising the economy – was an even more widespread international trend than democratisation during the 1980s–90s, and a change in economic structure may well have been sufficient to preserve these regimes' political structure.

If such were the case, the defiant dictatorships might be viewed in terms of the centuries-old notion of 'enlightened despotism' and the more recent notion of enlightened self-interest. For these despotic regimes had instituted the economic restructuring deemed by international conventional wisdom to be the only 'enlightened' economic policy for Communist regimes and for Third World regimes with a state-dominated economy. And in instituting this economic liberalisation the defiant dictatorships were acting out of enlightened self-interest. For the expected improvement in economic performance or prospects could also be expected to strengthen society's and regime personnel's commitment to maintaining political stability. (Their strengthened commitment to stability might arise from the regime's increased 'performance legitimacy', from gratitude for the regime's successful policy-making, from a desire to protect the new economic policy from disruptive political upheavals, or from a mixture of various reasons and emotions.) Economic liberalisation would seem to be a politically (self-interestedly) as well as economically 'enlightened' policy for a modern despotism.

In reality, however, by no means all the defiant dictatorships attempted any significant economic restructuring. Although China and Vietnam could be viewed as implementing a relatively radical economic liberalisation, North Korea and Cuba made only minor moves in this direction and not until the 1990s. As for the four Middle Eastern regimes, all implemented some liberalising measures but to a varying degree, and the most extensive liberalisations, those in Iraq and Iran, were not begun until the late 1980s and the early 1990s.

On the other hand, it is quite understandable why some of these regimes would be less enthusiastic than others about economic liberalisation. The implementation of 'enlightened' policies requires 'despotic' single-mindedness and power not only in order to overcome the inertia of outdated ideas and vested interests but also in order to cope with the decline in popularity, albeit only temporary or among privileged minorities, that such policies will likely produce.[5] It is not hard to understand why a politically enlightened (self-interested) dictatorship might view radical economic liberalisation as involving unacceptably high political risks, especially in a period when dozens of dictatorships were being overthrown. Furthermore, the regime's stability might be enhanced by a quite *limited* amount of liberalising economic reform if the reforms produced a significant improvement in economic performance or prospects without also producing a stability-threatening amount of discontent during its implementation.[6]

Consequently it is only to be expected that the defiant dictatorships would show a lack of uniformity in their approach to economic reform. Each regime would be dealing with not only different economic circumstances but also different potential threats to stability, degrees of political risk, and attitudes to political risk.

Obviously the investigation of economic policy as an alternative or supplementary explanation will have to be extensive and complex, investigating not only the extent of economic reform and success but also the reasons for reform and the political limitations on its extent (the ideological opposition, vested interests and the like). Even if it is discovered that not all the defiant dictatorships successfully undertook significant economic reforms, the investigation is likely to provide some supplementary explanation of these regimes' stability. Like the investigation of their structural and ideological changes, it should have much to contribute to the book's concluding assessment of the survival strategies of defiant dictatorships in a democratic age.

1 Defiance as a Stabilising Influence

DEFIANCE AS EXPLANATION AS WELL AS RESULT

The explanation which will be presented in this chapter as a *prima facie* plausible explanation for the eight dictatorships' defiant stability is based upon another 'defiant' feature that these regimes displayed in 1980–94. During this period each of them was for a substantial time publicly defying an external foe, whether an actual military enemy or only a political foe. Iraq was fighting a major war with Iran in 1980–88 and then the short war against the US-led coalition was followed by an era of rhetorically defiant defeat. Iran was of course fighting the same war in 1980–88 and was continuously engaged in rhetorical defiance of the US – the 'Great Satan'. Syria continued to be pre-occupied with a cease-fired war of liberation to recover the territory conquered by Israel in the 1967 war, and was bogged down in a military intervention in Lebanon that led to military clashes in the early 1980s with not only Israel but also the US. Libya faced political and economic pressure from the US (which occasionally escalated into military clashes) throughout the 1980s, and in the 1990s also defied United Nations' demands, backed up by sanctions, that it hand over Libyans suspected of complicity in the Lockerbie bombing.

As for the Communist regimes, Vietnam in the 1980s was engaged in a virtual proxy war with China in fighting Khmer Rouge insurgents in Cambodia and was also faced with the threat of a repeat of China's 1979 'punitive' invasion. In the 1990s what remained of the lingering political and economic pressure from the US was magnified into official anxieties about Western political/ideological machinations. North Korea continued throughout 1980–94 to see itself as still threatened militarily by the US and South Korean enemy that it had fought a generation earlier in the now cease-fired Korean War – a threat which seemed to be confirmed by the US economic embargo and refusal to formally recognise the existence of the North Korean state. Cuba, too, continued throughout this period to face political hostility and an economic embargo from the US, which was also still deemed to pose an at least latent military threat to Cuba.

China in the 1980s was the 'exception which proves the rule'. Of the eight regimes, the Chinese was the least committed to defiant rhetoric and by June 1989 was also facing the closest thing to a popular rebellion experienced by any of these regimes. Eventually repressed by the use of martial law and military force, the protest movement focused on Tiananmen Square almost forced a militarised restructuring of the regime like that seen in Poland in 1981–2 and in Burma in 1988. Moreover, the sacking of two successive holders of the post of General Secretary in the 1980s could also be pointed to as evidence of significant instability during this decade. In contrast, China in the 1990s saw its Communist regime publicly defying a supposed political/ideological attack by the West and also enjoying a new-found stability that had seen no further popular uprisings or sacked General Secretaries.

The stability-enhancing effect of a regime's public defiance of external foes arises from the additional loyalty this defiance elicits from both society and the regime's personnel, notably the upper ranks of the party, military and security organs. In particular, the need to display unity and stability in the face of the enemy is likely to discourage not only expressions of mass discontent but also moves within the regime to displace the present leadership. For example, even the generational 'changing of the guard' that took place within Vietnam's ageing collective leadership in the 1980s was affected by a determination 'to carry out the generational transition "gradually and slowly" to project an image of continuity and stability to the Chinese'.[1]

The 'defiance effect' obviously incorporates a degree of what is commonly termed a 'siege mentality'. The awareness of being threatened or pressured by an external foe – of being 'besieged' – is the basis for the increase in political loyalty. Therefore the defiance effect is less evident the less serious the external foe's 'besieging' threat or pressure, whether militarily, politically or economically. An example of how external threat or pressure is a precondition of the defiance effect was provided in 1982 by Argentina's humiliating military defeat by the British in the war for possession of the disputed Falkland Islands. Because the victorious British posed no 'besieging' threat to the mainland of Argentina, both Argentinian society and its military regime's personnel were free to indulge in 'disloyal' political responses to the disaster: the senior Generals quickly sacked General Galtieri as President and the country soon began the process of returning to civilian rule.

It is not difficult to find scholarly assessments of the eight defiant dictatorships which indirectly or partially confirm the presence of the defiance effect. For example, the 'besieged' basis of the defiance effect is very evident in assessments of Cuba and North Korea. By the end of the 1980s much of Cuban society had adopted a 'state of siege mentality', and in the 1990s a 'siege mentality' was 'characteristic of north Korean society'.[2] China in 1989 has been used as the example of how a combination of international and domestic factors 'can induce a siege mentality' in regime personnel.[3] (In the Chinese case these factors were the domestic challenge to the regime's legitimacy by the pro-democracy demonstrators, the international 'pariah status' of the Chinese regime after the massacre of demonstrators in Tiananmen Square, and the international decline of Communism as its rule was eroded in Eastern Europe and the Soviet Union.[4]) And 'the siege mentality became even stronger' after the dissolution of the Soviet Communist regime in 1991 left China as the lone Communist great power.[5]

The second, political stage of the defiance effect is visible in the 1985 assessment that 'the adversity of the West has helped to mobilise internal political support for Qadhafi'.[6] Similarly, the 1989 shooting down of Libyan warplanes by US carrier planes 'temporarily rallied the Libyan population behind the leader', and the United Nations sanctions imposed in 1992 left Qadhafi's position at the end of 1994 'more secure than before sanctions were first imposed'.[7] As for the loyalty of regime personnel, the Syrian nationalist struggle against Israel has provided the 'legitimating cement' of 'the regime coalition' and thus strengthened the (mutual) loyalty of the Syrian regime personnel.[8]

The most comprehensive indirect confirmation of the defiance effect comes from the Iran–Iraq war. The Iraqi invasion that started the war elicited a typical defiance effect from Iranians. There was 'a surge of patriotism' and 'the whole country rallied behind Khomeini'.[9] From the Iraqi perspective, the invasion of Iran was apparently seen as a defensive measure by the regime's leader and senior personnel, who felt threatened by the hostility shown to the Baathist regime and its leader, Saddam Hussein, by the new Islamic revolutionary regime in Iran.[10] But the invasion of Iran failed to arouse any sense of common purpose among Iraqis (as Saddam himself later admitted).[11] Only after their forces retreated from Iranian soil and Iraq was itself subjected to an Iranian counter-invasion did the Iraqis' mood change – now 'public morale became buoyant'.[12] Saddam was now able to enjoy the benefits of the defiance effect as he 'capitalized upon this perception of common threat to extend his own personal control and to assert his right to absolute obedience' as the regime's leader.[13]

Of particular significance in the Iraqi case was that the defiance effect seems to have been evident, albeit to a lesser degree, among the politically alienated or indifferent Kurdish and Shiite sections of society.[14] Kurds and Shiites were heavily represented among that large part of Iraqi society who had only a 'hazy' notion of the Iraqi nation but they also wished to avoid the 'direct misfortune' – the devastation and social chaos – of being subjected to a conquering Iranian army.[15] For many Iraqis the defiance effect therefore took the form of an 'expedient community of purpose' that conferred upon the regime's leadership 'a functional legitimacy, a right to command obedience in defense of the social order'.[16]

From this example it appears that if an external threat involves potentially drastic social implications, then even societies lacking national solidarity may experience the defiance effect to some degree. Furthermore, the Iraqi case indicates that these drastic social implications may include not just the devastation and social chaos brought by a conquering army but also the effects of a civil war triggered by the invading army's weakening of the state's power to repress ethnic, religious or other social strife.

The March 1991 uprisings by Kurds and Shiites in the aftermath of Iraq's military defeat is another 'exception that proves the rule' confirmation of the defiance effect, for obviously the threat of invasion and social chaos posed by the victorious US-led coalition was much less than that posed by the Iranians in 1982–8. But, more importantly, the fact that by no means all Shiites joined the uprising may indicate that many of them were concerned that the uprising might develop into a civil war and widespread social disintegration. This concern could also lead them to back the regime's leadership against any external threat that might weaken the state's capacity to prevent such social disintegration. As late as 1994 the Iraqi media was using 'the spectres of invasion and disintegration to boost support for President Saddam'.[17]

However, all the above assessments of the defiance effect in particular countries are only impressionistic or anecdotal. The very fact that these countries are dictatorships makes it impossible for anyone to carry out the sorts of research, such as opinion surveys, that would normally be looked for when assessing whether a particular policy stance has increased support for a government or regime. Therefore the evidence which will be presented in the remainder of this chapter will be of only a 'circumstantial' nature. Such circumstantial evidence will take the form of pointing to the presence of the regime's public defiance of an external foe that is said to be threatening or pressuring the country or regime – whether through military, political, or economic means. The regime's 'defiance' will involve the public identification of the foe and the explicit or implicit message that the regime and country will resist this foe and its threats or pressure. The regime's message of defiance may actually be developed into an explicit demand for loyalty, and the defiance posture may also be used to denounce domestic foes of the regime. But these are only accompanying, not essential, features of the basic regime-strengthening defiance effect.

THE INDIVIDUAL CASES

The *Iraqi* case has been covered earlier in the chapter and is the most straightforward in the sense that Iraq was at war or in a state of defiant defeat for all but a few years of the period 1980–94. The significance of the 1982 shift from offensive to defensive war in the conflict with Iran has already been pointed out. With the threat from Iran 'unmistakeable', Saddam could from then on 'portray the war as a heroic defense of the nation against a bigoted and aggressive foe who sabotaged efforts for peace'.[18]

When peace finally broke out in 1988, Saddam was left with the 'major problem' of how to compensate for the lack of such an urgent and comparatively uncontroversial mission as the defence of Iraq against Iranian invasion.[19] After only two years of peace the regime again resorted to invading a neighbouring country, but the conquest of Kuwait in August 1990 again brought the problem of an unpopular offensive war. Although Kuwait was conquered rapidly and almost bloodlessly, there was discontent in Iraqi society over the wider, international ramifications of Iraq's aggression.[20] The Iraqi people's lack of enthusiasm for the Kuwait affair was reflected in the regime's increasingly desperate propaganda, which resorted to using Arab nationalism and Islam rather than Iraqi nationalism in its attempt to portray the conflict with the US-led United Nations coalition as a defensive struggle against foreign intervention. The post-war Kurdish and Shiite uprisings were countered with a continuingly defiant propaganda line. The rebels were depicted as agents of the conspiracy that Iraq's enemies had resorted to after the failure of the 'aggression of the 30' (the US-led coalition of 30 countries) and of every other conspiracy in the revolution's history of confrontation with foreign enemies.[21] At the end of 1994 the regime was still defiantly proclaiming that the continuing UN sanctions against Iraq, and the US air-exclusion zones in the Kurdish north and Shiite south, were 'part of a plot to take control of Iraq's oil fields and provoke civil war.'[22]

Being on the other side in the Iran–Iraq war, the *Iranian* regime was engaged in publicly defying a military enemy for most of the 1980s. Following the Iraqi invasion, the Iranian leadership made it clear that there would be no peace with Saddam Hussein, 'the perpetrator of corruption', or with the other Islam-threatening Baathists, and soon Iran's official war aims demanded the 'punishment' or removal of Saddam and his Baathist regime.[23] Although by 1982 Iran was no longer fighting a clearly defensive war against Iraq, the war was depicted by the regime as being part of Iran's resistance to the threat posed by the ultimate external foe: the US. From the outset, the Iranian regime voiced not just suspicions but outright accusations that the US had instigated the Iraqi invasion.[24] The notion that Saddam had been acting as the 'deputy' of the US when he imposed the war on Iran 'was in part responsible for the Iranian decision to carry the war into Iraqi territory in July 1982' and to seek the deposition of Saddam as one of its official war aims.[25] During the ensuing long and bloody war, the Iranians continued to constantly accuse the US of supporting and assisting Iraq.[26] Other regional foes and opponents were also viewed in terms of the US threat, as when the Saudis were portrayed as American mercenaries; domestically, too, the regime's violent foes, the Mojahedin, were depicted by official propaganda as being US agents.[27]

The Iranian focus or fixation on the US foe and its machinations was a reflection of how political opposition to the US (the supporter of the Shah's former regime and of Israel) had been transformed into a theological/ideological opposition to the 'Great Satan', thereby ensuring that 'the essence of Iranian policy toward the United States became defiance and challenge.'[28] Such an approach was reinforced by the direct clashes with the US that occurred in the 1980s. The November 1979 storming of the US embassy and seizure of embassy staff as hostages led to a failed US rescue mission in April 1980, and Iranian assets held by American banks were not unfrozen until the release of the hostages in January 1981. Another direct clash came in January 1984 when the Reagan administration designated Iran a 'terrorist state' and imposed extensive controls on US exports to Iran.[29] But the most serious clash arose in 1987–8 with US intervention in the tanker war between Iran and Iraq. The US reflagging and protection of Kuwaiti tankers led to actual military clashes with some Iranian forces and to the accidental shooting down of an Iranian passenger plane by the cruiser *Vincennes*. Khomeini's response was to declare 'we must all be prepared for a real war and go to the war fronts and fight against America and its lackeys.'[30]

After the end of the Iran–Iraq war in 1988 and the death of Khomeini in 1989, there continued to be frequent expressions of radical anti-US rhetoric, even by the relatively pragmatic President Rafsanjani.[31] The outbreak of the crisis created by Iraq's conquest of Kuwait in August 1990 meant that now Iraq and the US were clearly on opposite sides. But it also led to a much more prominent US political and military presence in the Gulf. Although Iran was officially neutral 'between two equally "arrogant" and unjust states, Iraq and the United States', some leading figures in Iran launched rhetorical attacks against the US.[32] Such radicals as Khalkhali condemned the US as 'the number one aggressor of our era' and the regime's official spiritual leader, Ayatollah Khamenei, compared the effect of US actions in the Gulf region to the depredations inflicted by the Mongol conquerors in the medieval period.[33] In more level-headed fashion Khamenei warned the international community that 'the daily increasing American hegemony over them' was the real danger facing the nations of the world.[34]

By the mid-1990s President Rafsanjani's apparent desire for better relations with the US was still offset by the radical rhetoric coming from other parts of the regime. The new term for describing the US – the 'global arrogance' – may have been less extreme than 'global Satan', but the annual anniversary of the storming of the US embassy was still celebrated with mass demonstrations chanting 'Death to America' and burning the US flag.[35] And it probably meant little to defendants in the regime's political trials that they were now charged with the offence of 'siding with global arrogance' rather than 'siding with the Great Satan'.[36] When the US charged that the Iranian regime's support for terrorist activities around the world had made it an 'international outlaw', Rafsanjani responded by pointing out that US pressure only strengthened the Islamic Republic.[37]

By the beginning of the 1980s the *Syrian* regime had already for many years 'sought legitimacy through the struggle with Israel'.[38] Even the 1970 internal military coup that had brought Asad to power within the Baath regime had been politically and ideologically justified by the need to concentrate the country's energies on the struggle against Israel. (This internal military coup is the only instability in regime leadership or structure that Syria has experienced since the loss of the 1967 war began the mission to liberate the Golan Heights from Israeli occupation.) The conflict with Israel was portrayed as an historically epic event worthy of comparison with the Islamic world's struggle against the medieval Crusader state, as Asad himself referred to Israel as a 'neo-Crusader' state.[39] And the struggle against Israel was depicted as involving more than Syria's mission to recover the Golan Heights; there was also the need to resist the threat of further Israeli expansionism.

In the 1980s Asad would publicly portray Israel as a continuing threat to Syria and the Arab east not only politically and culturally but also territorially, as being 'bent on establishing a Greater Israel "from the Nile to the Euphrates"'.[40] He attempted to mobilise Syrian and Arab commitment to the anti-Israel cause by emphasising the need to restore the 'strategic balance' that had been upset by Egypt's retirement from the Arab coalition against Israel.[41] Concrete evidence of the threat posed by Israel was provided in June 1982 with the Israeli invasion of southern Lebanon. The invading forces were soon involved in clashes with Syrian forces stationed in Lebanon, and the Israeli air force inflicted a humiliating defeat upon the Syrian air force and SAM batteries.

The Lebanon crisis also provided Asad with more ammunition for his claims that Syria was threatened by the US as well as Israel. Syria had already formally aligned itself with the Soviet Union through a 1980 Treaty of Friendship and Cooperation and was receiving a huge new injection of Soviet arms paid for by soft loans. Asad had also already accused the US, and in March 1980 specifically the CIA, of encouraging subversion within Syria in order to overthrow him and dominate the Arab world in partnership with Israel. He responded to the 1981 US–Israeli strategic cooperation agreement by claiming that US forces were now directly aligned against Syria. Now in 1982 he depicted the Israeli invasion and the 1983 Israeli–Lebanese agreement as an American–Zionist plot to dominate the Middle East. His public suspicions were further aroused when American and other Western forces were despatched to Lebanon on a peacekeeping mission. And an actual military clash with the US had occurred by the end of 1983, with American ships and carrier planes making attacks on Syrian forces in Lebanon and two American planes being shot down on such a mission.[42]

Syria eventually triumphed in Lebanon, as the US peacekeeping forces withdrew in 1984 and the Israelis withdrew from all but a border zone in 1985. But the reduced immediacy of any threat from the US (the 'arch enemy') and of the strategic threat from Israel (the 'evil enemy') did not bring an end to Asad's belligerent speeches and frequent references to the need for strategic balance.[43] Only privately was there a reassessment of Syria's situation and approach now that Gorbachev's Soviet Union was becoming an increasingly unreliable source of support.

In 1991 the regime's new approach would become public when Syria fought alongside the US in the coalition to free Kuwait from Iraqi occupation. And a new attitude toward Israel was evident not only in Syria's willingness to take part in US-brokered multilateral peace talks in Madrid in 1991 and bilateral talks in 1992–3 but also in the tone of the Syrian media, which now used the word 'Israel' instead of 'Zionist entity' and the 'evil enemy'.[44] Yet although Israel was no longer being depicted as a threat to Syria and the Arab world, Syria adopted an uncompromising stance in the peace talks and little progress seemed to be made in ending the near-generation-old conflict.[45]

By the 1980s Qadhafi's *Libya* had already earned international notoriety and an outlaw image through its support of seemingly any and all revolutionary/terrorist groups, even the far-off IRA.[46] But whatever external pressure there had been on Libya before the 1980s was wholly insignificant compared to the pressure that would soon be exerted by the new, Reagan administration that took office in the US at the beginning of 1981. It immediately singled out Libya for special attention as a 'base for Soviet subversion', ruled by 'the most dangerous man in the world'.[47] For the next six years the US would conduct an intermittent campaign of political, economic and even military pressure against Libya. The political pressure took the predictable form of quickly severing diplomatic relations and constantly emphasising the threat to the international community posed by Qadhafi's outlaw Libyan regime. The economic pressure took the form of the 1982 boycott of sales of Libyan oil, the comprehensive economic embargo of early 1986, and attempts in 1982 and 1985 to persuade other Western countries to join the US boycott of Libyan oil. The military pressure took the form of the US Sixth Fleet exercising in the disputed waters of the Gulf of Sidra (Sirte), which Libya claimed as territorial waters but were viewed by the US as international waters. On several occasions this led to military clashes, as in August 1981 when two Libyan warplanes were shot down by US carrier planes and in March 1986 when Libyan missiles were fired at patrolling US carrier planes.

Qadhafi adopted an only mildly defiant stance in the early 1980s and strenuously denied that he supported terrorism, but he was not loath to point out that the US was using economic and political pressure against Libya.[48] In the mid-1980s he took to denouncing the US threat in strong language (calling the US not just imperialist and arrogant but also savage and barbaric) and he threatened to respond with suicide attacks and a war that would engulf the Middle East.[49] Such defiance was echoed by the ritualised chanting of 'Death to America' by audiences of his speeches and by members of the country's nearest equivalent of a parliament, the General People's Congress.[50]

On 15 April 1986 the pressure from the US increased dramatically with air raids on targets in Tripoli and Benghazi in response to evidence that Libya had been involved in a recent bomb attack aimed at US servicemen in West Berlin. After an initial burst of defiant rhetoric, Qadhafi began to adopt a more conciliatory stance in his foreign policy, notably in his attitude towards the US and the new, Bush administration (which did not reciprocate). But the new approach was interrupted by the January 1989 shooting down of two Libyan warplanes by patrolling US carrier planes, which produced a renewed bout of defiant anti-US rhetoric.[51] And in 1992 Qadhafi returned to the consistently defiant posture of the early and mid-1980s.

In 1992 the United Nations Security Council supported US and British demands that Libya extradite two citizens suspected of involvement in planting the bomb that destroyed a Pan Am passenger plane over the Scottish town of Lockerbie in 1988. Qadhafi defiantly refused to comply with the Security Council's Resolution 748 on extraditing the suspects and he adopted a yet more defiant tone when the threatened United Nations sanctions were applied.[52] The sanctions were nothing like the comprehensive economic measures taken against Iraq after its conquest of Kuwait; the most significant measures in the 1992 package were the severing of international air links and a ban on arms sales.[53] Such relatively mild pressure offered Qadhafi 'a relatively low-cost opportunity to play the nationalist card' and to adopt a defiant stance that bolstered his personal position and enabled him to pillory the opposition groups in exile for their connections with the US foe.[54]

At the beginning of the 1980s the *Vietnamese* regime was still engaged in military and political struggles against foreign foes, as Vietnamese Communists had been for much of the previous thirty years. The former military foe of the 1960s and early 1970s, the US, remained a strong political opponent, refusing to establish diplomatic relations and maintaining an economic embargo. The new military foe, China, had staged a limited, 'punitive' invasion of northern Vietnam in February–March 1979 in retaliation for Vietnam's December 1978 invasion of Communist Cambodia and removal of its pro-Chinese Khmer Rouge regime.[55] Anxieties and polemics were kept alive in the 1980s by China's cross-border military harassment and the continuing invasion threat.[56] In 1982 the Fifth Party Congress referred to China as 'the direct enemy of the Vietnamese people';[57] in the following year the Central Committee warned Party members that China still had a long-term ambition to annex Vietnam and had become yet more hostile; in 1984 tension and border clashes reached a new height, and in 1985 the two countries' polemics included a public threat from China to launch another punitive invasion.[58]

Vietnam was also fighting virtually a proxy war with China in Cambodia, where large numbers of Vietnamese troops were engaged in a counter-insurgency struggle against Khmer Rouge guerrilla forces supplied by China with military as well as political and diplomatic aid. Another pressure on Vietnam arising from the invasion and occupation of Cambodia was the international isolation and criticism bestowed on such a flagrant aggressor, despite its creation of a puppet government of Cambodians and its evidence of the former Khmer Rouge regime's atrocities. Vietnam's political, economic, and military alliance with the Soviet Union became its lifeline, confirming China's charges that Vietnam was the Asian equivalent of Cuba.[59]

The dangers of such isolation were confirmed after 1985 as the alliance with the Soviet Union was eroded by Gorbachev's desire to improve relations with the US and China, if necessary at the expense of Vietnam. In fact a more conciliatory Vietnamese approach to international relations began to be evident as early as the 1985 announcement that all Vietnamese troops would be withdrawn from Cambodia by 1990, and the Sixth Party Congress held in 1986 actually called for the normalisation of relations with China. The withdrawal of troops from Cambodia was completed in 1989 and Vietnam officially supported UN efforts (which finally bore fruit in 1991) to end the now civil war in that country.

But the more conciliatory approach in international relations had its setbacks and bouts of renewed defiance of external foes. The most notable occurred in 1988 when verbal conflict and exchanged threats with China over ownership of the disputed Spratly Islands culminated in the sinking of one or more Vietnamese naval craft and publicly exchanged accusations of belligerence. Relations with China were not formally normalised at a Party and state level until 1991. The normalising of relations with the US took even longer. The economic embargo was finally lifted in 1994 but the US still refused to establish full diplomatic relations (and grant the accompanying Most Favoured Nation trading status).[60] Moreover, relations with the US had been complicated by the regime's trenchant defiance of a new, political/ideological threat posed by the US-led 'imperialists'.

At the end of the 1980s the regime had discerned a new external threat that took a different, less straightforward form than the threats and pressures Communist Vietnam had faced in earlier years. The 1989 collapse of Communism in Eastern Europe and challenge to Communist rule in China led to the regime's official statements' increasingly displaying a 'tone of anxious defence against domestic and international forces' that were purportedly undermining the Communist regime.[61] Official propaganda adopted the Chinese line of blaming the collapse of Communism internationally on US-led imperialist and reactionary forces carrying out 'peaceful developments' aimed at eliminating all socialist regimes.[62] By 1990 the media was denouncing support for multi-partyism and pluralism by claiming it was the result of 'imperialist forces and their reactionary exiled henchmen'.[63] The Central Committee publicly expressed its concern about the 'wicked plots and manoeuvres of imperialism and reactionary forces inside and outside the country', and a sharp increase in political repression was justified in terms of national security and the threat to Vietnam's very survival.[64] The Politburo's words and behaviour expressed a belief that Vietnam 'was the target of a massive world wide conspiracy to destabilize the society and topple the government.'[65]

In the mid-1990s the Party was still warning the country to beware of the 'peaceful evolution' threat, and another national security alert was announced at the end of 1993.[66] Relations with the US were clearly improving but the Vietnamese leadership feared that the issue of human rights would become 'the new platform for U.S. pressure'.[67] Although relations with China had been soured by more disputes about the Spratly Islands, this had not led to a renewed bout of defiant anti-China rhetoric as apparently the Central Committee could not agree on whether to classify China as expansionist.[68]

Although *North Korea* had not been engaged in a shooting war since the 1950–3 Korean War, in 1980–94 the North Korean regime placed more propaganda emphasis than any of the other cases on the need to defy external foes. The country remained locked in a cease-fire, no-war/no-peace situation with its military enemies of a generation ago, who were still considered to be military as well as political foes. The US still deployed 40 000 troops behind the cease-fire line, refused to formally recognise the North Korean state, and maintained an economic embargo against it; the South Korean 'puppet regime' similarly refused to recognise or trade with North Korea and was building up powerful military forces. For decades the most important theme in North Korean propaganda (apart from the leader's personality cult) had been the threat posed by an alliance of the US, South Korea and Japan allegedly aimed at 'repeating' the 1950 aggression against the people of North Korea.[69]

During the 1980s there were continual expressions of apprehension by the North Korean regime about these US-led aggressive designs. Allegations of aggressive intent were particularly prominent during the annual US/South-Korean military exercises and the annual North Korean Anti-American Struggle Month, and they always dominated the meetings of the Military Armistice Commission at the cease-fire-line meeting point of Panmunjom.[70] Domestically, the regime portrayed North Korea as still being at war with 'imperialism' and as requiring 'iron-clad unity under leader-party-nation' to keep the nation safe from 'external predators'. [71] Even during the apparent relaxation of tensions accompanying the 1985 Red-Cross-supervised exchange visits between North and South, the regime maintained its media campaign against the 'US imperialists': journalists travelling south to Seoul were reported to have been 'stared at by the "bloodthirsty eyes" of "US imperialist aggressor wretches wearing helmets" and saw "offensive military installations for northward invasion" on every mountain ridge and in every valley.'[72]

By the 1990s a more moderate approach to international relations was evident as the regime apparently became worried about North Korea's increasing international isolation (especially when compared to the increasing international acceptance of South Korea). The refusal of nearly all other Communist states, including the Soviet Union and China, to join in North Korea's boycott of the 1988 Seoul Olympic Games was only an insult compared to the injury inflicted in 1989 by the collapse of a large proportion of the world's Communist regimes. Furthermore, relations with Gorbachev's Soviet Union had been deteriorating in the later 1980s even before the new decade brought the Soviet 'betrayal' of establishing diplomatic relations with South Korea. The actual demise of the Soviet Communist regime in 1991 was another case of injury being added to insult and left North Korea even more dependent upon the other neighbouring Communist power, China. Although there had been a warming of relations with post-Tiananmen-Square China, the new realities were confirmed when eventually China followed the Soviet lead and established ties with South Korea.

In response to this deterioration in its external environment the North Korean regime took steps to reduce its international isolation. In 1991 it cleared the way for joining the United Nations by at last accepting the 'two Koreas' notion of North and South Korea joining the United Nations as two separate states. And to compensate for the South's success in building ties with the Soviet Union and China, in 1990–1 it made a serious attempt at improving relations with Japan and the US.[73] (Although still indulging in anti-US rhetoric, the North Korean regime increasingly referred to the US as a particular state rather than as the leader of the international imperialist system.[74]) Combined with moves to improve relations with the South, these measures seemed to represent the beginning of the end of the defiance approach to international relations.

However, relations with the US were soon soured by the issue of North Korea's nuclear-power programme, which aroused US suspicions that North Korea was attempting to develop nuclear weapons. The nuclear issue saw mood swings from conciliatoriness to belligerence from both sides: US threats of United Nations sanctions in

1993 and again in 1994, North Korea officially putting itself on a war footing in 1993, and the aged Kim Il Sung emerging into the limelight in mid-1994 to hold the talks with ex-President Jimmy Carter that led on to the official Geneva Agreement signed by the two governments in October. The Geneva Agreement specified that, in exchange for freezing and in effect eventually abandoning its nuclear-power programme, North Korea was to receive not only two nuclear reactors and 500 000 tons of oil a year until the reactors were delivered but also diplomatic recognition and the reduction of barriers to trade and investment.[75] After the Geneva Agreement the North adopted a friendlier attitude towards the US, though not towards Japan or South Korea, and seemed to be finally winding down its long-standing campaign of defying the imperialist threat.

The *Cuban* regime was somewhat similar to the Libyan in seeming to attract a disproportionate amount of hostility from the US, but in Cuba's case this pressure had already been felt long before the 1980s – in fact for almost twenty years. The more than normal anti-Communist hostility shown by the US to Castro's regime was reflected in the lack of diplomatic relations and the maintenance of an economic embargo that dated back to even before the regime had become explicitly Communist and Soviet-aligned in 1961.[76] Such hostility actually increased in the 1980s with the inauguration of the strongly anti-Communist Reagan administration, which showed an undisguised desire to be rid of this disturbing Communist presence in its own backyard – only ninety miles from Florida. The new administration accused Cuba of supplying arms to leftists in Central America and 'intensified efforts to isolate Cuba', reimposing the ban on American tourist travel to the island and 'launching a new offensive against Cuba's export and financial dealings with third parties'.[77] The US pressure would be maintained throughout the decade by such measures as the inception in 1985 of Radio Marti broadcasts to the Cuban people.

Castro's regime had never been loath during the previous twenty years to indulge in defiant anti-US rhetoric and to maintain a relationship of mutual belligerence.[78] Now, in the 1980s, the message of defiance became more focused domestically on the reality of the US threat and on the means to combat it. The US was portrayed in the media as posing a very real military threat, especially after its invasions of Grenada in 1983 and Panama in 1989.[79] (Nor did the regime hide the fact that Gorbachev's Soviet Union would provide no form of protection for its old ally.[80]) The US threat was used to justify the creation of a huge new militia in the early 1980s and the re-emphasis of revolutionary consciousness incorporated in the 1986 Rectification shift in economic approach.[81] Even the leadership's failings in economic and social policy were blamed on the US threat. According to Castro, the leadership's attention had been distracted 'by the need to build up the defences of the country in the face of an increasingly hostile US administration.'[82] Furthermore, Castro contended that US encouragement was the cause of most political dissent or what he called 'counter-revolutionary' behaviour.[83] After the Sandinistas' loss of elections in 1990 to a US-backed political alliance, Castro warned the 1991 Party Congress that US imperialism would 'try to divide us in an attempt to find any pretext to justify its interventionist actions in our country.'[84]

In the 1990s the regime also portrayed its key problem, the economic consequences of a massive decline in imports, in defiant and virtually military terms. The cause of the economic disaster was the collapse of the nearly thirty-year-old supportive economic relationship with the Soviet block that had enabled Cuba to overcome the effects of the US embargo. But the regime shifted the focus of the problem from betrayal by old friends to surviving the US economic embargo. It was depicted as a form of economic warfare and even as a form of siege, as the country seemed to be facing the 1960 embargo situation all over again but this time without any hope of relief from friends and allies.[85] The fact that the emergency measures taken in response to the crisis were based upon plans for wartime needs, as indicated by the declaration of a 'special period (in peacetime)', strengthened the image of a country facing an economically enforced state of siege.[86] The US itself supported this image by passing the 1992 Cuban Democracy Act, aimed at foreign subsidiaries of US companies doing business with Cuba, which brought forth from Castro the predictable defiant calls for resistance to US pressure.[87]

During the 1980s *China* was the least defiant of the eight cases. At the beginning of the decade the only external foe was the Soviet Union, which was accused by the Chinese regime of seeking 'hegemony', and even the Soviet Union was no longer the ideological and border-clashing military enemy that it had been in the 1960s nadir of the Sino-Soviet dispute. In marked contrast to many of the other eight cases, China enjoyed an informal (anti-Soviet) alliance with the US and Most Favoured Nation trading status. By the mid-1980s the regime was changing its view of the US, increasingly viewing US foreign policy as hegemonist, and came to perceive the Soviet Union and the US as 'two hegemons of relatively equal threat'.[88] But Gorbachev's accession to power would bring a marked improvement in relations with the Soviet Union, and expressions of optimism about Sino-US relations continued to come from both countries. The US continued to be seen as a 'partner that would help China to achieve such goals as deterrence in the 1970s and economic modernization in the 1980s'.[89]

In 1989 the Chinese regime began to adopt a more defiant posture towards the US in reaction to what it saw as a new, political/ideological form of external threat which was potentially very dangerous to Chinese Communism. There was a growing propaganda emphasis on the threat posed by the West's 'peaceful evolution' method of undermining Communist regimes – a method which was succeeding so dramatically in Eastern Europe and seemed to be developing in China with the growth of the protest movement focused on Tiananmen Square. After the regime finally moved to crush the Tiananmen Square demonstrations, the regime's senior leader, Deng Xiaoping, expressed the view that the protesters had sought 'a bourgeois republic entirely dependent upon the West'.[90] Furthermore, he publicly put part of the blame for the 'rebellion' upon neo-imperialist plots to transform China into a vassal of imperialism.[91] In particular he and other hardliners blamed the US for supporting the demonstrations, if not actually directing them from the sidelines.[92] There followed 'an outpouring of anti-American invective' in the Chinese media and the 1989 demonstrations 'were repeatedly cited as "proof" of American infiltration into China'.[93] A siege mentality was evident in the regime's media pronouncements and there was even a plan to strengthen the people's 'national defence mentality' and increase their support for the military.[94] The military itself was subjected to an indoctrination campaign that portrayed the West as seeking a 'smokeless victory' through peaceful evolution.[95]

The defiant attitude towards the West was stoked by its condemnation of the Tiananmen Square massacre and by the US imposition of a range of sanctions. 'Washington canceled all high-level exchanges with China, cut off arms transfers and military-related sales, suspended financial credits and economic assistance' and declared that the removal of these sanctions would depend upon the Chinese regime's institution of political reforms.[96] Although the sanctions were relatively mild and did not remove China's Most Favoured Nation trading status, they and the continuing American expressions of concern about human rights were viewed by the Chinese regime as a weapon being brandished against Chinese socialism.[97]

In 1992–3 there was a temporary moderating of the regime's defiant stance. References to the 'peaceful evolution' threat, let alone to 'Western hostile forces' or 'US imperialism', were sharply reduced and there was a reduction in critical or antagonistic references to the US in the Chinese media.[98] (By the early 1990s Deng had begun taking a relatively moderate view of the 'peaceful evolution' external threat, largely because over-emphasising hostility to and from the West might bring an end to the 'open door' policy and damage China's economic development.[99]) But in late 1993 the campaign against 'peaceful evolution' began to be revived, perhaps because by then an ageing Deng was losing his control over events.[100] The revival of this theme suggested that the new, younger generation of collective leadership still had some doubts about whether they could dispense with the defiance appeal as China approached the potential instability of the post-Deng era. Already the notion of democratisation had been denounced in terms of not just peaceful evolution but also the more subtle claim that democratisation would lead to disunity and disorder and actually encourage the foreign aggression that had humiliated China in the pre-Communist era.[101]

2 Communist China

POLITICAL STRUCTURE

The Chinese Communist regime had maintained a relatively orthodox Communist political structure, with few unique or unusual features, in the generation from its founding in 1949 to the beginning of the 1980s. The personal rule enjoyed by Party Chairman Mao Zedong from the later 1960s to his death in 1976 was the most prominent unorthodox feature but was not as unusual as: the Politburo's having a small Standing Committee to handle weekly business and allow the larger body to meet only monthly; the dominant but unacknowledged role of factions (personal/patronage as well as ideological); and the existence of the Chinese People's Political Consultative Conference as a forum for the regime's no fewer than eight puppet parties. During the 1980s–90s there would be many changes to political structure, mostly only minor, but a few of real importance.

The first of these structural changes was the completion of the transfer of power to a new and unique form of regime leadership, which incorporated both a collective leadership and an individual, senior leader. By the beginning of the 1980s Mao's protégé and chosen successor as Party Chairman, Hua Guofeng, had already seen his pre-eminence undermined by a group of senior Party figures who wished to see their most famous member, the pragmatic and administratively expert Deng Xiaoping, become the senior leader of the regime. Deng's supporters had won a major victory in the watershed December 1978 Central Committee meeting which adopted Deng's pragmatic approach and emphasised the need for economic development rather than Maoist class struggle. Further progress had been made at the September 1979 Central Committee meeting and the way was clear for the transfer of power to be completed in a more formal fashion. In 1980 one of Deng's reformist protégés, Hu Yaobang, took over Hua's key Party post of General Secretary, and another reformist protégé, Zhao Ziyang, took over Hua's state post of Premier. Chairman Hua was left as a virtual figurehead and in 1981 lost even his (soon to be abolished) post of Chairman. China was now ruled by a combination of a) collective leadership by Party elders and the comparatively young Hu Yaobang and Zhao Ziyang, and b) individual leadership by Deng as the regime's senior leader.

Another important, though less obvious and more gradual, structural change was the strengthening of Deng's position as the senior, paramount, or pre-eminent leader. His personal prestige and influence eventually outgrew the need for any formal authority. In the early 1980s Deng was a member of the Standing Committee of the Politburo but did not hold the posts of Party Chairman or General Secretary, state Premier or President, that were normally held by the personal rulers or senior leaders of party-state dictatorships. He was already viewed inside and outside the country as the regime's senior leader or, to use a quasi-official term, the 'most authoritative' leader.[1] In the later 1980s he retired from his remaining posts: in 1987 from the Politburo and Central Committee, and in 1989 from the post of Chairman of the Central Military Commission. Yet his informal authority was such that apparently the Politburo in 1987 gave him the power to veto any of its decisions.[2] He remained 'the arbiter of last resort', with the right to intervene in any policy area and with the key role of balancing the factions in the Party's upper ranks through appointments to important posts and assigning functional responsibilities.[3]

Deng's programme of introducing economic reforms to stimulate development while maintaining political and social stability would suffer several policy and political setbacks during the 1980s. But after the most serious setback, the Tiananmen Square demonstrations and repression of 1989, he returned triumphantly to centre stage three years later to set a more radical economic agenda for the regime – and would see 'Deng Thought' enshrined as the regime's official guide to deciding China's future.[4] The Deng personality cult which developed from 1992 onwards was a unique case of a leader having a personality cult thrust upon him in his eighties and several years after his retirement from political office![5] By 1994 Deng appeared to have lost his mental and physical ability to determine policy, but the need for constant official denials of rumours of his imminent demise showed how important he was to the regime, even if only as a figurehead, in the remaining three years of his life.[6] In fact he could be argued to have acquired a degree of personal 'rule' as the equivalent of an ailing monarch.

The strengthening of Deng's position was associated with the decline in 1986–92 of the collective leadership that partnered his senior leadership. First the younger and more radical members of this deeply divided collective leadership were removed from power: the politically radical Hu Yaobang at the beginning of 1987 and the economically radical Zhao Ziyang in the middle of 1989. (In both cases the fall from power occurred when Deng joined his fellow-elders in the view that his too-radical protégé had become a liability to the regime.) Then the Party elders within the collective leadership lost an increasing amount of their influence in the 1990s as Deng's standing reached a new height and they suffered from the debilitating effects of their venerable age. Like Deng, they wielded great influence not through holding key political offices – like him, they retired from the Politburo and Central Committee – but through their prestige and personal contacts.[7] The institutional symbol of the elders' informal power was the Central Advisory Committee.[8] It was established at the 1982 Party Congress as a 'half-way house' for retiring elders that allowed them to continue attending Central Committee meetings and to tender advice; its abolition by the Dengist 1992 Party Congress indicated a move away from gerontocracy.[9] However, the evident decline in the 1990s of the power of the most senior elders, the eight or so elderly 'immortals', was 'less a function of political reform than of death, decrepitude and partial senility'.[10]

Whatever remained of a collective leadership accompanying Deng's individual leadership was coming, almost by default, to be dominated by the 'younger generation' of Party leaders, who held the regime's key formal posts of General Secretary, Premier, and membership of the Politburo. By 1994 they already seemed to be acquiring the dominant role in their partnership with Deng as he, too, apparently suffered from the 'decrepitude or partial senility' which had reduced his fellow-elders' influence over public affairs.

It is at least symbolically significant that the last remaining post which Deng had held in the late 1980s, Chairman of the CMC, was concerned with the Party's control over the military.[11] Although it appears that his retention of this post was at the military's request rather than because of the post's political significance,[12] the events of 1989 reaffirmed how vital the military was to the preservation of the regime. After June 1989 there were institutional as well as propaganda moves to strengthen Party control over the People's Liberation Army. The General Political Department of the PLA received more power and Party cells in military units were strengthened and given more authority to implement the new emphasis on ideological indoctrination.[13]

Furthermore, it can be argued that the massive involvement of the PLA in business activities in the 1990s may have acted as a new form of control over the military, through the use of 'economic incentives' to bind the officer corps to the regime and by 'fostering dependence upon civilian economic administrators and elites'.[14] Encouraged by the regime and by the need for more funds, particularly foreign exchange, for military modernisation, the PLA in the 1980s expanded its long-standing commitment to self-sufficiency in food and other basic needs into a commitment to also achieve a large degree of self-sufficiency in funding.[15] By the early 1990s the PLA was operating over 10 000 enterprises and had developed an external sector involving foreign trade, international hotels, manufacturing in the Special Economic Zones, joint ventures with foreign partners, and establishing overseas companies to raise investment funds.[16] The PLA's revenues from such activities 'were equivalent to two-thirds of the state defence budget', and by the mid-1990s the total profit may have been as high as $5 billion.[17] But such commercialisation also created new problems in maintaining control over the military.[18] The military's new, commercial perspective on what constituted its corporate interests was likely to provide new opportunities for disputes with civilians over the regime's economic policies. The abiding influence of the PLA within the Party and regime was emphasised at the 1992 Party Congress by the boosting of military representation in the Central Committee to a quarter of the membership and the inclusion of a military man, Liu Huaqing, in the Politburo Standing Committee.[19]

The 1992 Party Congress also implicitly confirmed that some planned structural changes announced at the 1987 Party Congress had been abandoned. At the previous Congress the then General Secretary, Zhao Ziyang, had put forward a programme of limited political reform that was primarily concerned with regularising the existing system and improving its administrative effectiveness but which included the radical structural change of separating Party and state into distinct spheres or roles, with the Party concentrating on political leadership and the state being left in sole charge of actually implementing policy.[20] Specifically, this meant phasing out the Party's 'leading groups' within state organs and removing the Party's factory committees' and secretaries' control over state enterprises. However, the implementation of these changes had been unofficially reversed in the post-June-1989 concern with strengthening Party control over the state. In his 1992 Congress speech, General Secretary Jiang Zemin now called for the further strengthening of Party bodies within state organisations and enterprises.[21] In similar vein the Party Congress adopted what has been called the (Party-state) 'cross leadership' approach that led to several members of the Politburo's Standing Committee taking on constitutionally important, if still largely ceremonial, state positions: the President, the Chairman of the National People's Congress legislature, and the Chairman of the Chinese People's Political Consultative Conference.[22]

The cross-leadership approach not only centralised the Party's hold on key constitutional posts but also boosted the prestige of these posts and the two 'representative' or 'democratic' institutions, the NPC and CPPCC, associated with them. The NPC legislature received more prominence under its powerful new Chairman, Qiao Shi, who argued that a socialist market economy needed a comprehensive and effective legal system; under his leadership the NPC passed a wad of economic statutes and regulations and also had a stronger influence on their drafting.[23] Nevertheless, by the end of 1994 the Chinese legislature had still not come close to the level of free debate enjoyed by its Vietnamese counterpart.[24] As for the CPPCC political forum, it had already been given more official prominence when the regime sought in the aftermath of June 1989 to display its 'multi-party' aspect to China and the world. But even under its powerful new Chairman, Li Ruihuan, the CPPCC remained little more than a useful 'think tank' containing a heavy representation of intellectuals and businessmen.[25]

A more significant but still only marginal move towards democratisation of the political structure was the introduction of 'choice' elections, where some choice was provided by the presence of more (approved) candidates than posts to be filled. Together with the use of secret ballots, this form of election had been introduced in the 1980s for elections to the Party Congress and to the Central Committee. It had also been introduced for elections to the NPC legislature, but this representative body was still elected indirectly by county and municipal assemblies – and under tight Party control. More significant democratising measures occurred lower down the political structure with the 1990s' moves to introduce 'choice' elections in the provinces and to devolve 'self-rule' to the villages, which did acquire some real autonomy in part because of the Party's decline at grass roots level.[26]

IDEOLOGY

By the 1980s the regime had acquired a large body of modifications of orthodox Marxism-Leninism that had been made by its recently deceased leader and been formally recognised as 'Mao Zedong Thought'. However, the new leadership was in the midst of arriving at a final assessment of how much of this Maoist inheritance was to be viewed as correct and ideologically orthodox, for many of the Party leaders had a distinctly negative opinion of Mao's more recent ideological innovations. His early modifications of Marxist-Leninist orthodoxy, notably his pragmatic emphasis on the peasantry as a potentially revolutionary class and on using practice as the test of theories about revolution, had been of benefit to the Party and had helped to bring it to power. But the upheavals of Mao's economically unrealistic Great Leap Forward and then leftist-populist Cultural Revolution had damaged the Party's credibility in the eyes of even its own members.

In his battle with Hua Guofeng and other Mao loyalists in the later 1970s, Deng Xiaoping had drawn upon the earlier, pragmatic strand in Mao's thought and had emphasised his dictum of 'seeking the truth through facts'. But after winning a crucial ideological victory for pragmatism at the December 1978 Central Committee meeting, Deng specified in March 1979 clear limits on pragmatism. His Four Basic (or Cardinal) Principles laid down a minimal core of dogma: 1) the socialist road, 2) the people's democratic (or proletariat's) dictatorship, 3) leadership by the Communist Party, and 4) Marxism-Leninism-Mao Zedong Thought, with the proviso that Mao was no longer officially deemed to have been infallible. To this new summary of ideological orthodoxy were joined the more positive and uncontroversial goals of the Four Modernisations – of industry, agriculture, science/technology and the military – that had been inherited from Mao's last years.[27]

The ideology did not undergo any marked *changes* in the early 1980s, certainly none approaching the magnitude of the changes that were occurring in economic policy. The Party's official evaluation of the Maoist heritage was completed in 1981 and concluded that Mao had made mistakes in his later years, deviating from the principles of his own Thought. Mao the person was to be distinguished from his Thought, to the extent that other leaders were credited with important contributions to Mao Zedong Thought, and only his 'correct' ideas were to be considered as part of his Thought. Having been cleansed of the Cultural Revolution leftism and other incorrect ideas, Mao Zedong Thought could now be safely maintained as orthodox doctrine. In 1981–3 there was also an attempt to promote a new ideal of 'socialist spiritual civilisation', but more attention seemed to be paid to the purely negative 1983 campaign against 'spiritual pollution', such as political ideas and pornography from the West.[28]

In 1986–7 the fear of spiritual pollution was overshadowed by a campaign against 'bourgeois liberalisation'. The new campaign attacked Western political ideas and individualism and was also exploited by conservatives to attack the overuse of material incentives, as exemplified by the semi-official dictum 'to get rich is glorious'.[29] Another negative element was added to the ideology in 1989 with the campaign against 'peaceful evolution'. The source of ideological anxiety was the West's (or rather the imperialists' and international monopoly capitalist class's) strategy of subverting Communist regimes through internal 'peaceful evolution' towards bourgeois liberal democracy – as was being seen so dramatically in Eastern Europe.[30] In the aftermath of the regime's June 1989 repression of the protest movement, ideological pronouncements focused upon the threat of 'peaceful evolution' and upon the confrontation between bourgeois liberalisation and the Four Basic Principles.[31] There were renewed and fervent rejections of Western-style multi-party democracy in favour of the people's democratic dictatorship and its consultative, not oppositional, multi-party system (as embodied in the puppet parties and their CPPCC forum).[32]

However, the doctrinally most important ideological changes of the 1980s were the belated justifications of the radical changes in economic policy. An official ideological doctrine justifying the regime's economic reforms finally emerged in 1985 with the publication of Deng's book of expository comments on *Building Socialism with Chinese Characteristics*. These special characteristics of Chinese socialism were deemed to be the diversified economic forms that were being employed to stimulate China's socialist economy into achieving the immediate revolutionary goal of improving living standards. Such diverse economic forms included private enterprise, the responsibility system, the use of market mechanisms, and the overall control still exercised by central planning. At the 1987 Party Congress official recognition was also given to the theory that China was in the 'primary' or 'initial' stage of socialism – the equivalent of the early, industrialising stage in the development of Western societies.[33] In the primary stage of socialism the main medium-term goal was to develop the productive forces and raise living standards, if need be through the supplementary use of markets and other methods that had been used by capitalist societies.[34]

The 1990s identification and legitimation of 'Deng Thought' provided the ultimate ideological recognition of the regime's economic restructuring. The Fourteenth Party Congress in 1992 saw 'the apotheosis' of Deng Xiaoping 'to join Marx, Lenin and Mao in the Communist pantheon' and the transformation of his ideas into holy writ or sacred revelation.[35] His concept of building socialism with Chinese characteristics was now incorporated (alongside Marxism-Leninism-Mao Zedong Thought) into the Party Constitution, which was also amended to define the essential nature of socialism as being 'to liberate and develop the productive forces, to eliminate exploitation and polarization and ultimately to realize common prosperity'.[36] Such formal recognition was bestowed, too, on the Dengist notion that China would remain in the primary stage of socialism for a hundred years – an ideological reassurance that the economic reforms would remain in place for generations to come.[37] The Congress also agreed with the Dengist argument that central planning was not a defining characteristic of socialism and that the market was not a defining characteristic of capitalism. In fact the centrepiece of the Party's economic programme was described as a 'socialist market economy', without any reference to planning, and soon the state Constitution would be amended to replace its commitment to central planning based on public ownership with a commitment to market socialism.[38] Furthermore, the Congress was followed by a nationwide propaganda effort to promote Dengism or 'Deng Thought', which seemed to be placed on an at least equal plane to Mao Thought.[39]

But Deng Thought could deal only with the economic changes and goals of the new China; it had nothing new to say about political and social matters. The regime was having to fall back on non-Marxist, atavistic nationalism as a means of securing political loyalty, as it had done in the immediate aftermath of the June 1989 repression. (Patriotism had been redefined by the Party elders to incorporate respect for China's traditional culture, there had been praise for such authoritarian aspects of Confucianism as discipline and collectivism, and it was claimed that Western-style democracy was incompatible with Confucianism and the other elements of Chinese culture.[40]) Although still falling far short of the prominence given to nationalism by the North Korean regime and ideology, Chinese nationalism was increasingly employed in the early 1990s to justify the regime's rule – 'the central appeal' was 'increasingly based on nationalism'.[41] Such nationalist grounds were also being used to justify the rejection of Western-style democracy, which would supposedly lead to disunity and disorder and encourage the foreign aggression that had humiliated China in the pre-Communist era.[42]

As for social matters, Deng himself identified in 1993 the need to maintain the 'spiritual purity' of the people by combating Western influence but he did not offer anything positive in the way of spiritual guidance.[43] By the mid-1990s the regime appeared to be falling back on nationalism as a means of strengthening social solidarity as well as political loyalty. Preparations were being made for a campaign of 'patriotic education', with an emphasis on 'consciousness of suffering' that described China's past humiliations and its present glories.[44] There was also a trend towards promoting a specifically Chinese identity, to the extent that the General Secretary began to include Confucian sayings in his speeches.[45] Other official spokesmen had asserted that over-Westernisation destroyed 'the dignity of the Chinese people and the cultural heritage of this great nation – words almost identical to those uttered by China's Confucian savants more than a century ago.'[46]

ECONOMIC POLICY

The regime's dramatic shift in economic policy that transformed a leftist version of orthodox Communist economy into a mixed, plan/market and state/private economy deserves special attention for several reasons. Apart from its directly affecting nearly a billion people and transforming a largely peasant economy into a prospective economic superpower, this transformation was the earliest move to liberalise a major Communist economy and therefore had a significant 'demonstration' effect on other Communist regimes. Furthermore, the fact that the successes of the economic reform programme were accompanied by political tribulations for the reformers raises some important issues about the extent to which – or manner in which – successful economic reform strengthens political stability.

Following Mao's death in 1976, there was agreement among senior regime personnel that restoring the Party's prestige after the disruptive leftist Cultural Revolution 'required improving economic performance and raising living standards' to demonstrate that the Party 'could deliver the goods'.[47] (Delivering the goods meant more than just a higher rate of economic growth, which had averaged a respectable 6 per cent a year in 1953–78; it meant a more efficient form of growth based on higher productivity, and a form of growth which would bring substantial increases in the people's living standards.[48]) Even the leftist Hua Guofeng had sought in 1977–8 to speed up the growth rate and improve efficiency by launching a 'Great Leap Outward' that aimed to acquire high-technology industrial plant from the capitalist world in return for oil exports.[49] The collapse of this strategy when excessively optimistic estimates of oil reserves were revised downwards had led to the rejection of his overall economic approach at the December 1978 Central Committee meeting and had provided an opportunity for new, liberalising policies to win acceptance.[50] But although this meeting of the Central Committee is usually seen as marking the beginning of the economic reform programme,[51] Deng and the other reformers were still only a minority within the coalition that was working to replace Hua with Deng.

With their political victories of 1980 Deng and his fellow economic reformers, notably General Secretary Hu Yaobang and Premier Zhao Ziyang, were in a stronger but not despotic position within the regime to implement what they saw as an 'enlightened' programme of liberalising economic measures. They still had to take into account the political risks arising from opposition within the regime to their programme of economic reform. The most politically dangerous opposition would come not from the defeated leftists but from the conservatives who had backed Deng's takeover and were now heavily represented in the regime's collective leadership. The conservative approach of retaining or rather reinstituting relatively orthodox Communist economic policies (after the disruptions of the Cultural Revolution) was to be widely found among the Party elders within the regime's collective leadership. Soon the economic expert among the conservative elders, Chen Yun, who enjoyed a degree of prestige and influence second only to Deng's, would become a rallying point for a loose coalition of opponents of radical economic reform.[52] 'Chen's more conservative [economic] strategy continued to attract substantial support and provide checks and balances throughout the reform decade.'[53] (His economic strategy differed from the reformers' in its concern with maintaining centralised financial and planning control of the economy, with instituting a more limited, cautious marketisation, and with avoiding any significant internationalisation.[54]) Another source of conservative opposition was bureaucratic and other vested interests, such as those of the privileged and influential heavy-industry sector. Their existence contributed to the reformers' tendency towards gradual and piecemeal reforms rather than a rapid and comprehensive restructuring 'that would threaten the vested interests of many groups' and be much more politically risky.[55]

An exception which proves the rule was the extensive restructuring that took place in agriculture in the early 1980s. Although 'there were strong *ideological* objections to dismantling collectivised agriculture', such restructuring 'faced less *bureaucratic* resistance' than reform of industry and consequently was introduced more rapidly, smoothly and comprehensively.[56] The restructuring involved not only some marketisation but also a sweeping privatisation that virtually returned Chinese agriculture to private farming (in a new, leaseholder form).

The agricultural reforms had already begun in 1978–9 with the approval of more generous state purchasing arrangements and of what was known as the '(household) responsibility system'.[57] By mid-1982 about 90 per cent of villages had adopted some form of the new system,[58] which replaced the communes' collective-farm methods by devolving responsibility for production down to the household level. The new system of literally 'full responsibility to the household' had originally taken a household contracting-for-workpoints form but by the 1980s had developed into a contracting-for-produce form. The contract involved a household's taking over responsibility a) for cultivating a specified piece of the commune's collectively owned land and b) for providing the commune with a specified amount of produce from this land.[59] In exchange for taking on these responsibilities, the household could retain for its own use any other, above-contract produce that it had cultivated from this allotted piece of land.

Furthermore, the household could sell its above-contract surplus in one of the rapidly growing number of market centres being set up in villages and urban areas. A 1983 decision to support officially the growing marketisation of agriculture spurred on the development of not only the peasants' retail markets but also wholesale agricultural markets, serviced by commercial dealers as well as state agencies. In the mid-1980s, too, the quota system that had been used by the state to extract large amounts of low-priced produce from the peasantry was replaced by a new system in which the compulsory aspect was disguised by negotiated contracts between the peasants and the state grain-purchasing agencies for the sale of agreed amounts of grain at better than the old quota prices.[60]

The increasing marketisation was accompanied by increasing privatisation as the responsibility contract was commonly transformed into a simple leasing arrangement. The household would pay a fixed amount in cash or kind to lease land from the commune for a period of years, which from 1984 onwards was allowed to be as much as fifteen years.[61] Such leasing arrangements were soon to be officially recognised as transferable and inheritable.[62] During the 1980s the peasantry was increasingly leading 'an owner-like life' despite the continuing absence of (ideologically problematic) landownership rights and the continuing use of state grain quotas.[63]

The degree of privatisation and marketisation instituted in agriculture seemed highly successful. Grain production grew by an average of nearly 5 per cent a year in the early 1980s, with per capita food grain output reaching a 'relatively comfortable' level of 362 kilograms, compared to only 314 kilograms in the late 1970s.[64] Production of other food crops (and industrial crops) actually tripled in the 1980s as a major diversification occurred in addition to the increases in production of basic crops.[65] The structural reforms were not the only factor accounting for the agricultural successes; other factors included the large increases in state purchasing prices, the legacy of high levels of state and collective investment in agriculture in the 1970s, and the relaxation of the former grain-first policy in favour of diversification.[66] Agricultural production and prosperity would stagnate in the later 1980s and the 1990s when state purchasing prices failed to keep pace with inflation, and levels of investment in agriculture declined dramatically.[67] But at least in the crucial early years of the reform programme there was indisputable evidence that the restructuring of agriculture had been successful, thereby providing more credibility for the reformers' plans to liberalise the urban economy.[68]

Although an early start was made on the (ideologically problematic) privatising of the urban economy, this took the cautious form of encouraging the expansion of the private sector without dismantling the state sector. (The most that would be achieved in the 1980s in the way of privatising the state sector was allowing some small enterprises, largely in the service sector, to be leased out to collectives or individuals and allowing larger enterprises to transform themselves into public companies with the state as their majority shareholder.[69]) Beginning in the late 1970s there was an explosion in the number of small businesses, from only 100000 in 1978 to nearly 6 million by 1983.[70] The burgeoning private sector was allowed to hire employees, accorded such standard property rights as inheritability, and provided with such material incentives as tax holidays and special loan funds.[71] In 1988, businesses with eight or more employees were formally recognised by the new legal category of 'private business' rather than 'individual enterprise'.[72] China's by then officially 14 million small businesses and 115 000 individually owned (as distinct from collectives) medium-sized businesses had established a significant presence in the service sector, especially in retailing.[73]

As businesses owned by collectives represented a half-way position between state and private ownership, the increasing number and size of these collective-owned businesses contributed to the privatisation as well as marketisation of the economy. Being a more ideologically palatable form of privatisation/marketisation than individually owned businesses, the collectives received more official backing and many entrepreneurs sought to register their businesses as collectives.[74] By the end of the 1980s urban collectives were employing 35 million people and were handling almost twice as much of the retail trade as the individually owned businesses.[75]

But somewhat paradoxically, it was in rural China that businesses owned by collectives not only had the most impact but also established a prominent role in industry – to the extent that by 1988 non-state firms were producing over 40 per cent of China's industrial output.[76] The 'most dramatic gains in the rural economy in the 1980s were registered not in agriculture but in rural industry, sidelines and commerce'; eventually the 'value of rural industry and sidelines substantially surpassed the value of agricultural production'.[77] They were employing an estimated 100 million villagers by the end of the decade and had proved a vital means of soaking up unemployed and under-employed labour in the villages.[78] Many of these rural businesses were household affairs, often operating under a form of the responsibility system, but most of the larger units were owned and operated by collectives.[79]

The reformers' general 'outflanking' approach of gradually creating 'new forms of economic activity alongside the traditional planned economy' was even applied to state industrial enterprises; the market aspect of their operations was gradually expanded while their place within the planned sector of the economy was maintained.[80] A profit-retention scheme introduced in 1980–1 gave state enterprises the right to sell any above-quota (above-Plan-target) production in the market sector of the economy and to obtain inputs for this production within the market sector.[81] As state-sector officials and managers therefore retained the security of the planning system while gaining 'access to the profitable opportunities of the market', they actually developed *new* vested interests in maintaining and even extending their freedom to operate in the *market* sector.[82] The same strategy of not just side-stepping confrontation with existing interests but also actually creating new vested interests in the reform process was also evident in the reformers' moves to internationalise the economy.

The early move to internationalise the economy was confined to particular geographical areas through the use of Special Economic Zones. In 1979 the first of four large SEZs was set up to attract foreign investment and expertise and act as laboratories in which to study and assimilate new economic methods.[83] The SEZs were initially established on the south coast 'not only to capitalise on links with Hong Kong and Southeast Asia, but to confine the SEZs' economic experimentation to locations away from established industrial areas.'[84] However, in line with the official 'open door' policy, gradually other parts of the country would be opened up to joint-venture foreign investment, especially in the mid-1980s, and eventually more than half of China's industrial enterprises had the right to take part in a foreign-investment joint venture – some 8000 of which were operating by the end of the 1980s.[85] In fact, coastal cities envious of the benefits accruing from foreign investment in the SEZs had actively sought to be classified as 'open' (to foreign investment) cities, and inland areas had sought to have the openness policy extended to them.[86] Provinces and cities competed to attract foreign investors both to acquire additional hard currency export earnings (a proportion of which local governments were allowed to retain) and to acquire the foreign technology that would improve their competitive edge in the domestic economy.[87] Internationalisation of the economy would involve many other measures than simply opening up the economy to foreign investment. Among them were: devolving the state monopoly of foreign trade onto several thousand competing trading companies; allowing some enterprises as well as local governments to deal directly with foreigners and retain some foreign exchange earnings; making frequent devaluations of the official exchange rate; and transforming the black market currency exchange into a semi-official swap market.[88] But even these other measures had their effectiveness enhanced by the creation of a new provincial/local vested interest in their success.

This was only part of the reformers' wider strategy of 'playing to the provinces' and giving 'provincial officials a vested interest in promoting and sustaining the reform drive'.[89] A crucial 1980 fiscal decentralisation of revenues and responsibilities to the provinces had ensured that many provincial officials would support the reform drive in order to protect their new degree of financial autonomy from a conservative recentralisation of funding and spending. The fiscal decentralisation had also created a vested interest in economic reform as the means of boosting the number, size and profitability of local enterprises and thus the revenues they could provide to provincial governments and officials.[90]

Such provincial support for economic reform was politically important as the conservatives' ideological opposition to the reform programme made itself felt on several occasions. There seemed to be a cyclical tendency for the reformers' initiatives to be met with conservative counterattacks which would force them to compromise or weather an anti-reform campaign before regaining their momentum.[91] As early as 1981 there was a conservative campaign 'to study the works of Chen Yun', with the implication that the Dengist economic reform programme should be replaced by Chen Yun's more conservative alternative.[92] The Twelfth Party Congress in September 1982 restored the reformist momentum, but little more than a year later the ideological campaign against 'spiritual pollution' was transformed by opponents of reform from a cultural rectification against imported pornography and philosophy into an attack on the capitalist or 'foreign' aspects of reform.[93]

The next conservative ideological counterattack, the campaign against 'bourgeois liberalisation', was approved by the Central Committee in September 1986 and led to a significant political defeat for the reform drive. The politically and culturally liberalising General Secretary Hu Yaobang proved reluctant to repress students who were opposing the campaign and supporting democratisation. Having lost the politically conservative Deng's support, Hu was removed from his post in January 1987. Although he would be replaced as General Secretary by the other member of the trio of leading reformists, Premier Zhao Ziyang, the reform drive had suffered its first serious political setback. Not only had a leading reformer been removed from a key post but also Deng had sided with conservatives in the collective leadership against his reformist protégé. And Zhao's former post of Premier was not given to another reformer but to a conservative technocrat, Li Peng.

However, the reformers soon seemed to have recovered their political momentum. At the 1987 Thirteenth Party Congress the torch was apparently passed to a new generation of Party leaders. Deng, Chen Yun and other elders retired from the Politburo and Central Committee. (Deng retained the post of Chairman of the Central Military Commission and Chen Yun was elected Chairman of the Central Advisory Committee.) Zhao was confirmed as General

Secretary and secured approval from the Congress for even a programme of limited *political* reform, albeit of a more administrative
than democratising nature. His keynote speech on advancing along
'the road of socialism with Chinese characteristics' had also secured
official recognition a) for the reformist formula that China now had a
'planned commodity [market] economy based on public ownership'
and b) for the reformist doctrine that China was still in the 'initial' or
'primary' stage of socialism. A confident Zhao proclaimed the
regime's intention to double GNP by the year 2000 in order to provide
a relatively comfortable standard of living for the masses.[94]

The success of their economic restructuring gave the reformers good
reason to feel economically and politically confident. Although the
restructuring was only partial or incomplete, it had already produced
some striking successes. In addition to the successes in agriculture,
industrial production was growing on average by some 12 per cent per
annum throughout the 1980s.[95] Significantly, this included a
remarkable growth in export manufacturing (10–15 per cent a year),
which by the end of the 1980s was contributing some 75 per cent of
exports and securing the country's trade surplus.[96] The most
important success from a political perspective, though, was attaining
the regime's goal of 'delivering the goods' to the Chinese people; the
1980s average annual growth in GNP, an impressive 9 per cent, had
produced average annual increases in per capita (real) income of 4.5
per cent in urban areas and over 9 per cent in rural areas.[97]

The success of the economic restructuring, however, could not prevent
a political crisis developing in 1989 that would lead to Zhao's political
disgrace and seemed to threaten the regime with the fate overtaking so
many other Communist regimes in that year. The 1989 political crisis
initially took the form of another round of the student protests and
demonstrations which in 1986–7 had inadvertently contributed to the
removal of Hu Yaobang as General Secretary. In fact the new round
of student demonstrations in the political heart of Beijing, Tiananmen
Square, was provoked by Hu Yaobang's death in April and the lack
of official respect paid to the memory of the only political liberal
among the reformist leaders. But the students and their supporters
were soon articulating a wide range of more concrete and politically
threatening grievances and issues. These went beyond such narrowly
student concerns as the need for educational reforms and included

attacks on inflation, corruption and nepotism, and calls for democratisation and Deng's retirement from public life.[98] More importantly,
the students were joined in street demonstrations by huge numbers of
residents of Beijing and other major cities – perhaps as many as a
million in the case of Beijing. Eventually protests about corruption
and other issues came to 'include almost all segments of the urban
population in Beijing and in China's other major cities'.[99] The Party
conservatives were especially concerned by the prospect of workers
mobilising themselves into a Polish (Solidarity)-style independent
trade union movement.[100] Worker discontent did in fact lead to the
establishment of independent trade unions in a number of cities, and
members of the Beijing example figured in the student-led demonstrations that brought the regime under such pressure in May.[101] That
these workers and their organisations would later be persecuted more
bitterly than the rebellious students is a reflection of the fear they had
aroused within the Communist regime.[102]

An indication of the seriousness of the crisis facing the regime was
the 19 May declaration that Beijing was under martial law. This also
brought to a head the problem of whether the regime could count on
the loyalty of its military personnel when facing massive civilian
discontent. The troops stationed near Beijing proved quite 'unreliable'
and other units had to be brought in from the regions to assault the
students in Tiananmen Square on 4 June. The commander of the
Beijing forces was only one of 21 senior officers later court-martialled
for insubordination, with another 89 officers officially reported as
having 'breached discipline'.[103]

Yet the most public and striking indication of problems *within* the
regime was the sight of General Secretary Zhao publicly showing
himself to be sympathetic towards the students. He and his personal
followers came to be perceived by the Party conservatives as actually
manipulating the students from behind the scenes in pursuit of Zhao's
own agenda.[104] In contrast, Deng joined other Party elders and
younger conservatives, notably Premier Li Peng, in adopting the
hardline stance which eventually culminated in the military massacre
of students in Tiananmen Square and the nationwide repression of
other 'counter-revolutionaries'. In the aftermath of the 4 June
repression Zhao would suffer political disgrace and removal from his
post of General Secretary – the second of Deng's reformist protégés to
lose this post in the late 1980s.

None of the other Communist defiant dictatorships would show
such instability within its regime leadership, let alone face such serious

discontent and opposition from its society. On the other hand, the Chinese regime, unlike so many Communist regimes, had at least survived. And it had also avoided the dramatic political restructuring that had recently been forced upon the Burmese dictatorship by the student and worker protests of mid-1988 – namely, the retirement from public life of Party Chairman Ne Win, the abandonment of the BSPP party-state façade, and the establishment of open military rule by a junta, the State Law and Order Restoration Council.

Therefore the economic successes achieved by the reformers do appear to have helped to preserve the regime's stability. Even the limited degree of instability that was experienced in 1989 may be accounted for in terms of the problems, glitches and failings of the reform programme. For example, it can be argued that the reformers faced the problem of having been *too* successful, in the sense that the rapid improvement in living standards during the 1980s had raised expectations to a dangerous degree.[105] Secondly, it can be pointed out that the reformers' run of economic success had actually come to a temporary *halt* in 1988–9 as the economy suffered an inflationary/deflationary crisis which frustrated or dashed the high expectations created in previous years.

Inflation seemed to be running out of control as it reached an official annual rate of nearly 18 per cent and an unofficial rate – fuelled by panic buying – of close to 60 per cent by August.[106] 'Precisely because of the way so many Chinese regimes have lost their legitimacy in a flood of worthless money, the inflation of 1988 was considered especially significant, both by officials and by ordinary citizens who wondered if the government would be able to maintain its "mandate of heaven".'[107] A more direct political problem for the regime was the obvious public discontent about the effects of inflation upon living standards; inflation was one of the grievances that would be widely shared among all groups of protestors in 1989.[108] What is more, the heavy-handed deflationary countermeasures instituted in late 1988 produced further economic pain.[109] A combination of price controls, a credit squeeze and the suspension or cancellation of many investment projects caused 'runs on the banks, local governments to have insufficient cash, local enterprises to collapse and unemployment to mount' as private, collective and even state enterprises went bankrupt or laid off workers.[110] Many members of the independent unions which sprang up in May 1989 were unemployed workers.[111]

It can also be argued that the only partial or *incomplete* nature of the restructuring had contributed to the 1988–9 crisis. For the earlier failure of the reform programme to proceed with further market-isation by replacing more of the administratively set prices with market-set prices had clearly contributed to the inflation crisis of 1988. The reformers had considered in 1984 and again in 1986 imple-menting a price reform that would have seen many more of industry's prices set by the market, but bureaucratic opposition (and the financial burden of compensating industries for increased costs) had aborted both these prospective price reforms.[112] This 'unfinished business' within the reform programme had exacerbated inflationary pressures in mid-1988 as the publicised prospect of a price reform finally being implemented had encouraged inflationary expectations and 'panic buying' until the September meeting of the Central Com-mittee officially deferred price reform for at least another two years.[113]

Furthermore, it has been argued that the reformers' system of coexisting plan and market sectors 'stimulated corruption as officials exploited their role as gatekeepers to the lucrative market sector.'[114] Provincial and local officials controlled 'access to lucrative market opportunities' through their 'authority to regulate access to the market and to redistribute fiscal benefits and burdens, investment funds, access to foreign investment and trade and so on'.[115] The unofficial revenue (or 'administratively generated rents') acquired by officials through their control over access to such lucrative opportu-nities was often used simply as a means of increasing their personal wealth in a classic case of blatant corruption.[116] The prevalence of corruption was another of the grievances that was widely shared among all groups of protestors in 1989 and, together with concern about inflation, had driven many ordinary citizens into protesting on the streets.[117]

Finally, the economic and political crisis of 1988–9 had starkly revealed how the reformers' outflanking strategy had developed dan-gerous economic side-effects which in turn had politically dangerous ramifications. The political strategy of 'playing to the provinces' and giving provincial officials a vested interest in local economic expansion had led to a chronic tendency for them to overheat their local economies, particularly through the abuse of the now decen-tralised state banking system.[118] The surges of overheated growth from the provinces 'caused shortages, deficits and inflation' and allowed conservatives to go 'on the attack against the "chaos" created by the reforms'.[119] The 1985 surge had led to the highest annual inflation (officially 9 per cent) China had experienced since the

1960s and, together with the resulting deflationary retrenchment policy, had prepared the way for the conservatives to win Party approval for the campaign against 'bourgeois liberalisation' – which in turn had indirectly led to the fall of Hu Yaobang.[120] In 1988 there was another inflationary economic boom in the provinces as provincial/local government and state enterprises took advantage of low interest rates (negative real rates) and expansively lending banks to create a construction boom and maintain the growth of their consumer industries.[121] This would make perhaps the largest contribution to the national inflationary crisis of that year and, as in 1985, would lead on to deflationary retrenchment, student political protests, conservative backlash, and the fall of a reformist General Secretary. But in 1989 the regime itself, not just reformers or the reform drive, had seemed in danger.

The reformers seemed a spent force after this dramatic evidence of the failure of their economic-reform programme to boost the Party's prestige. Deng remained as senior leader but with a lower profile and no obvious reformist allies within the collective leadership. In November 1989 he retired from his last post, Chairman of the Central Military Commission, handing it on to the new General Secretary, Jiang Zemin, the moderate (neither strongly reformist nor conservative) Party boss of Shanghai. Although Deng at least resisted the attempt by resurgent leftists and some conservatives to roll back the economic reforms of the 1980s,[122] he did not seek to revive the momentum of the economic reform programme.

Eventually, in 1992, Deng did move to revive at least the reformist emphasis on economic growth. The conservatives' concern to maintain economic stability had been reflected in the continuation of the anti-inflationary retrenchment programme into 1990 and in the 1991–5 Five Year Plan's annual growth target of only 6 per cent, significantly below what had been achieved in the 1980s.[123] Early in 1992 Deng began publicly espousing the need to return to an emphasis on high growth and evaluating economic policies and doctrines from the pragmatic perspective of whether they furthered economic growth. Deng used the standard reformist outflanking strategy by visiting several economically advanced southern cities in January–February 1992 in a publicity tour to promote his new message. In simple, propaganda terms the message would be summed up as 'speed up development' and 'faster pace and bolder steps'.[124] In more politically sophisticated terms Deng was warning the Party that it had to dramatically improve the people's standard of living or else suffer a similar fate to that of the Communist Party of the Soviet Union after the August 1991 failed coup.[125] The Fourteenth Party Congress of October 1992 accepted his message and not only institutionalised Deng Thought but also symbolically approved an increase in the Plan's annual growth target, raising it from 6 per cent to 8–9 per cent.[126]

However, the Dengist approach to economic policy sought only to maximise the growth-promoting *success* of the 1980s economic restructuring; it did not seek to revive the actual *process* of restructuring or economic reform. Relatively few reforms would be implemented in 1992–4 even when compared to the conservative years of 1990–1, which had at least seen China's first two stock exchanges established.[127] What is more, the most significant new set of reforms contained measures that represented a reversal – however justified economically – of the reformers' strategy of 'playing to the provinces'.

In 1993 Deputy-Premier Zhu Rongji, the regime's new economic strongman, put forward a sixteen-point plan for fiscal and monetary reform that contained such centralising measures as strengthening the central bank's control over lending and increasing the share of public revenues acquired by central government. And Zhu eventually succeeded in wringing a deal from the reluctant provinces that established a more favourable formula for dividing public revenue between central and local government – an albeit still minor reversal of the 1980 fiscal decentralisation. However, he was not as successful in achieving his plan's more immediate aim of creating a soft landing for an overheating economy. (Economic growth was running at the unexpectedly high level of about 13 per cent a year in 1992–3 and was pushing up the official inflation rate to nearly 20 per cent in large cities.[128]) His goal of reining in the economy was in effect abandoned in the last quarter of the year when the central government eased its credit squeeze on state enterprises, apparently in response to 'advice' from Deng that rapid growth should be maintained.[129]

The Dengist fixation on as much economic growth as soon as possible also precluded any attempt at such economically 'disruptive' reforms as fully marketising the operation of state enterprises. In the 1990s more than a third of state enterprises were still operating at a loss, especially in heavy industry, and were kept 'in business' only by extending them easy credit at interest rates below the inflation rate.[130]

Some of the loss-makers were being removed from the scene but normally through mergers rather than through the new bankruptcy provisions – each year there were thousands of the former but only dozens of the latter.[131]

Reform of state enterprises seemed for a time to be on the regime's public agenda. In 1992 state enterprises' autonomy was extended or confirmed in such areas as pricing and foreign trade, and there were plans to transform them into financially and legally independent corporate entities, with managers responsible to a board of directors representing the interests of the state and other shareholders in the enterprise.[132] In fact the November 1993 Central Committee meeting had 'proclaimed with great fanfare' the goal of not just corporatising but also actually privatising a large number of state-owned enterprises.[133] However, at the NPC meeting in March 1994 Premier Li Peng had nothing to say about privatisation and instead was promising additional funds to help large and medium state enterprises over their 'temporary' difficulties.[134] A new Corporate Law took effect in July but 'plans for extensive state enterprise reform... all but disappeared from the agenda'.[135]

Apart from the emphasis on immediate economic growth there were several other reasons why the regime avoided further marketisation – let alone the actual privatisation – of state enterprises. One reason was the fear of adding to China's already serious unemployment at a time, the close of the Deng era, when the regime wished 'to minimise sources of social unrest'.[136] Another reason was the long-standing problem of financial compensation for those industries unfairly disadvantaged by the replacement of administratively set prices with market-set prices. As for the long-standing forms of *opposition* to such reforms, the ideological conservatives' influence had waned in this officially Dengist era and as leading conservatives entered their twilight years. (The aged Chen Yun, for example, did not long outlive 1994.) But the bureaucratic vested interests in retaining the system of coexisting plan and market sectors were at least as strong as in the 1980s. Many state-sector officials and managers, even in heavy industry, had become supporters of state enterprises' having managerial autonomy and freedom to pursue profitable market opportunities, but they also desired to avoid risk by retaining the security associated with the plan sector.[137] Moreover, the very coexistence of plan sector and market sector had created new profit-making opportunities, such as selling off administratively priced goods at higher, market prices, that would be lost by further extension of the market.[138]

Officials and managers in industry were not the only bureaucrats with a vested interest in maintaining a limited and politicised market system. Provincial and local officials, too, still sought 'various ways to transform power into wealth' through 'a market system in which goods and services are less important than power and prestige'.[139] Despite the regime's periodic anti-corruption campaigns, officials were still able to exploit the fact that business and peasant entrepreneurs needed to secure an official's patronage or favour if they were to prosper in such a politicised market system.[140] In addition to gifts, kickbacks and other standard forms of corruption, officials were provided with non-investing partnerships in businesses and with free shares in companies (known colloquially as 'power shares' because power rather than money was being invested in the company).[141] This tendency for the social stratum of Party and state officials to virtually merge into the business class was highlighted by the manner in which leading Party figures' children, known colloquially as 'princelings', were allowed to exploit the deference shown to their parentage as a highly effective business asset.[142]

Therefore many of the regime's economic and political personnel had developed personal vested interests in maintaining the economic *status quo* of a mixed economy with a heavily politicised market sector. The regime's military personnel, too, had presumably developed a corporate vested interest (and some cases of personal vested interests) in maintaining an economic environment in which the PLA was thriving commercially. Clearly the political limitations on further economic reform were more extensive and complex than simply a combination of the waning influence of ideological conservatives and the fear of endangering the current levels of economic growth and employment.

On the other hand, these vested interests also enhanced the survival prospects of the regime in the sense that they had an interest in preserving not only the economic but also the political *status quo*. In return for the freedom to transform their political/administrative power into personal wealth, officials at provincial, county and town level extended their loyalties upwards to higher authority and could be counted upon 'at least formally to work to maintain the political status quo'.[143] Similarly, the regime's military personnel had reason to maintain a political environment that had allowed them to develop into a dynamic economic force. Within society, too, the new business class created by the economic reforms were tied to the political environment as the backdrop to their commercial success and the guarantor of the economic system in which they had prospered.

By the mid-1990s the general direction of the regime seemed to be towards a system reminiscent of the Kuomintang regime that the Communists had replaced in 1949. Corruption had reached a level comparable to that of the final years of the Kuomintang regime.[144] Like the Kuomintang, the Communist regime was based economically (and increasingly politically) upon the internationalised coastal provinces and cities, such as Guangdong province and Shanghai. Relatively 'advanced' provinces like Guangdong had most of their enterprises operating outside the Plan, had implemented radical price reform and 'user pays' principles, and had been very successful economically – in Guangdong's case contributing more than 20 per cent of China's exports.[145] They were opposed to the amount of revenue being siphoned off from them by the central authorities to spend on the 'backward' interior provinces.[146] In return, these more conservative and less successful interior provinces resented the privileges granted to the coastal provinces, which were also seen by some in the interior as being 'sites of depravity'.[147]

But the most striking evidence of the tendency towards 'Kuomintang-isation' was the benign neglect being shown towards the peasantry. Agriculture had seen no significant new reforms since 1984, and the produce prices paid to the peasants by the state's purchasing agencies had not kept pace with the rising prices of consumer goods and farm inputs – in fact the government gave agriculture such a low spending priority that the peasants were often paid in IOUs.[148] What made the situation even worse for the peasantry were the increasing costs and declining benefits emanating from public authorities. The array of new taxes and informal exactions levied by local government came to be known as the 'peasants' burdens', while rural social services, especially health and education, deteriorated to the point of near collapse in many parts of the country.[149] By the mid-1990s there was evidence of an increasing amount of rural unrest and violence, with peasants taking out their frustrations on visiting officials.[150] The most likely source of political instability, albeit only at a local level, was no longer the students, workers and other urban residents of the 1989 protest movement – who were now enjoying a degree of Dengist prosperity – but the peasantry whose discontent had provided the basis for the successful Communist movement of nearly half a century earlier.

3 Communist Vietnam

POLITICAL STRUCTURE

Before 1980 the Vietnamese Communist regime had such an orthodox Communist political structure – whether as North Vietnam in 1954–75 or reunified Vietnam thereafter – that its orthodoxy was actually a distinctive feature of the regime. In particular, the Vietnamese carried the Leninist commitment to collective leadership to the furthest lengths seen in a Communist regime. After the death of the founding leader Ho Chi Minh in 1969, all the other Politburo members elected at the 1960 Party Congress continued to serve together as a collegiate and outwardly unified collective leadership until the 1980s.[1]

The regime's political structure continued to be a model of Communist orthodoxy until 1987. Then a new generation within the regime's collective leadership seemed to be pushing through a political 'renovation' that appeared likely to produce a distinctly unorthodox, semi-democratised form of Communist political structure. In December 1986 the Sixth Party Congress had elected the southern reformer Nguyen Van Linh to the post of General Secretary left vacant by the death in July of the veteran Le Duan. The new General Secretary had only recently been brought into the Politburo as part of the Party's 1985 shift in favour of economic reform, and his election as General Secretary 'could be construed as the triumph of the pragmatist-reformist wing of the old guard'.[2] Moreover, the Congress had seen the second stage of the regeneration of the Politburo. The Party had already begun at the 1982 Fifth Party Congress the process of regenerating its elderly collective leadership with the retirement and replacement of six members of the Politburo, including the military hero, General Giap. The 1986 Party Congress saw the retirement of a further six Politburo members, including three of the Party's most famous leaders. (However, these three distinguished retirees of 1986 were retained as official advisers to the Central Committee and were given the right to participate in Politburo meetings and to resolve problems on behalf of the Politburo.) At the head of a largely new generation of collective leadership, the new General Secretary immediately launched a campaign for political and economic 'renovation' and more 'openness' by the regime.[3]

The new strategy for renovating the Party went beyond reinvigorating the internal disciplinary/control mechanisms and aimed to deploy the media, the mass organisations and the ordinary citizen as watchdogs to monitor the Party and denounce the failings of its cadres, especially their corruption and abuse of power. The General Secretary himself led a public campaign against such failings, and over a thousand Party cadres were put on trial for corruption in 1988. A less public purge that removed the majority of provincial and district Party leaders also ensured that the process of regeneration and renovation was extended down the Party hierarchy.[4]

However, the new central leadership was seeking to renovate the political structure as a whole, not just the Party, and this involved redefining and limiting the role of the Party. It would continue to provide policy direction and guidelines – as the 'conscience of the revolution' – but would no longer be concerned with policy details or implementation. The new approach meant not only a reduction in the Party's overly powerful supervisory role at central and local levels but also a change to the Party's electoral role. In the lead-up to the 1987 elections to the National Assembly legislature, the Party was publicly advocating that it should play only a minimal role in selecting or approving the list of candidates. The nomination of candidates was officially organised by the Vietnamese Fatherland Front as a 'united front' of parties and social organisations, and presumably it was to have much more autonomy in selecting candidates. (Although the two puppet parties, the Socialist and Democratic parties, dissolved themselves in 1988, the Fatherland Front continued with its electoral duties as a united front of social organisations.) An element of choice was also introduced into the elections themselves by the presence of 70 per cent more candidates than there were seats to be filled.[5]

The supposedly changing electoral role of the Party was part of the wider change of allowing the people's elected representatives much more independence. The new independence of the National Assembly was most graphically revealed in the June 1988 session, when the Assembly was permitted a choice of candidates for the office of Premier. The official candidate, Do Muoi, was elected comfortably with 296 votes but the alternative (more reformist) candidate, Vo Van Kiet, won a surprisingly large 168 votes.[6] During the December 1988 session the Party implemented its new approach of setting 'only general orientations on policy and allow[ing] the assembly to legislate without direct interference'.[7] The Assembly was also allowed to assert its constitutional right to hold the Council of Ministers accountable by questioning and criticising individual Ministers. The following year's December session, now televised live to the nation, saw heated debates and divisions over legislation as members defended their constituents' interests, formed voting alliances (with informal geographical blocks emerging), and displayed divisions reflecting those within the Party.[8]

The likelihood of the regime's moving any further toward democratisation ended in 1989. The collapse of Communism in Eastern Europe and its apparent weakness in China and the Soviet Union provoked the Vietnamese regime into a new political conservatism which halted any further political renovation and openness.[9] Vietnam was one of the few countries to praise the Chinese regime's Tiananmen Square repression of 4 June 1989, and a Politburo member was expelled in February 1990 for having publicly raised the issue of whether Vietnam should consider the idea of a multi-party system.[10] The shift back towards a politically more conservative approach seemed to be symbolised by Nguyen Van Linh's retirement at the 1991 Seventh Party Congress, but even he had faithfully reflected the new political conservatism by denouncing 'extreme democracy' and the 'misuse' of democracy, and by describing pluralism as 'a scheme of imperialism'.[11] He was replaced as General Secretary by the more conservative Do Muoi, whose post of Premier was in turn taken over by the southern economic reformer and specialist, Vo Van Kiet, in a display of the continuing commitment to economic renovation.

There was no move to reverse the changes brought by political renovation. The 1992 elections to the National Assembly had a slightly lower candidate-to-seat ratio than in 1987 (despite two 'independents' now being allowed to stand) and the majority of the incumbent members were excluded from the official list of candidates. Nevertheless, the more independent role of the Assembly was allowed to continue, with the new members proving no less assertive than their predecessors. The debates continued to reflect constituency concerns, regional orientations, sectional interests, and divisions within the Party.[12] The new Assembly had plenty of topics to debate as the 1991 Party Congress had decided to change the regime's traditional method of running the country; the use of Party directives was to be replaced with 'government by law'. In part this was a recognition that foreign investors and a market economy required an extensive and effective legal framework in which to operate. (There were some practical problems to be overcome, though, before the promised 'rule of law' could be applied properly to the host of business laws that were emerging from the Assembly.) But in part it was also a legacy of political renovation and showed a continuing willingness to 'fine tune' the political structure.[13]

An amendment of the Constitution in 1992 replaced the Council of State with an individual post of state President, who was to be Commander-in-Chief of the armed forces and Chairman of the National Defence and Security Councils. A military man, General Le Duc Anh, was given the new Presidency and the number two position in the Politburo, while another military man, the Defence Minister, was promoted to the number five position in the Politburo.[14] On the other hand, the Party sought to reassert control over the military, the People's Army of Vietnam, through a series of moves which suggested serious concern about whether the PAVN would prove 'reliable' if a Tiananmen Square situation arose in Vietnam. The Party implicitly abandoned the 1980s plan to shift to an orthodox Soviet-style 'one-commander' system, in which the military commander exercises sole and ultimate authority over his unit. Instead, there was a continuation of the unique Vietnamese system of combining the 'two-commander' system (in which a unit's political commissar exercised veto power over the orders of its military commander) with a Chinese-style bestowal of ultimate authority upon the unit's Party committee. Other measures apparently aimed at ensuring the reliability of the military were 1992 constitutional amendments stipulating that the PAVN was 'duty-bound to defend the socialist regime' and that the military was the backbone of not only national defence but also 'public security'.[15] However, the question of control over the PAVN had been complicated by the fact that, as in China, the military had been allowed to engage in business ventures. The number and scale of these business ventures had greatly expanded in the 1990s, employing a significant proportion of army regulars and including ventures with foreign companies. Although still falling well short of the PLA's level of involvement in business, the PAVN's expanding commercial role was likely to have similar implications to the Chinese case.[16]

IDEOLOGY

By the 1980s the Vietnamese regime was as distinctive for its ideological as for its structural orthodoxy. The Vietnamese Communists 'claimed to be the most faithful followers of doctrine, the only ones fully practising the principles that Moscow and Beijing have claimed to apply', and in fact the Vietnamese 'seemed to take these texts literally'.[17] Founding leader Ho Chi Minh had never sought to be a theoretician and had not produced a corpus of theory modifying or adapting Marxist-Leninist ideology to fit his Party's needs.[18] In particular, although nationalism had been 'the primary springboard of the Vietnamese revolution',[19] the Vietnamese never found it necessary to develop a nationalist adaptation of Marxism-Leninism like the North Korean concept of Juche. Ho found in Leninist doctrines relating to imperialism and colonialism all the ideology that he needed for a nationalist struggle to free Vietnam from foreign control.[20]

At the 1976 Party Congress, though, there was an attempt to provide a new (additional) ideal for the new, united and socialist Vietnam. The concept of 'the people's collective mastery', which embodied the idea of 'the people's mastery over society, over nature, and over themselves', was said to have originated in Marxist-Leninist writings. But it appeared quite novel when the Congress paired it with the hackneyed Marxist term 'proletarian dictatorship' in describing the preconditions for completing the socialist revolution in Vietnam. The new Constitution of 1980 emphasised 'the people's right of collective mastery' and envisaged that it would be expressed through the National Assembly and the People's Councils at regional and local levels.[21]

In the 1980s the Vietnamese did make some significant ideological *changes* but seemed to be modelling these changes on those of first the Soviet Union and then China. Gorbachev's *perestroika* and *glasnost* were matched by the new Vietnamese principles of *doi moi* (renovation) and *cong khai* (openness) which were enshrined at the Sixth Party Congress in December 1986.[22] Then with the swing back to political conservatism at the end of the decade, the regime seemed to be copying the Chinese ideological approach: emphasising the distinctiveness of the Vietnamese road to socialism, warning of the foreign-inspired threat of 'peaceful evolution' from socialism to bourgeois democracy, referring to 'Ho Chi Minh Thought' in apparent imitation of Mao Zedong Thought, and espousing what seemed a Vietnamese version of Deng's Four Basic Principles – 'the socialist path, the unquestioned leadership of the VCP, the dictatorship of the proletariat, and Marxism-Leninism-Ho Chi Minh Thought '.[23] As late as 1994 a Party Conference called in typically Chinese style for vigilance against 'hostile forces' seeking 'peaceful evolution' towards democracy.[24]

Furthermore, as in China, a lack of commitment to political reform did not affect the commitment to *economic* reform. In 1989 political renovation was implicitly dropped from the 'new way of thinking' but the commitment to economic renovation continued on into the 1990s. The 1992 revisions of the Constitution were specifically required to be in harmony with (economic) *doi moi*, and the revised Constitution mandated a 'socialist-oriented multi-sectoral economy driven by the state-regulated market-mechanism' – which was more precise than the notions of seeking 'prosperity along the path of socialism' and being in 'the transition to true socialism'.[25] Such economic liberalisation was still being confirmed as official doctrine in 1994, when the Party Conference committed itself to continue economic restructuring and to establish a free-market economy.[26]

However, the Vietnamese regime did not develop an equivalent of Dengism in the sense of a new, reformist ideological contribution attributed to the senior leader. The Vietnamese were content with an increasing cult of 'Uncle' Ho Chi Minh, their deceased founding leader, which seems comparable to the continuing Mao cult in China. But a marked difference from the Mao cult was the portrayal of the hero's humility, unpretentiousness and benign, 'member of the family' character – a depiction encapsulated in the Party's use of the description 'Uncle Ho' even when applying his authority to an admonition or instruction.[27] More importantly, Ho did not leave behind a theoretical and often radical body of work like Mao Zedong Thought; the Vietnamese Communists could use Ho's name to legitimise policy without having to deal with the sorts of complications raised by Mao's ideological legacy. Thus many moderates and economic reformers had referred to Uncle Ho to legitimate the new policies associated with *doi moi*.[28]

Apart from its avuncular aspect, there was little to distinguish the Ho cult from its counterparts in other countries. The mausoleum with its constant queues of devotees paying respects to the embalmed body in a glass coffin was probably modelled more on the Soviet Union's Lenin cult than on the Chinese Mao cult – as were the banners proclaiming that Ho would live forever in Vietnam's cause. The omnipresent portraits and the birthplace shrine were standard features of the personality cults of even such living leaders as North Korea's Kim Il Sung and Iraq's Saddam Hussein. So, too, was the use of the cult figure's name and words to promote rectitude in the Party and the policies of the regime. In fact the Ho cult may be better analysed from the perspective of political structure than of ideology. For it could be seen as the personality-cult component of a shift in the regime's leadership structure to a more personal, individual form of leadership at a purely symbolic level which posed no threat to the existing collective leadership.[29]

Although the Vietnamese regime never propounded a theoretical equivalent of the 'socialism with Chinese characteristics' doctrine, by the 1990s it was affirming that each country has a unique history and evolution towards socialism.[30] Such an argument can easily develop into what seems to be a nationalist as much as socialist ideology. The Vietnamese regime's ideology has, in fact, always contained a minor and largely implicit traditionalist-nationalist strand. Some aspects of its beliefs had little to do with Marxism-Leninism and were 'more closely derived from indigenous cultural traditions', such as the Confucianism imported from China centuries ago; the 1980 Constitution's commitment to the family as the 'cell' of society is clearly more Confucian than Marxist.[31] (It has also been argued that the avuncular depiction of Ho was 'consistent with traditional family-oriented and patriarchal Confucian ideas.'[32]) The Party has emphasised the need 'for a specifically *national* Vietnamese culture' and there has been a 'somewhat xenophobic approach to defining and promoting a national culture'.[33] Whether the Vietnamese Communists' traditional commitment to Marxist-Leninist orthodoxy would contain this nationalist potential was still a moot point in the middle of the 1990s.

ECONOMIC POLICY

The North's military conquest of the South in 1975 had reunified this Vietnamese nation of almost 60 million people but had also created a bifurcated national economy. Although the nation shared a common poverty and low level of industrialisation, in the north there was a typical Communist economy and in the south a typical capitalist economy (to the extent that the old landlord class had largely been replaced by middle-class and peasant owners). The 1976–80 Five Year Plan attempted to unify the economy by an (albeit hesitant) programme of nationalising southern industry and collectivising southern agriculture, but these policies had produced an economic and social crisis by 1979. Industrial production had stagnated, the distribution system was ineffective, agricultural production fell well short of targets, food shortages were leading to the spread of actual hunger, and southerners were discontented with the fall in their standard of living as well as with the socially disruptive effects of nationalisation and collectivisation.[34] The country was also facing an external crisis created by Vietnam's invasion of Cambodia in 1978 and China's short counter-invasion in February 1979. The August–September 1979 Central Committee meeting decided in response to the crisis to shift the emphasis in economic policy from socialism to pragmatic economic development. The private sector was to be allowed a role in the economy wherever it was better suited to a task than the socialist sector, and the southern collectivisation campaign was to be wound down. Later it was also decided to allow collective farms to introduce a household-based 'contract' system of production.[35]

However, unlike in China, the first half of the 1980s did not see the policy changes of the late 1970s carried forward into an extensive programme of economic reform. The ideological orthodoxy for which the Vietnamese Communist party was well known soon began to reassert itself. There was no equivalent of Deng Xiaoping to act as the political and ideological standardbearer behind whom a reformist group could advance. Nor was there a committed and powerful reformist coalition or faction. (Southern leaders, though, tended to be more in favour of economic liberalisation, or the preservation of southern economic freedom, than were their northern counterparts.) The tendency in Vietnam seems to have been for 'reformers' and 'conservatives' to benefit from shifting currents of opinion within a Party mainstream that was relatively conservative but willing to consider new solutions to crises and problems facing Party, regime and country. Finally, in Vietnam there was a long-standing emphasis on inner-Party consensus which meant that a controversial decision a) would be fudged into vagueness or ambiguity and/or b) would be allowed to be modified, delayed or simply ignored by lower-level authorities at the implementation stage.[36] The emphasis on preventing despotism within the regime made it difficult to implement any significant changes in policy, however enlightened.

Even the apparently decisive 1979 Central Committee meeting had been unable to decide on methods of implementation.[37] For example, although the Central Committee had approved a quite radical reform of state enterprises, most enterprises did not bother – and were not forced or induced – to experiment with the new methods.[38] Similarly, there was no guidance on *which* of the various models of agricultural 'contract' system should be adopted as standard. (There were several such models being unofficially experimented with in different parts of the country.) Ideological opponents were able to delay until 1981 the nationwide implementation of even a quite limited form of household contract system – a much less radical form than the system being introduced in China. The Vietnamese 'product-based' or 'end-product' system only allowed a) a collective farm to contract remuneration with individual households according to the quality and quantity of their crop-tending and b) a collective farm to sell above-quota production to the state at negotiated prices close to those prevailing in the free markets.[39]

The 1981–5 Five Year Plan reflected the relatively conservative climate of the early 1980s in reviving the goal of transforming the south into a socialist society. Once again southern industry was targeted for conversion into joint-venture or state enterprises and again southern agriculture was slated to be collectivised. However, the implementation problems that had hampered the 1979 'liberalisation' also ensured that the 'socialisation' of the south would fall far short – especially in collectivising agriculture – of the official claims to have achieved the Plan's socialising goals.[40]

Moreover, 1985 marked 'the end of conservative resurgence and the beginning of a new drive for reform'.[41] The economy was suffering from a continuing inflation problem and industry was not achieving the Plan's quantitative targets, let alone with acceptable quality and efficiency. In fact since 1984 it had been the central authorities' policy to decentralise decision making in the state sector and to reform wage and price setting. This had given confidence to a number of provinces in both north and south to adopt openly the 'Long An model', which was based upon Long An province's experiments since 1980 with removing rationing, price subsidies and the 'two-price' system – the system of coexisting market-set and administratively set prices.[42] But the shift in emphasis from conservative caution to reformist experimentation was not finally agreed upon until the June 1985 Central Committee meeting. It sought to establish 'socialist economic accounting by business methods' (allowing decisions on production, pricing, and wage setting to be made by managers of state enterprises) and to abolish 'bureaucratic centralism and subsidy-based management'.[43] Subsidies were also to be removed from food and consumer goods, and there was to be a shift towards a 'one-price' or 'unified' pricing system where there would be no disparity between state and market prices.[44]

However, these reforms were undermined by an inflationary crisis that was caused partly by the measures themselves and partly by their being combined with a botched introduction of new banknotes and with a continuation of the regime's very loose monetary policy. With a) subsidies removed from food and other consumer prices, b) huge compensatory wage increases that also contributed to a record budget deficit, c) managers given flexibility to raise prices in the 'one-price' era, and d) a backdrop of very loose monetary policy and a botched currency reform, the inflation rate blew out to unheard-of levels for a Communist regime – reaching no less than 700 per cent in 1986. The final blow to the 1985 programme was that the Central Committee decision to reform the state enterprises had not been fully implemented. The ideological opposition and vested interests to be found among central administrators had produced a lack of decisiveness in the follow-up pronouncements they issued about the reform, and this indecisiveness had provided room for manoeuvre by the reform's opponents when it was actually implemented at the local or enterprise level.[45]

The 1985 reform programme was probably the most unsuccessful restructuring attempted in any country during the 1980s. Its dramatic failure not only brought a sharp decline in living standards that had already been in steady decline for several years but also provoked 'a severe and widespread crisis of confidence among the people – including Party members and cadres – as regards the Party leadership'.[46] Within the Party itself there was discontent over dashed expectations, as even this relatively privileged sector of society had been affected by the fall in living standards and by the failure to make good a 1976 promise that in ten years' time each family would have a radio, a refrigerator and a television set.[47] However, the 1985–6 crisis, unlike the one in 1979, led to the formal and ideological recognition of the need for change, with the 1986 Party Congress expressing support for political and economic reform and the encapsulation of the reform programme in new ideological principles. The similarity of these principles of *doi moi* (renovation) and *cong khai* (openness) to Gorbachev's recent pronouncement of a programme of *perestroika* and *glasnost* was too obvious to be denied by Vietnamese officials. But their claims that the renovation and openness campaign 'had emerged essentially from local conditions' had some plausibility.[48] The promise of renovation and openness by a largely regenerated collective leadership, headed by a new and reformist General Secretary, must have done much to defuse the discontent and disillusionment found within society and regime.

Yet it seems quite incongruous that the campaign for renovation incorporated a *liberalising* renovation of the economy that would involve a more sweeping set of reforms than those attempted and botched in 1985. Although the Party leadership had publicly accepted responsibility for the 1985 economic débâcle, it was displaying a commitment to press on with 'more of the same' in the sense of another attempt to implement these economic reforms.[49] The official view appeared to be that the 1985 programme had been correct in seeing the need for economic liberalisation and had failed only because of bungled implementation at the central as well as local level. In 1986 the emphasis in economic policy had had to shift towards anti-inflationary measures, which reduced the inflation rate to 'only' 400 per cent in 1987.[50] But the economy was also still facing the longer-term problems that had provoked the 1985 experiment with economic reform – for example, agricultural and industrial production were still falling short of Plan targets.[51] Therefore it appears that the regime viewed the political risks involved in long-term failure to meet economic aspirations as being greater than the risks involved in again attempting – and again possibly botching – a programme of economic reform. The campaign for (liberalising) economic renovation signalled to regime personnel and to Vietnamese society that the Party would persevere with a major attempt to put the economy on a sound basis for meeting the expectations aroused a decade earlier.

Therefore the 1985–6 economic and political crisis had in a sense strengthened the political foundations for an economic reform programme. The regime itself, not just a reform group or faction, had made an open commitment to economic renovation and had staked its credibility on successfully restructuring the economy. The remainder of the 1980s would see an actual decline in the average annual growth rate compared to the 1981–5 period.[52] But the regime would press on with implementing a reform programme that in some areas, notably agriculture and price reform, went further than the Chinese reform programme begun a decade earlier.

In agriculture the new emphasis on reform was initially reflected in the regime's tolerance of southern farmers' subverting the largely nominal collectivisation of agriculture (officially completed in 1985) and soon only a small proportion of southern rural households were still members of a collective farm. In 1988 the Chinese-style 'net product' or 'package' contract system was introduced in the collective farms; now there would be long-term allotment of land to the household, with lease-like contract quotas paid in cash or kind. In some respects Vietnamese agriculture was actually more extensively liberalised than its Chinese counterpart. The relationship between state and peasantry was put on a purely taxation basis, without any form of output quotas, and the marketisation of rice prices in 1989 also removed price control over this key crop. But although the 1988 reform was colloquially referred to as the New Land Reform, the peasants' lack of legal ownership rights in this 'redistributed' land still imposed 'constraints on the full liberalization of agriculture'.[53]

The urban economy did not experience a massive expansion of the private sector like that seen in agriculture. As in China, there was no attempt to privatise the state sector but rather an 'outflanking' strategy of encouraging the growth of the private sector. The new approach would stimulate a rapid growth in the number of small businesses; by the mid-1990s there were over 330 000 of them, employing nearly a million workers.[54] But the number of medium and large private-sector enterprises had not increased to more than 450 by 1991 and then actually declined.[55] The failure to develop many medium and large-scale enterprises was in spite of the regime's offering such encouragement as officially allowing the private sector to engage in large-scale industry and trade, to hire any number of workers and to set up partnerships or companies to draw on investment funds from more than one source.[56] (The 1991 Law on Private Enterprises also gave them such standard capitalist legal rights as inheritability.[57]) Another failure of the privatisation policy was that entrepreneurs tended to be attracted towards construction, agricultural processing, and export arts-and-craft but not towards manufacturing.[58] Clearly the newly encouraged private sector was not going to make a significant contribution to industrial development, especially in the crucial area of export manufacturing.

However, the urban economy did see a massive expansion of the market sector with the successful implementation of the 1989 price reform aimed at establishing a single pricing system based upon market forces. Not only did the 'two-price' system come to an end as the prices of state goods and services were brought in line with market prices but also controls on market pricing were lifted.[59] Although many observers had feared that such an extensive price reform would increase the already triple-digit inflation rate, there was actually a fall in inflation in 1989 to only some 35 per cent.[60] For the regime had learnt from its 1985 mistake and had accompanied the price reform with a tough anti-inflationary programme. Based upon a tight monetary policy, it involved higher interest rates (well above the inflation rate), lending restrictions, and a halt to printing new currency. However, the anti-inflationary package, in combination with the adjustments made by state enterprises to cope with the price reform, produced a recession and unemployment increased sharply throughout the economy. Perhaps because of the seriousness of the recession, monetary policy was loosened in 1990 and there was even a revival of the old policy of keeping interest rates below the rate of inflation. Inflation increased to rates of around 67 per cent a year in 1990–1 before being brought down to 17.5 per cent in 1992 and 5.2 per cent in 1993 by a return to higher interest rates and a strengthening of 'central bank discipline', with the bank no longer being used to cover the government's continuing (large) budget deficit.[61]

There were also moves in the late 1980s to internationalise the economy, such as the devaluation of the currency down to a free market rate and the scrapping of the complex system of multiple exchange rates. The adoption of an 'open door' policy toward trade and investment was embodied in the 1987 generous law on foreign investment, which allowed foreign ventures to be wholly owned and operated by the investors. In 1988–92 over 500 foreign investment projects were approved and by the end of this period foreign direct investment totalled more than $4 billion.[62]

The internationalising aspect of the economic reform programme seems to have been encouraged by a fear of the country's falling too far behind in technology and in participation in the international economy if Vietnam remained tied too closely to the Soviet Union's economy. There was also a determination not to let Vietnam become too economically dependent upon the Soviet Union – not to become truly the 'Asian Cuba'. The Soviet Union had been very generous not only in its economic aid but also in its favourable trade arrangements. By 1986 over 70 per cent of Vietnam's trade was with the Soviet Union and the Vietnamese were also piling up a massive rouble debt as their trade deficit with the Soviets continued to increase.[63] But the dependency problem was becoming increasingly acute as the Soviet Union became increasingly reluctant to subsidise the Vietnamese economy. In May 1987 both countries publicly committed themselves to the new principle of 'mutual benefit' in economic relations.[64] Soviet economic aid, which had been running at around $2 billion a year, actually came to an end in 1990, while Vietnamese–Soviet trade shifted to a hard currency basis in January 1991.[65] That same year a new law authorised the creation of Export Processing Zones with attractive incentives for export-oriented foreign investment, and in 1991–2 EPZs were set up in Saigon (Ho Chi Minh City), Haiphong, and Da Nang province.[66]

A similar momentum was not apparent in other aspects of the economic reform programme in the 1990s. For example, in the 1991–2 discussions of amendments to the Constitution 'conservatives successfully fended off calls to legalize private ownership of land'.[67] Farmers had to be content with the relatively liberal 1993 land law, which allowed land use 'to be transferred, exchanged, leased, inherited, and used as collateral', and also confirmed that such land-use rights were of twenty-year duration for rice and fifty years for long-term crops.[68] Another instance of lack of momentum was the manner in which the promised privatisation programme was delayed by foot-dragging implementation. There were frequent references to the regime's intention to privatise many state enterprises, and as many as 400 of the 700 centrally run state enterprises in industry had apparently been identified as candidates for eventual privatisation.[69] But first there was to be an experimental pilot programme and by June 1992 five of the chosen seven trail-blazers or guinea-pigs had been allowed to opt out of the programme.[70] In early 1994 an experimental 'equitisation' (to use the official term) was completed, with 40–50 per cent of the shares being sold to the new company's employees and the remainder being partly retained by the state and partly sold to state officials and the public.[71] However, there was no indication that now the floodgates would open and a wave of privatisation sweep through the state sector.

Such caution was also evident in the implementation of plans for establishing a stock exchange. Despite the official importance attached in 1993 to this project, it became clear that even an 'experimental' small-scale stock exchange would not be established for several years. One of the reasons for the lack of urgency, though, was the stymieing of the privatisation programme. For although the private sector had been allowed to set up dozens of joint-stock companies, the total value of their shares was still quite low. Without a substantial equitising of state enterprises there was no pressing need for a stock exchange.[72]

But the most revealing example of 1990s caution was in dealing with the problem of fully marketising the state sector of the economy. It did not raise the same ideological issues involved in legalising land ownership, privatising the state sector or establishing a stock exchange, and during much of the 1980s there had been plans to make state enterprises more business-like and market-oriented. As late as the 1989 price reform another attempt had been made to push state enterprises into operating as profit-seeking entrepreneurs in competitive markets.[73] Yet despite all the plans to free state enterprises from the 'bureaucratic-subsidy system' and even to close/merge persistent loss-makers,[74] the state sector had clearly not yet fully adapted to the market economy. In 1992 about 4000 of the 12 000 state enterprises were virtually bankrupt and many others were operating at a loss.[75] (In fact the drain on the state budget arising from the need to cover these losses was one of the reasons given for the privatisation programme.[76]) A programme of 're-registering' state enterprises would soon be liquidating thousands of enterprises, mostly small loss-making units, by merging them with more efficient enterprises, leasing them to private businessmen, or simply selling them off to meet debts.[77] However, as many as 30 per cent of all enterprises were still operating at a loss, and although subsidies to loss-making enterprises were being phased out, they were being replaced by subsidised credit from the state banks.[78]

The political limits on economic liberalisation that became apparent in the 1990s were in part a result of reaching the limits of ideological tolerance. As in the case of land ownership rights, there was ideological opposition to such moves as the privatisation or marketisation of the state sector, which were viewed as constituting an unacceptable weakening of the socialist economy.[79] But vested interests were also involved in the attempts to preserve the *status quo*. The 1993 debate over legislation on bankruptcy and other reforms of state enterprises came up against 'entrenched political forces with a vested interest in resisting change'.[80] State economic officials at the central level had much to lose and so, too, did the managers of state enterprises, whose career success had been based in part upon such non-market strengths as maintaining close personal connections with the higher ranks of Party and state.[81] Although in the 1980s these managers and some central officials had sought more autonomy for state enterprises, by the mid-1990s it seemed that many of them were quite happy with the existing situation and were 'afraid of losing their privileged positions'.[82]

There was some similarity here with the Chinese situation. Although the 1989 price reform had marketised the state sector to a greater degree than in China, many controls and privileges remained within the newly marketised system and provided 'informal' earnings and revenues for managers and officials at central, provincial and local levels. The regime was wary about senior officials' engaging in business activities, and state officials and military officers were legally banned from owning businesses. But while Vietnam lacked the

Chinese phenomenon of powerful officials (and princelings) taking a personal stake in business enterprises, there was no lack of the abuse of powers for personal gain – the seeking of informal commissions and other kickbacks by state and Party officials had 'always been substantial' and appeared to be increasing.[83]

Nevertheless, whatever the political limits on a further restructuring in the 1990s, the reforms implemented in the 1980s had been successful in improving economic performance and providing a sound basis for meeting the people's aspirations. The economy had grown by more than 8 per cent a year in 1992–4.[84] In particular, rice production had grown by 40 per cent in 1988–92 and by 1993 Vietnam had become the world's third largest rice exporter. Perhaps the most impressive result of economic restructuring had been the economy's weathering of the collapse of trade with the Soviet Union. Exports had been increasing at nearly 25 per cent a year on average in the 1990s and manufacturing exports had increased dramatically (300 per cent) in the mid-1990s. Further growth of manufactured exports seemed assured by the success in attracting foreign investment – $2.8 billion worth of projects were approved in 1993 and more than $3 billion in 1994.

However, unemployment remained a serious problem and was doubtless another reason for the foot-dragging over privatisation and marketisation of the state sector. The unemployment level was 10–12 per cent officially but 20 per cent on unofficial estimates, and the limited restructuring of state enterprises in 1990–3 had already produced more than 800 000 lay-offs.[85] (Rural society was suffering from serious unemployment and under-employment partly because it lacked the rural industries which had become so prominent in the Chinese countryside in the 1980s.[86]) Even those in work had to cope with the dismantling of the 'old safety net' as the state sought to reduce its social spending; it was also moving to a user-pays approach that involved charging for post-elementary schooling and for hospital treatment.[87] The peasantry was in a particularly difficult position as the social services once provided or subsidised through the now virtually defunct collective farms were inadequately supplied by the state and on a largely user-pays basis that had reduced usage of education and health services.[88]

As in China, the problem of rural relative deprivation was becoming more acute as the urban areas benefited disproportionately from liberalisation.[89] By the mid-1990s the GDP per capita of the rural population was still only about $200 per annum compared to estimates of $1000 for residents of Hanoi and as much as $1600 for residents of Saigon (Ho Chi Minh City).[90] The income gap between northern Hanoi and southern Saigon in turn reflected a further inequity, as the flow of resources into the south had 'far outstripped' the flow into the north.[91] Foreign investment patterns as well as residual 'capitalist instincts' in the south were producing a similar distinction to that found in China between 'coastal' and interior provinces.[92]

But within the context of Vietnamese history the more significant similarity to China was the tendency to display characteristics of the period preceding the Communist takeover of the country. The decline in the already 'limited authority' of the central state and Party authorities, and the south's tendency to go its own way, were endangering national unity and revived memories of pre-1975 divided Vietnam.[93] Like the other economically restructuring Communist regimes, the Vietnamese Communists were facing the problem not so much of democratisation as of historical regression and irrelevance.

4 Communist North Korea

POLITICAL STRUCTURE

The political structure of the North Korean Communist regime had developed some distinctly unorthodox features before the 1980s. The most important was Kim Il Sung's personal rule, which in its degree or strength was unusual for a Communist regime and in its longevity was unusual for any regime. Kim Il Sung had come to power in the late 1940s as the puppet ruler installed by the Soviet forces that had occupied the northern part of formerly Japanese-ruled Korea in the aftermath of the Second World War. He had been the leader of a Korean partisan band that had fought the Japanese in the 1930s before retreating into the Soviet Union and returning to Korea with the Soviet army in 1945. When the Soviet forces withdrew at the end of 1948 from the newly proclaimed state of North Korea (formally the Democratic People's Republic of Korea), they left Kim ensconced as leader of a typical Communist regime.

As founding leader and Party Chairman (from 1945) or General Secretary (from 1966), Kim had completely dominated the Party since the late 1950s, when he had purged the last remaining factions not personally loyal to him. In other respects the structure of the Korean Workers' Party was quite orthodox despite the fact that it had become a uniquely 'mass membership' form of Communist party which incorporated as much as 16 per cent of the population.[1] There is some evidence that the Party was performing an unusually strong supervisory role: its political commissars (the Political Committeemen/ Guidancemen) within the military had veto power over military commanders' orders, and the post of provincial Governor was often held by provincial or city Party leaders. Similarly, the Party's performance of its electoral role seems unusually thorough. In association with two puppet parties (the Korean Social Democratic Party and the religious Chondoist Chong-u party), the Party delivered a 100 per cent 'yes' vote for the official candidates in the elections to the Supreme People's Assembly – and with an apparently 100 per cent turn-out.[2]

Kim had used the state organs as an almost equally important instrument of his personal rule and had adapted them to suit his purpose. Therefore the state structure of North Korea had developed

some unusual features for a Communist regime. The office of state
President had been given powers by the 1972 Constitution that were
comparable only to those of the Cuban Communist regime's Presidency. Elected by the legislative Supreme People's Assembly, the
President had decree powers, commanded the military, convened and
led the State Administration Council (the government of Ministers)
and, most importantly, nominated, chaired and 'directly led' the
powerful new Central People's Committee that had been created by
the 1972 Constitution.[3] The small Central People's Committee, also
elected by the SPA, was a unique state organ with very extensive
powers. As the 'highest leadership organ of state power' it set the
state's policy and controlled, coordinated and supervised the
executive, legislative and judicial branches of the state.[4] The CPC
exercised executive power through appointing/removing the Premier
and Ministers and through issuing directives to them; it exercised
legislative powers by having been given the powers of the SPA legislature's Standing Committee.[5] The President and CPC together
deployed powers that rivalled those of the Party's Politburo and in
fact 'many of the party's policy-setting functions were taken up by the
Central People's Committee'.[6] At first all members of the Politburo
were given membership of the CPC, but in the later 1970s the CPC
was reduced in size from 25 to 15 members and not all of the
Politburo were allowed dual membership.[7]

Kim's personal hold on the military, the Korean People's Army,
was secured by not only his Party and state powers but also his
(propaganda-inflated) military reputation as a partisan-band leader
and his possession of the highest military rank, that of Marshal.
(When the rank of Marshal was conferred both on his son and on
Defence Minister O Jin U in the 1990s, the elder Kim maintained his
pre-eminence by giving himself the new rank of Grand Marshal.[8])
Another important basis for his personal hold over the military was
Kim's use of his old partisan-band cronies to hold key military as well
as Party posts.[9] The most prominent military crony was General O Jin
U, who was Kim's long-standing Defence Minister and would become
in the 1980s the third most important political figure in the regime.

Kim's personality cult was the most extravagant of any Communist
dictator's. The cult of Kim as the Great Leader had eclipsed that of
Stalin and Mao 'in scope, magnitude and fervor'.[10] Kim Il Sung
'seemed to have been called by every honorary title imaginable' and
to have had every imaginable virtue ascribed to him.[11] The ubiquitous
statues, monuments, museums, household portraits, and lapel badges

were complemented by the constant praise which ascribed all good things to his actions or guidance. In particular, much was made of his military reputation as an anti-Japanese partisan leader (which was so magnified that he seemed to be the founding-father of the country) and his ideological reputation as the originator of the Juche idea (see below, p. 72). Moreover, the impact of the personality cult was strengthened by his security services and the Party's ensuring that the people were protected, to a perhaps unique degree, from any 'disturbing' sources of information from within or outside the country.[12]

Another common aspect of personal rule, the use of family members to hold key posts, was also evident in unusual degree in Kim's North Korea. Younger brother Kim Yong Ju became Party Secretary for Organisation in 1966 and was seemingly the heir-apparent until he faded into obscurity in 1973–4. His powerful Secretariat post was taken over by the ruler's son, Kim Jong Il. Two other relatives held the key Party and state posts for administering the capital city, a nephew was Chairman of the SPA legislature, and several other relatives held important political posts, such as his wife heading the Women's League.[13]

The most important *change* to the regime's political structure in the 1980s and 1990s was Kim Il Sung's move to achieve the most extreme form of nepotism and of personal rule – hereditary succession by his first-born son. At the 1980 Sixth Party Congress Kim Jong Il was informally invested as his father's heir-apparent. He was given very high rank on all three of the Party's key executive organs: fourth-highest on the newly created Presidium of the Politburo, third-highest on the Party's central military committee and second-highest on the Secretariat. Kim Il Sung also instructed the Congress delegates to support his son.[14] That the younger Kim seemed to have burst on the scene from obscurity was due to the cautious manner in which his rise to power in the 1970s had been concealed, as through the use of the cryptic term 'the Party centre' when referring in public to the increasingly powerful younger Kim.[15] Now it could be revealed that he had become Secretary of Organisation and Propaganda as early as 1973 and had been a member of the Politburo since 1974.[16] Among his newly revealed ideological triumphs was the coining of the term 'Kimilsungism' and the creation of the 'seed theory' which provided implicit legitimation for his hereditary succession.[17]

During the 1980s Kim Jong Il took over an increasing amount of the administrative burden from his father, who went into virtual semi-retirement and made few public appearances after his seventieth

birthday in April 1982.[18] By 1985 the elder Kim was referring to the
'Kim Jong Il era', and in the later 1980s he allowed his son's personality cult to rival his own – as when the young Kim, too, had a
flower named after him.[19] The dual personality cult of Kim the father,
officially the Great Leader, and Kim the son, now officially the Dear
Leader, became one of North Korea's unique contributions to the
history of personal dictatorship.

The attempt to secure the succession for Kim Jong Il also explains
many of the other structural changes of the 1980s and 1990s. The
creation of an only five-member Presidium (standing committee) of
the Politburo in 1980 seems to have been for power-enhancing rather
than policy-making reasons, as by 1985 the Presidium had shrunk to
the triumvirate of the two Kims and Defence Minister O Jin U.
Although little is known about the higher operations of the Party,
it appears that the now much-enlarged Politburo was probably less
important than the two smaller Party executive organs – the
powerful Secretariat headed by the two Kims and the Party's central
military committee headed by them and O Jin U.[20] Although all
Party organs had been overshadowed after 1972 by the combined
President-CPC entity, the succession politics of the 1980s brought a
decline in this entity's practical role as President Kim went into semi-
retirement and allowed his Secretariat-based son to take over day-to-
day policy making. By the 1990s the younger Kim was 'apparently
firmly in control of day-to-day affairs' and in 1992 his father stated
that Kim Jong Il was 'now "fully responsible" for running the
country'.[21] In the 1990s the elder Kim actually relinquished some
of his formal presidential powers in order to strengthen Kim Jong
Il's position. The 1992 revision of the Constitution transferred the
President's powers over the military to a newly authoritative and
independent National Defence Commission which was soon headed
by Kim Jong Il. The presidentially-linked CPC was confirmed by the
revised Constitution to be the highest organ of state power, but the
nature of the CPC's membership indicated that it was probably now
a largely ceremonial body. While in the 1980s its membership had
still included the top Party and state figures, now the membership
seemed to be an *ex officio* one of the President, the four Vice-
Presidents, and the twelve provincial Governors. In fact even the
Presidency itself seemed to have taken on something of a ceremonial
or figurehead role.[22]

However, the elder Kim was unable to share his military prestige
with his son, who had never even served in the military. The various

attempts to strengthen Kim Jong Il's formal position in relation to the military were an indication of the heir-apparent's vulnerability in this area. Before becoming Chairman of the National Defence Commission, he had already been given the rank of Marshal and the military post of Supreme Commander of the KPA. His long-standing control over the Party's powerful Secretariat should have provided him with sufficient power in a supposedly Party-ruled regime; the Constitution specified that the state was to 'undertake all its activities under the guidance' of the Party.[23] But after decades of being used as just an instrument of personal rule, the Party was unlikely to be able to provide a strong support base for a weak leader. (A prominent indication of the Party's lack of corporate integrity and independence was the fact that no Party Congress had been held since 1980.) In contrast, the military had developed by the mid-1990s into a powerful corporate body with vested interests that went beyond purely professional concerns. For example, the military constituted 'an economy within an economy, with lucrative sidelines of their own – such as selling Scuds to Syria and Iran'.[24]

A new, informal structural feature that was likely to favour the younger Kim's ambitions was the existence of a whole generation or cohort of fellow beneficiaries of political nepotism. These 'young scions of the vast Kim clan and of the father's anti-Japanese partisan followers' were 'beginning to move into high posts in the party, military, and state bureaucracies.'[25] A prominent example was the post-1992 Premier, the influential economic specialist Kang Son San, who was the son of one of Kim's partisan-band comrades.[26] On the other hand, a new potential threat had arisen from the elder Kim's 1993 decision to politically resurrect his brother Kim Yong Ju, his second wife Kim Song Ae, and his son by her, Kim Pyong Il – the latter two having disappeared into obscurity in 1983 after a rumoured family dispute.[27] Although the public reappearance of these family members may have been staged in order to present a Confucian image of family harmony, in a succession struggle they would pose the same sort of threat to Kim Jong Il as such 'extraneous' family members have done to heirs apparent in other shaky monarchical systems.

When the long-prepared succession was finally set in motion by the elder Kim's death in July 1994, there seemed to be few problems in securing a smooth succession. However, Kim Jong Il did not take over the two political offices that his father had never relinquished – state President and Party General Secretary. At the end of 1994 these offices remained unclaimed, raising doubts about the succession despite the public declarations of loyalty to Kim Jong Il by the military and the Party. Residual loyalty to Kim Il Sung was still being used to strengthen loyalty to his son, and by the end of the year it seemed that Kim Jong Il was ruling as a proxy for his dead father.[28] The 'devoted' civilian population was apparently privately cynical about the regime's triumphs,[29] and Kim Jong Il's elderly military patron, O Jin U, would succumb to his terminal illness early in the following year. Yet more than two years after Kim Il Sung's death, his son was still the country's official leader – and had still not occupied the Great Leader's posts of President and General Secretary.

IDEOLOGY

As in the case of political structure, the ideology of the North Korean regime had already seen major departures from Communist orthodoxy before the 1980s and again these unusual features had been introduced by Kim Il Sung. The term 'Kimilsungism' was officially coined by Kim Jong Il to describe the contributions of his father to the Marxist-Leninist ideology on which the regime was purportedly based.[30] Certainly the elder Kim had added as much as Mao had done to Marxism-Leninism. Modesty or prudence prevented him from claiming credit for one of the most striking additions – the emphasis on leadership by an historic individual rather than by the Party's collective leadership. (For the masses apparently needed guidance by the 'correct leadership' of not just the Party but a 'revolutionary leader', such as Marx, Lenin or Kim Il Sung, possessing the 'art of leadership'.[31]) However, there were many other innovations that could be more openly ascribed to him.

Kim's other additions included identifying the anti-imperialist type of revolution and the need for a continuing ideological revolution. The latter was required in order to remould the peasants' thought as part of a process of what Kim called 'proletarianisation' or 'working-classisation'. (Eventually this process would also require replacing collective farms with state-owned farms, on which the former peasants would work as agricultural wage labourers.) However, such leftism was balanced by an inclusive approach that in the meantime sought a class alliance of workers, peasants and intelligentsia. The inclusive approach was depicted in the Party symbol's combination of writing brush, hammer and sickle, and was embodied in a Party membership that was open to all 'patriots'.[32]

The core of Kimilsungism, though, was the concept of Juche. Kim's own working or practical definition of Juche was 'solving for oneself all the problems of the revolution and construction in conformity with actual conditions at home, and mainly by one's own effort'.[33] But the concept of Juche had developed deeper and wider ramifications. Its usual translation into English as national 'self-reliance' and/or 'independence' also captured only some aspects of Juche, and national 'self-identity' may be a better translation of the concept.[34] The term Juche was first used by Kim in 1955, became a central theme in the 1960s and had developed into quite an elaborate political philosophy by 1967. In relation to foreign policy it expressed and justified the regime's determination not to become dependent on the Soviet Union or China. (Thus North Korea sought only 'selective participation', not full membership, in the Soviet Comecon economic block and rejected the 1968 'Brezhnev doctrine' that the Soviet Union could intervene to protect socialism in Czechoslovakia and other Communist countries.) As for domestic policy, the significance of the new concept extended far beyond its justification of self-reliant economic policies. For Juche doctrine was also applied to such cultural areas as music and architecture, and by the 1980s the Party aimed to model the whole society on the Juche idea, with Juche-oriented policies to be found in every field, from linguistics to agriculture.[35]

Kim and other regime spokesmen vehemently denied that Juche embodied any form of nationalism, as distinct from patriotic loyalty to a socialist fatherland. Their claim that Juche did not conflict with Marxist proletarian internationalism was supported by North Korea's strong public commitment to the Third World and the Non-Aligned Movement. Nevertheless, there was an obvious nationalist aspect to the notion of Juche and to its varied applications. The nationalist aspect could also be seen in official arguments that only Korea had the necessary historical and geopolitical preconditions for originating the notion of Juche. This Juche-linked nationalism was in turn supported by and contributed to a pervasive nationalist orientation that was very evident in such areas as the depiction of Korean history. The regime's historians emphasised the important role Korea had played in world civilisation as a nation with a supposedly 5000-year history. There were also positive evaluations of historical, pre-20th century examples of Korean nationalism, including the Korean monarchy's policy of isolation which had first led Westerners to coin the term 'the hermit kingdom' that they now applied to Kim's North Korea.[36]

An obvious expression of the regime's nationalism was the strong commitment to the reunification of Korea. North Korea has been depicted since the Korean War as being an unfinished and incomplete nation unless and until reunification is achieved. However, the goal of reunification was also presented in more orthodox ideological terms. With South Korea being depicted as a US colony, reunification could be depicted as the completion of the anti-imperialist revolution and the first step to a working-class revolution in the South.[37]

A similar attempt to avoid too obvious a contradiction of or separation from Marxist-Leninist orthodoxy was the portrayal of Juche as being simply an application of Marxism-Leninism to local conditions. But such ideological modesty was not to be found in official claims that Juche offered a solution to the problems facing many Third World countries, and a substantial effort was made to propagate the Juche faith internationally. More importantly, Juche had been developed into a philosophy containing abstract and apparently universally applicable ideas. The essence of the Juche philosophy was the supposed human desire and capacity for mastery over oneself and nature; in Kim's words, man 'desires to live and develop independently as master of the world and his own destiny' and to be 'free from the fetters of nature and society'.[38] Such 'human determinism', as it was called, was hardly Marxist; North Korean ideologists had to acknowledge that even Marx had been unaware of this 'eternal truth'.[39] On the other hand, Juche's voluntarist rather than materialist philosophy complemented the regime's emphasis on mass mobilisation and moral incentives as a means of economic development. So important and characteristic were these mobilisation techniques that they have been viewed as one of the components of Kimilsungism.[40]

The first mobilising techniques were developed in the later 1950s and early 1960s. The most famous was the Chollima Movement, which used the image of Korea's legendary winged horse that flew great distances at great speeds to the land of happiness. The Chongsanri Method combatted bureaucratism by sending officials to work with the people, and the Taean Work System gave workers control over production decisions in their factory through their factory Party committee. By the 1970s a more technologically oriented approach was evident. The Three Revolutions Team Movement mobilised teams of educated young people (including Party officials) to provide technical guidance and revolutionary inspiration to workers in the factories and to renovate the middle-level Party hierarchy. Kim Jong Il soon took charge of the Team Movement and used it to further his own political ambitions, but he also developed some new mobilisation methods aimed solely at boosting production. The Three Revolutions Red Flag Movement used moral, honorific incentives to spur on production by work units, while the Learn from the Example of Hidden Heroes Movement discovered unsung work heroes. Finally, by the 1980s the Chollima Movement was being replaced by a more modern equivalent, the 'speed battle', which transformed an economic task into a battle to be completed in a specified number of days, such as the 200-day battle to increase production in the lead-up to the country's fortieth anniversary in 1988.[41]

The two most significant *changes* in ideological content in the 1980s–90s were a) the development of a theoretical justification for Kim Jong Il's hereditary succession, b) the implicit triumph of Juche over Marxism-Leninism, and c) the increasing use of traditional Confucian themes. Ideologically justifying hereditary succession in a Communist regime was a daunting task. But the theory of the 'unfinished' or 'perpetual' revolution was used to argue the need for a 'reincarnation' of Kim Il Sung to carry on the revolution after his death. To this theory was added the younger Kim's 'seed' theory, which argued that the seed of a cultural work (or, by implication, of a revolutionary leader) contains its thought and message.[42]

The triumph of Juche over Marxism-Leninism was a reflection of how much the North Korean regime was relying in the 1990s on nationalism instead of Marxism-Leninism for ideological legitimation.[43] Marxism-Leninism was not even mentioned in Kim Jong Il's 1991 ideological tract on socialism, which also credited the elder Kim with having invented a completely *new* ideology.[44] The elder Kim himself had proclaimed in his 1991 New Year's message that Juche socialism was 'unique and the most superior system in the world'.[45] Juche's triumph over Marxism-Leninism was confirmed and completed in 1992 by the deletion of the reference in the Constitution to Juche's being an 'application of Marxism-Leninism'.[46]

But Juche itself, formally the 'guiding principle' of Party and state, was increasingly being overshadowed by traditional Confucianism.[47] Although originally imported from China, Confucianism had a long and influential history in Korea. In medieval times Korea had become more Confucian than China itself, with the common people as well as the intellectuals adopting Confucian ethics. The breadth and depth of Confucian influence had been reflected in the Communist regime's reluctance to challenge the Confucianist familial values in its cultural and social policies. The Confucian influence was also apparent in the references to Kim Il Sung as 'fatherly leader' and 'our father', to the Korean Workers Party as 'Mother Party', and to society as 'a big revolutionary family'. By the 1990s the central Confucian virtues of loyalty and filial piety were being used to praise both Kim Jong Il's and the people's support for Kim Il Sung. Such Confucian themes permeated Kim Jong Il's official ideological statement, 'Socialism is Science', of November 1994. It contained references to a) the (Confucian) virtues of benevolence, loyalty, gratitude and harmony, b) the use of familial symbols in describing the father-like leader, mother-like Party and harmonious family-like society, and c) expressions of concern that the leader be a 'man of virtue'.[48] Although this tract also contained expressions of commitment to socialism, the combination with Confucian language rendered them quite incongruous – as when socialist politics were described as being in essence 'benevolent politics'.[49]

ECONOMIC POLICY

As Kim Il Sung had established such a despotic regime and had shown such little regard for orthodoxy in ideological matters, there might seem to be every prospect of his regime's implementing 'enlightened' economic policies. Certainly in the decades prior to the 1980s his regime had shown a willingness to use extreme methods to ensure rapid economic growth and a willingness to change policies to meet the changing requirements of this process of economic growth. In the 1950s and 1960s the North Korean economy had been one of the most leftist versions of a Communist economy. Although structurally orthodox, it had placed great emphasis on mass mobilisation and on moral rather than material incentives to attain very ambitious Plan targets. A massive effort by the North Korean population had produced remarkable growth rates in the later 1950s, with dramatic progress being made towards industrialisation. However, in the 1960s it proved impossible to maintain such high growth rates and there were embarrassing Plan revisions. Consequently the 1971–6 Six Year Plan showed not only a greater emphasis on technologically based growth but also a new desire to increase trade with the capitalist world in order to import its technology and industrial plant. This internationalising and technology-centred approach proved successful in terms of economic growth but not in trading terms. Unable to earn enough from its exports to cover the Plan's needs, North Korea had by 1976 built up a large hard-currency foreign debt and actually defaulted on the servicing of this debt, thereby ending any prospect of continuing with a technologically based growth strategy.

Therefore the drafting of the next Plan, the 1978–84 Seven Year Plan, was delayed a year and had to incorporate less ambitious targets. Denied imported capitalist technology, the regime had to rely on its by now outworn mobilisation methods. In addition to urging the people to use the 'speed of the 80s' to surpass previous production records, the 'media conjured up an image of a nation under siege, threatened by the United States, South Korea and Japan, and operating in a wartime atmosphere.'[50] (In fact the regime had long used militaristic language in its economic slogans, such as 'shock attack' and 'exterminatory attack'.[51]) Although officially completed on target, the Plan ran into problems in the 1980s after the industrial plants imported in the early 1970s had reached their full capacity.[52]

However, there would not be as innovative a response to the economic problems of the 1980s as there had been to the problems of the 1960s. Having squandered the 'quick fix' solution of using imported plant, the regime seemed to have little option but to institute a drastic economic restructuring, but in fact its response to the need for change would be hesitant and half-hearted. The regime's worries about the economy were not displayed until the mid-1980s, with the resort to a two-year 'adjustment' period in 1985–6 and the introduction of new economic methods. Some of these changes could be categorised as liberalising, albeit on a very limited scale. For example, private handicraft production was permitted and peasants were allowed to sell produce from their tiny (200 square-metre) private plots at local farmers' markets. The greater use of material incentives might also be categorised as a form of economic liberalisation. Such incentives were increased by allowing industrial enterprises to redistribute above-Plan-target earnings to their work force and by rewarding work teams financially for above-target production. To ensure that such financial rewards would be effective incentives, there was also a campaign to improve the supply of consumer goods available for purchase. Finally, there appears to have been a copying of the East German 'combine' system, known in North Korea as the 'associated enterprise' system, which linked together industrial enterprises in vertical or horizontal integration to form larger management units.[53]

The most striking change in policy – and also the most clear-cut liberalisation – were the minor internationalising measures that were introduced in the search for more hard-currency foreign exchange. Now the country known internationally as 'the hermit kingdom' even planned to open itself up to foreign tourists. More important from a purely economic perspective was the 1984 foreign-investment joint-venture law, which was apparently modelled on its Chinese equivalent and offered generous terms to attract foreign investors. However, in addition to all the other factors discouraging foreign investors, North Korea's reputation for unreliability in debt repayment ensured that such enticements were given a cool reception. The regime had to fall back on calls for its own outdated industries to increase exports and on new trade agreements with its traditional trading partners, the Soviet Union and China, who at least did not require payment in hard currency.[54]

Nevertheless, it is surprising that the minor liberalising economic reforms of the mid-1980s were *not* developed further in the Seven Year Plan for 1987–93. The Plan instead relied on prioritising and extolling a 'technological revolution' involving computers, robots and auto-mation – even though these were not available domestically or able to be acquired from foreign sources.[55] In reality there was nothing new in the Plan and nothing that could have been expected to pull the economy out of its historically low growth rates of about 3 per cent a year in the mid-1980s and take it back to the growth levels of the early 1970s.[56] A mobilisational emphasis on the 'speed of the 1990s' and an All People Drive to Increase Production campaign were unlikely to make much difference.[57] They could not compensate for an inefficient and technologically backward industrial sector whose isolation was excused as much as encouraged by the Juche glorification of economic self-reliance.[58] As for agriculture, the only reform of the collective-farm system that was envisaged at the end of the 1980s was that farmers were to be rewarded for extra work days.[59] There seemed to be a degree of complacency about the fact that the 'use of high-yielding seed varieties, expansion of the irrigation system, and the heavy use of fertilizers' had succeeded in making the country 'largely self-sufficient in grain production' in accordance with the Juche emphasis on economic self-reliance.[60] Although agriculture had received increased attention and resources in the 1980s, there seemed to be no appreciation of the problems – economic and environmental

– associated with an over-concentration on intensive grain farming and an over-emphasis on the use of fertiliser.[61] Instead of addressing such questions and the issue of efficient use of resources within the collective farm, the new Plan was more concerned with the ideological social goal of converting the peasantry into a rural or agricultural working class by converting the collective farms into state farms.[62] Therefore it can be argued that the 1987–93 Plan was seeking a more statist, not more liberal, economy, and in fact the transformation of the peasantry into agricultural workers would have left North Korea with the world's most statist economy.

The beginning of the 1990s saw the regime's economic problem shift from low growth to fully fledged 'recession'. (The Plan's traditional economic methods had not been able to prevent a further decline in economic growth to 2–3 per cent a year in the late 1980s.[63]) According to foreign estimates, the economy actually *shrank* by more than 3 per cent in 1990, more than 5 per cent in 1991, and more than 7 per cent in 1992.[64] The recession was largely the result of a crisis in the country's external economic relations. First the export markets in formerly Communist Eastern Europe were lost and then the Soviet Union demanded a shift to hard-currency trading relations and refused to supply any more subsidised oil. China at least deferred the implementation of its decision to adopt a similar hard-headed approach to trade with North Korea. But the new Soviet attitude had been a devastating blow, affecting some 50 per cent of North Korea's total trade, and it was largely to blame for the crisis in external trade being severe enough to provoke a more general economic crisis.[65]

The North Korean economic crisis was broad and deep. The fall in oil imports coincided with a fall in domestic coal production to create an energy crisis (which included a halving of electricity supplies) and when combined with the shortage of imported inputs needed by industry, created a steady decline in industrial output in 1991–3.[66] Agricultural production was also badly affected by the energy crisis and shortages of imported inputs, such as fertiliser and insecticide, and proved very susceptible to climatic and other physical problems.[67] In fact the biggest fall in production occurred at the outset of the recession – a fall of 12 per cent in 1990 that reduced the yield to 1.6 million tons less than what was needed to feed the country's population.[68] With production continuing to decline in subsequent years, the regime resorted to increasingly heavy food imports but these still failed to meet the population's basic needs.[69] The regime's main response to the food shortages still seemed to be the Two Meals a

Day and One Foodless Day a Month campaigns.[70] If lack of successful economic reform reduces a dictatorship's prospects for political stability, then the North Korean regime was being undermined by both a critical lack of economic success and a lack of economic reform.

Kim Il Sung did not offer North Koreans any change in economic approach in his few speeches of the early 1990s, despite the regime's official acknowledgements that the adverse international events had created economic 'problems'.[71] In his 1992 New Year's Day speech Kim promised the people 'steamed rice, meat soup, silk garments and tiled-roof houses' but the people seemed even further from that paradise on earth than when Kim had promised them exactly the same wonders in a speech thirty years earlier.[72] The regime was content with very limited and *ad hoc* changes narrowly focused on the crucial problem of foreign exchange, whose acquisition was publicly declared to be a matter of 'survival'.[73] (The country's main source of hard currency was not exports but the funds remitted by members of the large Korean community in Japan; foreign estimates of these contributions ranged from $600 million to $1.8 billion.[74]) Characteristically, the 'new economic regime' introduced in 1992 involved giving more freedom to provincial governments and industrial enterprises in the areas of, respectively, foreign trade and production of export-oriented goods.[75]

The most obvious measures that were taken to acquire foreign exchange were a further development of the 1980s move to attract foreign investment. New laws relating to foreign investment not only provided more generous terms for joint ventures but also now allowed full foreign ownership. To encourage foreigners to site their industries in North Korea, a zone of 'free economy and trade' was created and planning began for a cross-border economic zone, the ambitious UN-supported Tumen River project, which would incorporate some Chinese and Russian as well as North Korean territory. However, the overall approach was epitomised by reports in 1994 that a fifty-mile fence was to be built around the Rajin-Sonbong free economic zone, apparently to seal off this externally affected territory from the rest of North Korean society.[76] The regime's strategy was to minimise the amount of economic liberalisation, confining it to the limited internationalisation required for survival, and to seek to quarantine this internationalised element of the economy from the rest of the country.

However unenlightened this strategy may have been economically, it was a (self-interestedly) politically 'enlightened' approach for a despotic regime that had isolated and tightly controlled its society for decades. Kim Il Sung's assessment of political risks presumably compared those involved in a Chinese-style or Vietnamese-style economic restructuring with those involved in trying to ride out the downturn with minimal concessions to economic requirements. The decision to opt for a conservative rather than a reform strategy seems quite rational in the light of what has happened historically to other long-established, 'monarchical' despotisms that have opted for reform. However, Kim's policy may have been motivated by something other than just political self-interest, perhaps by a personal commitment to the ideology and its goals. For he announced in early 1994 an intention (not pursued by the regime after his death) to convert the peasants' collective farms into 'all people's ownership' (state) farms.[77] This had been an ambition of the 1987–93 Plan but apparently had been pragmatically postponed when agriculture ran into difficulties. Clearly Kim must have felt agriculture could now cope with the disruptive realisation of his ideological goal of transforming the peasantry into a rural working class. Or he must have been determined to see this goal achieved, at whatever economic and human cost, before his now inevitably imminent death. In either case this was an example of how despotism may have the ability to ignore opposition to enlightened policies but also has the ability to pursue policies based on personal misconceptions of reality or delusions of ideological grandeur.

Kim had also announced, in his 1994 New Year's Day speech, that 1994–6 was to be another one of those 'periods of adjustment' (as in 1977 and 1985–6) when the regime was not prepared to commit itself to a new economic Plan.[78] And he had gone on to declare that priority would be given to agriculture, light industry and foreign trade, not the heavy industry beloved by orthodox Communist economic planners. On the other hand, the economic downturn appeared to be bottoming out by the end of 1993,[79] and the regime had discovered some relatively 'safe' means of internationalising part of the economy, notably through contract manufacturing for export. Here North Korea had found a competitive niche in labour-intensive, high-value-added forms of light manufacturing, such as the textile industry's capture of 10 per cent of the Japanese market for men's business suits.[80] Moreover, the regime's political strategy was producing some important economic spin-offs. As was seen in an earlier chapter, the regime's intransigent stance over the nuclear issue had led to the US agreeing to provide North Korea with 500 000 tons of oil a year – a significant proportion of North Korea's needs. Furthermore, China's desire to maintain stability on the Korean peninsula at least partially explains its favourable attitude towards trade with North Korea; China was now supplying most of North Korea's oil and food imports and was allowing much of this trade to be conducted on a barter basis.[81] Political self-interest in other countries seemed likely to underpin the North Korean regime's decision to stick to orthodoxy and a bunker mentality.

5 Communist Cuba

POLITICAL STRUCTURE

The political structure of the Cuban Communist regime was relatively orthodox and most of the unusual features it displayed at the beginning of the 1980s were the legacy of its conversion in the 1960s from a nationalist-populist revolutionary military regime into a purportedly Communist regime. A revolutionary guerrilla army, the Rebel Army, had overthrown the country's military regime at the beginning of 1959 and its young leader, Fidel Castro, had taken the posts of military Commander-in-Chief and Prime Minister of a provisional revolutionary government. By the end of 1961 he had declared himself to be a Marxist-Leninist and Cuba was beginning a protracted conversion into a 'typical' Communist regime. But the continuing domination of regime and country by Castro and other former leaders of the Rebel Army left Cuba with a unique, military-party type of Communist regime which was only gradually transformed into a more orthodox Communist regime. The 1970s process known as 'institutionalisation' saw the 1975 First Party Congress's formal establishment of Party rule and the 1976 Constitution's replacement of the provisional revolutionary government with a relatively normal Communist state structure. However, Castro remained the regime's leader as not only First Secretary of the Party but also from 1976 onwards the holder of a powerful new state Presidency. His continuing possession of the military post of Commander-in-Chief and his propensity for military garb kept alive the image as well as the reality of rule by a military man – 'in many ways, the ultimate Latin American *caudillo* [military leader] of the twentieth century'.[1]

Another unusual feature of the regime's political structure was the populist and 'hands-on' style of personal rule for which Castro became famous in the 1960s. During the institutionalisation of the regime in the 1970s Castro had lost some of his personal power and had changed his style of rule, coming 'to rely more on listening, choosing and mediating than on shouting, initiating or imposing.'[2] The 1980 Second Party Congress continued the process of institutionalisation – or 'orderliness' as Castro called it when addressing the Congress. He himself was acting not as an instigator of policy but as a judge or arbiter settling disputes over policy and organisational matters. There was a continuing tendency throughout the regime to shift away from rule by 'heroic' leaders like him towards rule by leaders of organisations and towards such unheroic politics as the development of personal followings, known as 'buddy socialism', that were sometimes based upon the more material forms of patronage.[3]

But despite his setbacks and lesser prominence, Castro retained much of his public standing. His personality cult was unusual in both its relative moderation and its genuineness. Not only was he the leader and hero of the revolution but also he possessed great oratorical skills, an ascetic character, and a populist approach and affinity with the people which 'made ordinary people feel a sense of dignity and importance'.[4] In addition to his public standing he also held a state Presidency with unusually strong powers for a Communist regime.[5] Elected by the National Assembly legislature, the President headed not only the Council of Ministers but also the Council of State, which acted as the standing committee of the Assembly and thereby provided the President with various legislative powers in addition to his executive powers as head of state and government. To these were added his powers as First Secretary of the Party and as the military Commander-in-Chief of the Revolutionary Armed Forces. Another important aspect of his personal rule was that his younger brother, General Raúl Castro, was his deputy and official successor. Having been one of the senior commanders of the Rebel Army, Raúl Castro became Minister of the Revolutionary Armed Forces when they were established as the new Cuban military in 1959, and he later also acquired the posts of Party Second Secretary and state First Vice-President.

As for the rest of the regime's political structure, the only unique institution was the multi-role neighbourhood Committees for the Defence of the Revolution, which had lost some of their roles and significance by the 1980s.[6] But the municipal assemblies (the lowest level of the Organs of People's Power pyramid of elected assemblies created in 1976) were more democratic and powerful than their equivalents in other Communist countries – for example, they required that at least two candidates stand for each seat.[7] Otherwise the Cuban regime was a quite orthodox example of a Communist regime.

The most obvious *change* to the political structure in the 1980s was the return of Castro to centre stage as instigator and director of the Rectification economic programme. He initiated each new turning point in the Rectification campaign and there was a marked increase in his public appearances, whether in person or (almost daily) on television.[8] He may not have reacquired the almost absolutist degree of personal power he had enjoyed in the 1960s.[9] But he had restored his 'hands on' personal influence over even lower-level economic decisions, and the revival of a very personal form of rule was evident in the existence of a 'Commander-in-Chief's advisory committee', a personal Coordinating and Support Group and the abundance of anecdotes about Castro's personal 'micromanagement' of the economy.[10] Irrespective of whether the mid-1980s change in Castro's position was more a change of style than an increase in power, the revival of a publicly very personal form of rule was a marked change from the 'orderliness' and institutionalisation of recent years.

In contrast to the renewed prominence of its Commander-in-Chief, the military as an organisation saw a further decline in its role within the regime. The 1980 Party Congress had reduced the representation of the active-service military in the Central Committee to less than 15 per cent, and the 1985 Party Congress again reduced that representation and clearly asserted the civilian role in Party leadership.[11] Even within its own professional sphere of national defence the military was being pushed into the background. The formation of the MTT part-time militia (which by 1985 had grown to 1 million active members) was accompanied by a new 'war of all the people' doctrine of irregular war waged by the entire population against a presumably American invader.[12] The political and popular-morale requirements of such a people's war justified an increased, if not leading, role in national defence for the Party – a point that was emphasised by both Fidel and Raúl Castro. The Party launched an intensified indoctrination programme within the military (though there was still no move to give the Party a strongly supervisory role in place of the existing Soviet-style orthodoxy). Moreover, the Party's local first-secretaries were given control of the 1300 defence-zone councils that were established to lead the people's struggle against any invader. At the end of the 1980s the military suffered another blow to its prestige when the celebrated commander of the Cuban expeditionary forces in Angola, General Arnaldo Ochoa, was court-martialled and executed on charges of corruption, abuse of power and attempting to organise a drug-smuggling ring with Colombian drug barons.[13] The economic crisis of the 1990s meant that the military suffered the humiliation of having to parade with bicycles and having to grow food for its own and civilian use – becoming more concerned, in Raúl Castro's words, with 'beans than cannons'.[14] The agricultural deployment of the army in the fields was part of a wider policy of making the military not just self-sufficient but an actual contributor to the economy. By the end of the 1980s the military's Revolutionary Armed Forces Ministry already operated food-processing and clothing factories, construction firms, and even tourist facilities. In fact by the mid-1990s the military's presence in such commercial areas as the hard-currency-generating tourist industry (where it owned hotel chains and tour operations) suggested that it might be heading down the same road as the PLA in China and PAVN in Vietnam.[15]

As for the Communist Party, it did not benefit as much as might have been expected from the new emphasis on the Party's role not only in defending the country but also in leading its economic development. One of Castro's constant themes during the Rectification campaign of the later 1980s was 'the preeminence of the party over technocrats'.[16] He and other Party leaders declared that the Party was taking on a more prominent role after its loss of influence and mobilisational capacity in the early 1980s. But the Party was also to be 'improved'. By the end of 1987 over 40 per cent of grassroots-level Party secretaries had been replaced, thousands of members had been expelled from the Party, and about a quarter of the membership had been censured for various failings. After such an extensive purge, the Party was not in any shape to challenge Castro's revived personalism and the direction in which he was taking Cuba.[17]

The early 1990s saw several significant but not major changes in political structure, as when the Party reduced the size of its bureaucracy and later actually eliminated its Secretariat as a distinct Party organ. The Party also showed signs of a degree of democratisation with the introduction of secret ballots and 'choice' elections (with more candidates than posts) for Party elections. Other, seemingly more significant signs of democratisation of the political structure were the introduction of direct elections to the National Assembly, and the decision that the Party, as an organisation, would no longer participate in nominating candidates. However, the official Candidacy Commissions selected only *one* candidate per district, and the Commissions themselves were composed of representatives from the Party-controlled mass organisations. (The elections to the National Assembly also took on an apparently plebiscitary and quite nationalist atmosphere, with calls to vote 'yes for Cuba', and the selection of candidates seemed to have been tailored for such an approach, having included sporting and cultural figures and even religious leaders.) Signs of more popular participation in policy making appeared with the input in the 1991 pre-Party-Congress 'convocation' of local public meetings to air opinions and complaints (within limits), the greater role of the National Assembly in dealing with and even opposing the proposed austerity measures of 1993–4, and the 1994 'parliament in the workplace' meetings to consider such measures.[18] However, there was no indication that these were becoming institutionalised or were more than just *ad hoc* expedient manipulations of the populist tradition of the Cuban revolution.[19]

Castro's personal position seemed to have weakened in the 1990s. He could no longer rely to the same extent on his personal standing as leader, which seems to have declined markedly, especially among the young.[20] Perhaps for this reason, he maintained his military image by continuing to wear military garb, even to the United Nations Earth Summit Conference in Brazil in 1992.[21] But his constitutional position was strengthened when one of the 1992 constitutional amendments established a National Defence Council that was to be headed by the President and was to deal with internal-security as well as defence crises; it was to run the country during a state of emergency as well as in wartime, and the President was given the right to declare such a state of emergency.[22] Moreover, in the true hereditary style of monarchical personal rule the succession was being prepared – in the absence of any male offspring – for Castro's younger brother Raúl, his long-standing official successor. By 1994 the younger man was becoming increasingly prominent in public life and seemed to be taking over the day-to-day administration of the country.[23] But unlike Kim Jong Il in North Korea, Raúl Castro had for decades been securing his hold on the military. He was the last active-service General surviving from the revolutionary era and had been Minister of the Revolutionary Armed Forces since the post's inception. Therefore it appeared very likely that even after the demise of Fidel Castro, the Cuban Communist regime would continue to be headed by a military man.

IDEOLOGY

Long before the 1980s the Cuban regime's ideology seemed a typical case of orthodox Marxism-Leninism's being modified by a regime's leader or personal ruler, to produce in this case Castroism or Fidelismo. Castro acknowledges that the Cuban revolution started in 1956 with a *nationalist* orientation, developed a class orientation only during the revolutionary struggle of 1956–9, went on from there to become socialist, and finally became Marxist-Leninist in 1961.[24] What is of greater importance is that the nationalist element continued as part of Castroism even *after* the revolution became officially Marxist-Leninist. In particular, Castro continued to be an avowed follower of the nineteenth-century Cuban nationalist theorist and revolutionary, Jose Martí, who was killed in 1895 fighting against Spanish colonial rule and became known as the Apostle of Cuban independence. Castro viewed Martí 'as an anti-imperialist reformer, some of whose ideas epitomize the Cuban ethos and must be incorporated into Cuban socialism'.[25]

The official description by the 1970s was that Castro had 'effected a juncture between Martí and Marx'.[26] The most important idea or theory contributed by Martí – apart from the basic commitment to Cuban nationalism – was his warning that the United States would replace Spain as the new imperial power in relation not only to Cuba but also to Latin America as a whole. From 1959 onwards the regime had also emphasised the revolutionary and socially radical elements of Martí's writings, and during the regime's Marxist-Leninist heyday of the 1970s and early 1980s this approach developed into an official depiction of Martí as the link between Marx's thought and Cuban Marxism-Leninism. Not only in Castro's own speeches and writings but also at official congresses of the regime's various organisations Martí would seem to have been mentioned at least as much as Marx – and every village displayed a bust of Martí.

To introduce a nationalist element into Communist ideology through the medium of a nineteenth-century nationalist theorist was a unique and apparently incongruous move, but the combination of Martí and Marx does not appear to have caused ideological problems. This may have been because of Castro's emphasis that Cubanness was not to be a narrow-minded form of nationalism which sought the national interest at the expense of other countries.[27] Martí-ist nationalism did not prevent the Cuban regime from espousing a truly internationalist Marxism-Leninism which was expressed in tens of thousands of Cuban troops fighting in Ethiopia and Angola, a massive programme of civilian assistance to developing countries, and a very active role in the United Nations and the Non-Aligned Movement.[28]

As for unorthodox features within the Marxist-Leninist component of the regime's ideology, there were more than might be expected considering Castro's reputation for being an orator rather than a theorist.[29] The success of the Cuban revolution produced a new theory of Communist revolution, emphasising the rural guerrilla band and the

peasantry rather than the party and the proletariat.[30] A further ideological innovation was the notion that the guerrilla band would
continue (like the vanguard party in Leninist theory) to play a leading
role after the revolution.[31] A more esoteric modification of Marxism-
Leninism was the new doctrine of the parallel or simultaneous rather
than consecutive development of socialism and (full) communism.[32] It
was argued that instead of first concentrating on developing in a
socialist fashion the technological and economic productive capacity
for an eventual shift to a fully communist society, a communist *conciencia* (conscience/consciousness) should be instilled in the masses at
the same time as – parallel or simultaneous with – the development of
this productive capacity. Or, as Castro put it, 'communist awareness
must be developed at the same rate as the productive forces'.[33]

The emphasis on *conciencia* provided the basis for the indoctrinating
campaign to create a 'new communist man' and also for the emphasis
on the use of moral rather than material incentives to stimulate production. In practice, moral incentives took the form of honorific
collective rewards, voluntary labour, and 'fraternal competition'
between work groups – described as socialist emulation. The influence
of Che Guevara, who was second only to Castro in fame as a Rebel
Army leader, was very apparent in pushing through this approach, but
after Guevara's death in Bolivia in 1967 the banner of moral incentives
was taken up by Castro, who combined it with his strong commitment
to egalitarianism. Nevertheless, the 1970s shift to a more orthodox
economic approach was accompanied by an official admission that the
doctrine of parallel development had been mistaken. There was now a
retreat to the orthodox doctrine of progressing through a distinct
socialist stage before attaining communism, and the introduction of a
new system of material incentives was justified in 1973 by reference to
the socialist distributive ideal of 'to each according to his work'.[34]
However, the emphasis on *conciencia* would return with the Rectification campaign of the 1980s.

The Rectification campaign stands out as the obvious ideological
change of the 1980s–90s but it is difficult to discern in Rectification
any new ideological themes as distinct from the revival of 1960s
concerns. Rectification was often seen as reviving Guevarist thinking,
such as the emphasis on moral incentives and voluntary work, and
Castro reasserted his long-standing opposition to economic
inequality. There was also a revived ideological focus on *conciencia*,
especially in opposition to money-making and self-interest (though
this was phrased more often in terms of revolutionary consciousness

than a parallel communist consciousness). While not as significant as the Rectification campaign, several quite new ideological themes were also discernable in the 1980s–90s. A less hostile attitude to religion became apparent as Castro moved in 1985 to find common ground with Catholicism and other religions; by the 1990s Christmas and Easter services were being broadcast, the Party had relinquished its commitment to atheism and allowed 'believers' to become Party members, and the Constitution now guaranteed religious freedoms.[35] As part of the inclusive approach adopted in the 1990s, the Constitution and the Party discarded the use of the Marxist term 'proletariat' or 'worker' in favour of 'people'.[36] And the downplaying of Marxism-Leninism in favour of nationalism was so marked that it seems virtually a new theme within the regime's overall ideology.

Nationalism, predictably, was used to depict the siege-like 'special period' response to economic crisis as being one more battle in Cuba's long struggle for true independence.[37] The Martí nationalist heritage, in particular, was given such prominence, at the expense of Marxism-Leninism, that it became perhaps the most important ideological theme of the 1990s.[38] The 1991 Fourth Party Congress proclaimed the Party to be 'the sole party of the Cuban nation, *martiano*, Marxist and Leninist'.[39] And Castro justified one-party rule not in Leninist terms but by referring to the single party founded by Martí to pursue the independence war against Spain.[40] Marxism-Leninism seemed of little relevance or interest to the regime. The adaptation of Marxism-Leninism to fit present needs (for example, reinterpreting 'internationalism' to mean maintaining the Cuban revolution as a bastion of socialism[41]) had not proved as meaningful as the appeal to the nationalist tradition. What remained of official Communist theory was focused on Castro's pronouncements, and although sloganising 'socialism or death', labelling himself an 'inflexible socialist' and proclaiming Cuba to be 'the last bastion of socialism', Castro himself did not use Marxism-Leninism to analyse such key questions as the international collapse of Communism or the nature of the 'special period'.[42] The revolution had apparently returned to the nationalist, populist and socialist attitudes of pre-1961.

ECONOMIC POLICY

By the 1980s the Cuban economy had become a quite orthodox, Soviet-style Communist economy, built upon sugar exports and the generous trading relationship that it enjoyed with the Soviet Union and the rest of the Comecon economic block. (The agricultural sector, though, was an incongruous and unique combination of large state farms, often sugar plantations, small to medium-sized private farms, and a relatively small number of collective farms.) In the 1960s the Cuban regime had developed a more leftist form of Communist economy, with the use of moral incentives and relatively egalitarian material rewards. The 1970 failure of mass-mobilising methods to reach the vaunted propaganda goal of a 10-million-ton sugar harvest had provoked a shift to more orthodox Communist methods, such as the use of bonuses and other material incentives, and in 1976 the first Five Year Plan was begun. The shift to orthodoxy had also been encouraged by the failure of the short-lived move back to extensive trading ties with the capitalist world when international sugar prices boomed in the early 1970s. The collapse of sugar prices a few years later left Cuba with a large hard-currency foreign debt and a need to earn hard currency through exports, foreign investment and tourism in order to service this debt – and a renewed dependence on the Soviet Union. The Soviet model's influence upon economic policy was apparent in Cuba's adoption of a new system, SDPE, that copied the Soviet economic reform of 1965 in using decentralisation and profitability to improve enterprises' efficiency. The shift to the right in economic policy was also apparent in the later 1970s in the removal of rationing from many consumer goods and the legalisation of self-employment in construction and service industries.

The 1980s opened badly for the regime, with unavoidable evidence that it was not meeting the expectations of a large segment of its society. The 'Mariel boatlift' occurred when the regime was provoked into authorising the mass emigration of disaffected citizens through the port of Mariel, from where they were picked up by thousands of small boats manned by Cuban exiles. The number of people who took advantage of the boatlift, some 125 000, was a shock to the regime and was a worrying indication of how little support it enjoyed. The regime's upper ranks have been described as 'shaken', 'disoriented' and as having experienced a 'traumatic event'.[43] One of the byproducts of the Mariel boatlift was the move to improve the supply of fruit and vegetables by allowing farmers to sell their produce to the public in (free) 'farmers' markets'.[44]

However, few other significant changes in economic policy were made in the early 1980s, probably because the economy seemed to be operating reasonably well under the new, orthodox approach of the

Five Year Plans. While the rest of Latin America was experiencing actual declines in economic output, the Cuban economy was exceeding the Second Five Year Plan (1981–5) targets with a growth rate averaging more than 7 per cent a year.[45] Whatever changes in policy that did occur can usually be seen as continuing the shift towards an orthodox Soviet-style Communist economy and away from the leftism of the 1960s. The state's parallel markets (where normally rationed consumer goods were freely available at much higher prices) were expanded to compete with the farmers' markets, and private plots were reintroduced on state farms.[46] The state farms were enlarged to an average 14 000 hectares and the still voluntary collectivisation process was speeded up, rapidly reducing the number of private farms still in existence.[47] Most importantly, the implementation of the SDPE system was completed. Formally introduced in 1977 as part of the first Five Year Plan, many of the SDPE's core elements were not introduced until 1979–80 and (like the systematic use of material incentives in the workplace) were not fully operational until the 1980s.[48] The new system sought to encourage greater efficiency by decentralising more decisions to the enterprise level, by rewarding profitability rather than just quantitative production, and by encouraging the use of markets in some areas of an enterprise's operations.[49]

By the mid-1980s, though, there were obvious problems with the economy and major changes were in the offing. In 1985 high-ranking discontent with the direction of the economy was indicated by the sacking of the head of the Central Planning Board. He was dismissed because there was 'insufficient plan discipline and too much reliance on the market' and because his policies appeared to have produced serious balance of payments problems.[50] There had been continued efforts in recent years to promote export growth and diversification and to attract foreign investment, notably through the quite generous terms of the 1982 investment code. Yet the country's current account in hard currency had plunged from a comfortable surplus to an almost equally uncomfortable deficit in 1983–4, which in turn had more than doubled in 1985.[51]

The Third Party Congress, postponed until February 1986, saw the dismissal of many other high-ranking economic specialists and a scathing attack by Castro on economic policy and performance in his report to the Congress. In addition to a litany of complaints about long-standing failings, such as poor quality goods, he attacked some of the side-effects of the SDPE, such as the pricing policies adopted by enterprises in their attempt to increase profitability. He argued that simply raising prices was not a meaningful way of increasing an enterprise's efficiency and profitability (particularly in light of Cuba's lack of market-set pricing). As for the SPDE as a whole, he criticised the slavish copying of foreign (that is, Soviet) experiences and the failure to adapt the system to Cuban conditions. Castro's view seemed to be that there was indeed a need to improve economic efficiency but that decentralisation and the use of markets was the wrong method of doing so – at least in Cuban conditions. However, the Congress ended without conclusively dealing with this economic issue because Castro 'either had trouble imposing his views... or he had not made up his mind altogether'.[52] He was either unsure about his despotic position and the political risks involved in forcing the issue or unsure about what would be the enlightened solution to the problems he had highlighted at the Congress.[53]

Whether Castro's hesitation was owing to a lack of political self-confidence or a lack of intellectual self-confidence, the political and economic *opportunity* for him to impose his own views was greater now than at any time since the 1960s. 'Castro's ability to override opinions that contradicted his own was at its most limited in the early 1970s' as the regime began its shift to more orthodox economic policies; by the mid-1980s, with some of these policies 'faltering', he had 'the opportunity once again to redirect the course of the Revolution personally.'[54] He could more easily override vested interests and ideological belief in the existing, orthodox economic policies the more obviously these policies failed to solve the country's increasing economic problems. And during 1986 the country's trading problems were being transformed into a fully fledged foreign exchange crisis. Castro had warned the Party Congress in February that Cuba was facing a serious shortfall of hard-currency earnings, in large part because of a fall in world prices for two of the country's principal exports.[55] The 1980–5 decline in sugar prices had cut hard-currency earnings from sugar exports by 80 per cent and during 1986 there would be a calamitous 50 per cent fall in Cuba's earnings from the re-exporting of surplus Soviet oil imports, which in recent years had contributed almost twice the amount of hard-currency earnings that sugar exports had produced.[56] Thus Cuba's overall hard-currency export earnings would be almost halved in 1986, and the country would be unable to secure a new hard-currency loan.[57] By July Cuba would be forced to suspend interest as well as principal payments to its Western creditors.[58]

Only two months after the inconclusive Party Congress of February 1986, Castro moved to impose his own, leftist, solution to the country's problems. Whether as a more intellectually self-confident despot or a more securely despotic ruler, Castro was intent on implementing a new economic approach that was very different from the 'enlightened' liberalising approach being adopted in so many other parts of the world in the 1980s. In a speech in April he returned to his Congress themes and in more extreme language. The depth and breadth of his attack on the present approach to economic policy (and implicitly on any liberalising approach) was revealed in his claims that the revolution's glories had not been based on money and that market mechanisms only built capitalism. He again attacked managers for seeking to increase profitability by simply raising prices and he also accused them of bureaucratic sectionalism (promoting their industry's interests without regard for national interest), of corruption, and of corrupting workers, too, through the over-use of incentive bonuses. This was only the first of five very aggressive speeches in which he would call for a shift in the country's approach to economic policy – for a 'strategic counteroffensive' against the recent 'liberal-bourgeois' period of 'bitter experiences'.[59] The first shots fired in this counter-offensive were aimed at the epitome of market money-making by capitalists. The farmers' markets were abolished in May and new limits were put on the privatising self-employment measures of the 1970s. Soon a more technical, economic target emerged. Attention was increasingly focused on the wasteful use of resources, the lack of coordination among sectors of the economy, and even labour indiscipline and overstaffing. The Party, the media and public meetings, especially workplace meetings, were used to expose waste and other mismanagement practices as well as actual corruption. But the ideological and social, the moral and revolutionary, dimensions of the campaign would not be lost as it took on a more formal status.[60]

In his May speech announcing the reversal of the decision to allow farmers' markets, Castro had talked of the need for the 'rectification' of such errors of judgement, and by mid-year his new campaign was being termed one to 'rectify errors and negative tendencies'.[61] The title became truly official when a second session of the Third Party Congress was held in December to approve the Rectification of Errors and Negative Tendencies campaign – and to call for the renewal of 'moral principles and *conciencia*'.[62] For the campaign was also re-emphasising such 1960s ideas as *conciencia*, moral incentives and voluntary labour.[63] The moral incentives largely took the banal form of 'exhorting everyone to raise their revolutionary consciousness and to let the general social interest guide their behaviour.'[64] But the renewed prominence of moral incentives and of *conciencia* in general could also be seen in the reintroduction of defunct types of voluntary labour, notably the construction mini-brigades, and in calls for voluntary labour on community projects.[65] Another move reminiscent of the 1960s was the new policy of holding down middle-class income in favour of the lower classes, as Castro had claimed that 'stretching the wage scales too much was intolerable and resembled capitalism'.[66] Such egalitarianism was also seen in his condemnation of the increasing inequality that had been caused by not just self-employed activities and the farmers' markets but also the awarding of excessive bonuses to managers and workers.[67] The use of material incentives in this fashion was accused of tending to produce capitalist levels of inequality and selfishness/greed, and of undermining political and social consciousness and commitment.[68]

However, Castro was not calling for simply a return to the policies of the 1960s, 'which he and other revolutionary leaders still considered a period of idealistic illusions'.[69] Moreover, even in the apparently most ideological elements of Rectification it was also possible to discern, as Castro himself indicated, a practical dimension directly related to the exigencies of the economic crisis.[70] The apparently egalitarian increase in the minimum wage compensated the low income groups for the disproportionate effects on them of the austerity programme.[71] The egalitarian/moral cutback and crackdown on managerial and worker perquisites and bonuses, the emphasis on moral rather than material incentives, and the use of voluntary (unpaid) labour can all be seen as money-saving elements of the austerity programme. They were providing a more moralistic or altruistic complement to the cutbacks in production of consumer goods, the increase in their prices and the increased charges for transport and other public services.[72] Such practical or expedient aspects seem to overshadow any leftist aspect to such policies as: tightening central control of the economy in order to allocate and minimise the use of hard currency; strengthening the tourist industry in order to acquire more hard currency; and instituting an austerity programme to cope with the reduction in Western imports, to free up more 'surplus' consumption for export, and to ease the pressure on the state's budget.[73] Similarly, it is difficult to see any leftist aspect in some of the more technical concerns of Rectification. Amongst its wide-ranging technical–economic goals were 'high productivity, commitment to quality, labor discipline...efficiency, conservation of resources, honest professional management, and respect for the consumer-public'.[74] To take one example, there was a strong interest in copying American and Japanese methods of efficiently and flexibly organising the use of labour, with Castro calling for administrators who had mastered 'the science of organization and management'.[75]

Therefore the Rectification campaign was more than a Castroist ideological revival; it was also putting forward a 'practical' economic alternative to orthodox Communist economic policies and to a liberalising economic restructuring. Rectification was an unsystematic, Castro-determined 'programme' which did not offer long-term solutions to Cuba's problematic economy.[76] But it was also something more than the 'bunker' approach that would be adopted by the North Korean regime, and it was the only alternative approach to liberalising economic restructuring/reform that was ever developed and implemented in the 1980s. From a politically self-interested perspective, Rectification was a high-risk strategy for Castro and his regime, as he had linked his credibility and that of the Communist regime very publicly to this untried and unfashionable or 'unenlightened' approach. As in the case of Kim Il Sung in the 1990s, it seems that a personal ideological commitment may well have played a large part in the decision to reject the internationally prevalent option of liberalising economic reform and in this case to attempt a very different type of reform.

Rectification proved to be a short-term success in so far as a slight surplus in the hard-currency trade balance was achieved in 1987–8, but it came at the cost of a large increase in (suppliers' credits) foreign debt, the virtual stagnation of the economy, and the decline in living standards associated with the austerity programme.[77] Moreover, Rectification's lack of longer-term solutions to such basic underlying problems as dependence on sugar and the Soviet Union would soon be displayed when a far worse external blow hit the economy at the end of the 1980s. In addition to the collapse of trade with formerly Communist Eastern Europe, Cuba saw no less than 70 per cent of its trade endangered by the Soviet Union's winding down of its generous trading arrangements; Castro would later describe the loss of Soviet preferential trade and other aid as a 'treacherous, devastating blow'.[78] Castro stated in 1991 that Soviet exports to Cuba were less than 40 per cent of the agreed amount, and the crucial oil deliveries may have fallen to an even lower level.[79] With the disintegration of the Soviet

Union itself at the end of the year, the former Soviet trade virtually evaporated, leaving Cuba to survive in 1992 on only a quarter of the imports that it had enjoyed in 1989.[80] By the following year the economy had shrunk to only 60 per cent of its 1989 size.[81] In fact the sheer enormity of the new crisis, together with its external origins and political implications, probably obscured in most people's minds any question of whether Rectification had been a success.

The regime responded in 1990 to the new crisis by declaring 'a special period (in peacetime)', virtually a war economy in peacetime, and even mentioned in September 1991 the possibility of the 'Zero Option' of existing without imports.[82] The use of Five Year Plans was abandoned in favour of a yet more stringent austerity programme and desperate attempts to earn foreign exchange. Although by the end of 1994 it would appear to a foreign observer that the regime was very slowly implementing a typical IMF structural adjustment pro-gramme,[83] the Special Period seems much more like an *ad hoc* emergency response within the context of Rectification. The Special Period measures 'were seen as piecemeal reforms arising out of the emergency created by the loss of the Soviet connection; as in time of war, economic decisions had to be improvised.'[84] Any liberalising economic reforms were 'the product not so much of new thinking about the economic system as the regime's sheer need for survival.'[85]

The austerity programme included such predictable measures as reintroduction of rationing for virtually all foodstuffs and consumer goods. But it also included such extreme measures to increase food production as encouraging the creation of urban vegetable gardens and reassigning under-employed factory workers, civil servants and Party bureaucrats to working in agriculture. Other austerity measures were: cutting the electricity supply by several hours a day, cutting back television broadcasting hours, reducing private petrol supplies by half, making large reductions in bus and taxi transportation, and encouraging people to use bicycles and horse-drawn transport. Some of the austerity measures were simply a matter of necessity, such as the lack of imported inputs forcing half of the country's factories to shut down or operate at much reduced capacity.[86]

Attempts to acquire the desperately needed foreign exchange pre-dictably included offering more generous terms to attract foreign investment, with foreign investors now allowed a majority share-holding in joint ventures. That tourism proved the most attractive area for foreign investment was partly because of Cuba's competitive advantages (beaches) but partly, too, because of the problems of running a business within the Cuban economy and of coping with the US economic embargo against Cuba. The failure to attract extensive foreign investment even led to talk of allowing Cuban-American investment, and the 1993 legalisation of US dollars was presumably an attempt to beat the black market to the pool of remittance money sent from Cuban-Americans to their relatives, which was estimated to exceed the net revenue from tourism. A combination of foreign-currency needs and pressure on the state budget seems to have motivated the 1993 shift to self-financing and more autonomy, parti-cularly in hard currency and exporting, for about a quarter of the state enterprises. The conversion of thousands of state farms into collectives also seems to have been a budget-driven measure, as col-lectives did not receive the same scale of subsidies as state farms. With the budget deficit about three times as great in 1993 as in 1989, there was even talk of charging for some of Cuba's vaunted social services.[87]

Yet there were still obvious ideological limits on the direction, extent and speed of these emergency responses to the crisis. Despite their proven ability to improve the food supply, the reintroduction of farmers' markets was not included in the relatively radical measures introduced in 1993, such as the renewed expansion of legalised self-employment.[88] The new year did not bring any further liberalisation; there was actually a crackdown on self-employed street vendors and restaurateurs.[89] But later in 1994 a delayed programme of budgetary measures brought more reductions in subsidies to industry and agri-culture and there was finally approval for the ideologically fraught reintroduction of farmers' markets.[90]

However, the reintroduction of the farmers' markets in September seems to have been less a concession to the need for economic reform than a 'knee-jerk' political reaction to the 5 August Havana riots, in which the rioters had ended up chanting for food and looting shops.[91] The riots were on a small scale and had broken out apparently only because of frustration about being thwarted in an attempt to use the regime's main safety valve for popular discontent – joining the increasing exodus of 'raft people' seeking a better life across the Florida Straits in the United States.[92] In a sense Cuba was back to the situation of the 1980 Mariel boatlift and the liberalising intro-duction of farmers' markets that it had provoked. But the economic situation was now far worse and the regime had so far responded with only hesitant, *ad hoc*, limited and as yet unsuccessful reforms. The lack of massive publicly expressed discontent – and of any form of political instability – again suggests that successful economic reform is by no means a necessary condition for a stable dictatorship.

6 Baathist Syria

POLITICAL STRUCTURE

By the 1980s the Syrian political structure was in most features quite close to the orthodox Baathist model of a party-state regime, with its virtually Leninist or Communist-style political structure (see Appendix II). The main deviation from orthodoxy was that the regime was headed by a military man and was actually a military-party regime. A 1970 coup had brought Defence Minister (General) Hafiz al-Asad to power, after years of factional squabbling within the Baathist regime that had been established after a 1963 military coup. The struggle for power in the 1960s between rival military-civilian alliances within the new Baathist regime had already led to an internal coup in 1966 that had brought a left-wing faction of Baath officers to power – establishing what is sometimes referred to as the 'Neo-Baath regime'. But in 1970 a moderate member of the Neo-Baathists, the aforementioned General Asad, had staged what was to be the last act of instability within Syrian Baathist rule for more than 25 years.[1]

He had also brought about another major deviation from Baathist orthodoxy by establishing a degree of personal rule. It was in turn based on such unusual features for a Leninist political structure as the existence of a very powerful state Presidency. Created by Asad in 1971 and strengthened by the 1973 Constitution, the Presidency incorporated the powers of head of state and of an overarching head of government responsible not only for appointing/dismissing the Prime Minister and other members of the Council of Ministers but also for establishing the state's general policy and supervising its implementation. The President's legislative powers went beyond a right of veto to include the right to legislate between parliamentary sessions and whenever the national interest made it necessary.[2]

The President was also constitutionally the 'supreme leader of the army and armed forces',[3] with appointment powers that Asad used to control the transfer and promotion of officers to key posts.[4] (He was also able to supervise the regime's policy of reducing the likelihood of coups by exacerbating divisions between different types of unit and officer.[5]) Therefore he had relinquished little real power over the military when he retired in 1972 from his post as Defence Minister and from active-service in the military.[6] Moreover, although he

usually wore civilian clothes, he retained the rank of Lieutenant-
General and remained the only holder of such high rank within the
Syrian armed forces.[7] In accordance with his professional military
background, Asad had not used the Baathist ideal of an 'ideological
army' as a basis for using the Party to control the military. Although
the great majority of the officer corps were Party members, Asad had
actually reduced the Party's activities within the military, and the
army's Political Department and its military-trained political officers
were concerned solely with ideological indoctrination.[8]

The Party performed a stronger supervisory role than this in relation to the civil service, and also had the important role of ensuring
that Asad would continue to be nominated as President by the
People's Assembly and to win the more than 99 per cent 'yes' vote
from the people in the confirming referendum.[9] Asad was assured of
being nominated by the Party as he held the leadership posts of both
(international) National General Secretary and (national) Regional
Secretary and had carried out a Stalin-like centralisation of control
over the Party which ensured it was an obedient instrument of his
personal rule.[10] The Party's Politburo-like Regional Command, comprising key governmental, military and Party figures, was still, though,
the only collective body with which Asad met on a regular basis to
discuss and decide policy – over which, of course, he had the final
say.[11] (Its formally vital position in the political structure was symbolised by its constitutional role of recommending a presidential
nominee to the People's Assembly.[12]) Even in the 1990s the Regional
Command continued to meet weekly to discuss policy matters but
were now being joined only rarely by the President, whenever he
wished to consult with them on important policy issues.[13]

In addition to being buttressed by his Party, Asad's personal rule
was supported by a modest but successful personality cult. It was
founded upon his impressive leadership in the 1973 war with Israel
and the economic prosperity and political stability that the country
had enjoyed under his low-key, measured and moderate form of
rule.[14] Party leaders hailed his exemplary leadership of Syria domestically and internationally, and he came to be depicted as a leader of
the Arab world and a statesman of truly international stature – an
evaluation shared 'by a great many Syrians (and many other
Arabs)'.[15]

An unorthodox but hardly unusual feature of the structure of Asad's
personal rule was the role played by his religious/ethnic minority, tribe
and family. Asad belonged to the Alawite sect of the Shiite branch of

Islam, which comprised about 12 per cent of the Syrian population (most Syrians being members of the Sunni branch of Islam).[16] Even before Asad's 1970 coup, Alawites dominated the military's officer corps, and although he made an effort to appoint more Sunnis to senior and junior posts, by the 1980s they were still outnumbered by Alawites.[17] The Alawites had also historically had a disproportionate presence in the Baathist movement, only in part because of their dominance of its military wing.[18] But Asad ensured that Sunnis were properly represented in civilian posts at the top of the Party and particularly in the government – all his Prime Ministers and most of his Ministers were Sunnis.[19] In contrast, Alawites filled most of the positions in his many military and civilian security/intelligence networks and organisations.[20] Asad also relied on members of his tribe, one of four within the Alawite community, and on members of his family to hold key posts in his security and intelligence network and to man key bodyguard/security military units. His small al-Matawirah tribe contributed the heads of the Presidential Intelligence Committee and of Military Intelligence as well as a large number of the ordinary members of the 1000-man Struggle Companies and 12 000-man Defence Companies; his brother Rifat commanded the Defence Companies (in which another brother and two nephews held important posts) and his cousin Adnan commanded the Struggle Companies.[21]

There were few, if any, *changes* to the regime structure in the 1980s–90s. The gradual transition from military rule seemed to be continuing, with a further reduction in the role of 'political' officers in top Party and government posts. More subtle indications of gradual demilitarisation were a) the military's declining importance as a recruiting ground for senior regime personnel and as a means of upward social mobility for minority groups, and b) the tendency for sons of the military elite to avoid a military career in favour of civilian, especially business, opportunities.[22] But the decline in the military's political role did not lead to a stronger governing role for the Party. Instead, the Party was gradually removed not only from the centre of policy making but also from the public domain, being increasingly 'forced to keep a low profile, most conspicuously so during the presidential campaign of 1991 from which it was virtually absent'.[23] An obvious symptom of its declining prestige was the lack of a Party Congress after 1985, and another symptom was the continuation into the 1980s of the rapid expansion of Party membership to mass levels that were quite contrary to the Baathist ideal of an elite vanguard party.[24]

The 1990s brought signs of a degree of democratisation. Some twenty years earlier Asad had set up the representative assemblies/councils required by the Baathist notion of popular democracy. He had also allowed a degree of supposed multi-partyism by establishing the National Progressive Front, composed of the Baathists and three other 'progressive' parties: the Communist Party, the (Nasserist) Arab Socialist Union, and the Arab Socialist Movement.[25] The Baath-dominated Front had from then on chosen the official candidates for election to the People's Assembly. But the 1990 elections saw the Front leave 30–40 per cent of the 250 seats 'open' to competition among non-Front parties/groups and independent candidates.[26] Even the Front-allocated seats were made more representative by the expansion of the Front to include three other political groups, one of them with an Islamic orientation.[27] The independents who won election included a number of businessmen, which rectified the previously marked underrepresentation of the private sector.[28] However, all candidates had to be officially approved and the independent forming of parties, even if fully committed to Asad, was not tolerated, as was illustrated during the elections when three such parties were forced to dissolve themselves.[29] In any case, the reserving of virtually two-thirds of the seats for the Front's selected candidates meant that the system was still not even semi-competitive. The 1994 elections saw no further progress towards such a semi-competitive democratisation; businessmen strengthened their representation among the independents but the Front was still allocated two-thirds of the seats.[30] This lack of progress confirmed suggestions that, for all Asad's emphasising of the importance of the Front and the People's Assembly, the supposed democratisation was only cosmetic or a safety valve.[31] Moreover, what has been described as the Assembly's 'new consultative-participatory function' was confined to issues relating to 'the economy and the daily affairs of the people'.[32] Even in this limited sphere only individuals or groups, not the Assembly collectively, have opposed the government's bills, and the Assembly's amendments require in practice government consent.[33]

Counterbalancing the marginal degree of democratisation, the regime was also moving towards an almost monarchical degree of personal rule.[34] A sympathetic biographer of Asad acknowledges that in the 1980s he became 'more an object of orchestrated adulation than he had been in the 1970s' as, for example, the portraits and invocations of his name became yet more common.[35] Although the actual titles or honorifics bestowed upon him by the personality cult were not very extravagant, the most significant were 'our leader into eternity' or 'our leader forever',[36] as they unconsciously raised the key question of who would succeed him. And here the monarchical aspect of Asad's personal rule became very obvious. In the early 1980s it seemed that his younger brother Rifat was a likely successor, but his premature move to take over from a sick Asad in 1983–4 removed him from consideration, leaving attention to be focused on Asad's eldest son, Basil. Although 'never officially named as successor', this young officer seemed to be being groomed for the succession.[37] He became involved in affairs of state, enjoyed his own personality cult, and developed a following in the security services after being put in charge of security at the presidential palace in 1986.[38] He was also building a strong military profile as a member of the General Staff and (in the 1990s) *de facto* commander of the military's large 'praetorian guard', the Republican Guard.[39] The contrast with his lack of any significant Party role indicated that while all other military aspects of the regime may have evaporated, there was still a need for Asad's potential successor to be a military man rather than a civilian Party leader. In January 1994 Basil was killed in a car accident, but the monarchical aspect of the regime was soon dramatically confirmed when attention was shifted to Asad's second son, the 29-year-old Bashar, who appeared to be becoming the new heir apparent. Although trained as an ophthalmologist, Bashar graduated from the military academy later in 1994 and so he, too, would be able to continue the tradition of military leadership of the Syrian Baathist regime.[40]

IDEOLOGY

By the 1980s Asad's regime had shown little obvious inclination to stray from Baathist ideological orthodoxy. Even the one significant and officially recognised ideological innovation, the Corrective Movement, purportedly returned Baathism to its true or pure course. Asad ideologically justified his 1970 coup against the left-wing Neo-Baathist regime by accusing it of having deviated from the true Baathist path and by claiming that he had taken power in order to return the Baath party to its 'pure' course.[41] At the 1971 (international) National Party Congress he officially characterised the coup as a 'corrective movement' carried out within the revolution and seeking only to restore the revolution to its true path.[42] (See Appendix II for explanation of international National Baath Party and national

Regional Baath Parties.) But the Congress did incorporate a new
element into the Syrian interpretation of Baathism by also explicitly
affirming that the struggle against Israel was to have the highest
priority.[43] The (national) Regional Congresses of 1971 and 1975, too,
'formally approved this major ideological revision', arguing that the
key social contradiction was the national one between the Arabs and
Israelis, and that 'the main priority for which "all resources must be
mobilized" was the recovery of the occupied territories, and hence all
lesser social contradictions had to be subordinated to this national
aim'.[44] Asad did not use this virtual 'blank cheque' to reverse,
rather than just halt, the leftist momentum of the 1960s. But from
now on any economic measures which went beyond 'correction' of
Neo-Baath leftism were easily justified by Asad as a more efficient
mobilisation of resources for defence and as a strengthening of
national unity by offering the commercial classes a place in Syria's
future.[45]

As such concern with national unity and strength in the struggle
against Israel could be viewed as an example of the 'Syria first'
deviation from Pan-Arab Baathist orthodoxy, the regime was careful
to claim that a 'unified Syrian people would in turn constitute a solid
basis for Pan-Arab unity' and for 'the struggle against Zionism,
imperialism and reactionary Arab regimes'.[46] Asad was able to make
much of Syria's front-line status in the Arab struggle against Israel,
particularly after Egypt's withdrawal from the struggle.[47] Nevertheless, a form of more narrowly Syrian nationalism began to develop
as an implicit part of the regime's ideology. The emphasis on
Syrianness, irrespective of Arabness, was reflected in the prominence
given to archaeological finds revealing the antiquity and glories of
Syrian civilisation, such as the excavation of the 4500-year-old site
at Ebla. In addition to providing a means of matching Israel's
claims to ancient heritage and legitimacy, the official promotion of
Syria's archaeological heritage contributed to nation-building and
boosting national pride. 'The often heard theme that history had
placed Syria at the centre of the world was an indirect way of saying
that it lay today at the centre of regional power and decision-
making.'[48]

An even less official form of Syrian nationalism was the notion of
Greater Syria. The term 'Greater' was not chauvinist but geographical
in nature. It referred to the goal of politically uniting the sovereign
states and territories lying within the extensive geographical region
known as 'historic' Syria that has existed as a recognised geographical

region ever since the word 'Syria' first originated thousands of years ago, in ancient Greek.[49] Although it has never yet existed as a political entity, historic Syria would now incorporate the states of Syria, Jordan, Israel and Lebanon, the Palestinian territories of the West Bank and Gaza Strip, and a part of south-eastern Turkey. A moderate form of Greater Syrian nationalism could readily be accommodated within Baathist Pan-Arab ideology, and Asad appears to have implicitly taken this step in the later 1970s. In rhetorical conflict with Israel over the Golan Heights he declared that Palestine was itself 'a principal part of southern Syria', and during a political tiff with King Hussein he referred to Jordan as 'a territory carved out of Syria by the British'.[50] That the notion of Greater Syria had been 'quietly absorbed' by Asad's regime became most evident, though, in its use to legitimise the Syrian military intervention in the Lebanese civil war.[51] It is not surprising that some foreign opponents and analysts claimed that Asad was actively seeking to establish a Greater Syria in the region.[52]

In the 1980s and early 1990s the regime's ideology saw few significant *changes*. The notion of Greater Syria continued to be evident in the early 1980s in relation to propaganda in Lebanon and in the domestic schooling of the next generation.[53] But thereafter the notion seemed to have lost favour. Asad in 1985 made it clear that his regime recognised Syria and Lebanon as two separate states inhabited by the one (Arab) people, and his favoured Western biographer declared that 'Asad was no convert to pan-Syrian romanticism'.[54] Syrian nationalism was restricted to the existing state of Syria and to relying on such well-established themes as Syria's role as the leader and main burden-bearer of the Arab struggle against Israel.[55] Even foreign analysts who continued to see Greater Syria as Asad's ideological goal in the region acknowledged that such a goal no longer involved territorial unification but only a federation of states or dominion over Greater Syrian satellite states.[56]

Although Asad had never been a doctrinaire socialist,[57] neither did he show any enthusiasm for a major revision of Baathist economic doctrines to accompany the liberalising economic reforms introduced in the 1980s and 1990s. For example, it was representatives of the business sector, not Asad, who began to talk of an economic *infitah*, an 'opening up' of the economy.[58] Asad's ideological conservatism was evident in his claim that he had already instituted a Syrian form of *perestroika* (that is, the Corrective Movement) in the 1970s, long before Gorbachev's *perestroika* restructuring campaign, and therefore by implication that Syrians should not expect anything more from him.[59] The official media took a dismissive or negative attitude towards the Soviet Union's *perestroika* and the economic reforms occurring in the Third World. The Soviet economic restructuring was deemed irrelevant to Syria because the local brand of socialism had always retained a large role for the private sector in agriculture and commerce.[60] The Third World economic reforms were denounced as Western attempts to penetrate developing countries' economies with 'international capitalist monopolies'.[61]

However, the collapse of Communism in Eastern Europe and the Soviet Union weakened the position of ideological opposition to economic liberalisation,[62] and some adjustment to new international and domestic realities became evident in the 1990s. The 'official ideological bias toward the public sector was replaced by a recognition of the importance of all sectors', with the new term 'economic pluralism' all but replacing the old Baathist concept of the 'leading role of the public sector'.[63] These ideological revisions extended to re-emphasising the politically and economically more liberal aspect of Baathist ideology that had been pushed into the background in the 1960s.[64] Even Asad himself in 1992 publicly conformed to the increasing use of the new term 'pluralist' democracy rather than the old Baathist term 'popular' democracy.[65] He also told the People's Assembly that the Syrian form of democracy – as distinct from other countries' concepts of democracy – was in essence a combination of political and economic pluralism.[66]

ECONOMIC POLICY

The avowedly socialist Syrian economy of the 1980s incorporated extensive state ownership of finance and large industry as well as tight state control over the whole economy. A sweeping nationalisation of banks and industry had been carried out in 1965 by the first Baathist regime. Agriculture had seen a redistributive land reform years before the Baathists came to power, and they had planned to develop land reform into a system of cooperatives and then, ultimately, collective farms. This plan had been implicitly abandoned after Asad took power, and in the 1980s only a third of cultivated land was cooperatively (let alone collectively) farmed, but the state maintained control over agriculture through state procurement and pricing.[67] Agricultural production, especially cotton exports, played a more important part in the economy than in such oil-based (and much wealthier) economies as Libya's and Iraq's.[68] Nevertheless, the oil industry, run by the state-owned Syrian Petroleum Company, earned the majority of the country's foreign exchange and was a lucrative source of public revenue. Increases in world oil prices and Syrian oil production in the 1970s, together with aid grants from oil-rich Arab states, had fuelled rapid economic growth, with annual rates of close to 10 per cent in the mid-1970s.[69]

But the 1980s would provide a much more difficult environment for growth as sources of foreign exchange dried up. While per capita GDP had almost doubled in the 1970s, it would decline by nearly 20 per cent during the 1980s in what has been described as 'a lost decade for the country's social and economic development'.[70] Although the regime would respond with a programme of economic reform, the reform process would not build up any momentum until late in the decade.

By the end of 1985 a few minor economic reforms had been instituted in order to cope with the developing foreign-exchange problem but there was no indication that any major economic reforms were envisaged. An austerity programme, publicly described as belt-tightening or self-reliance, had been forced on the regime by shortages of foreign exchange. The foreign-exchange problem in turn stemmed in large part from the decline in the volume and prices of oil exports, which contributed some 60 per cent of export earnings in the early 1980s.[71] (Aid grants from oil-rich Arab states and funds remitted by expatriate Syrian workers had also passed their peak and were declining in the mid-1980s.) But apart from such austerity measures as reducing the subsidising and importing of consumer goods, the only economic reforms had been the granting of some modest concessions to encourage private-sector exports and foreign investment.[72]

In 1986, though, the foreign-exchange problem became a crisis as the world price of oil plunged. Syria's earnings from oil were halved and export earnings now covered little more than 40 per cent of the country's imports – Syria was 'on the brink of foreign-exchange bank-ruptcy'.[73] The foreign-exchange crisis in turn forced a curbing of imports, including raw materials, that resulted in the economy shrinking by officially 5 per cent in 1986.[74] There were 'grave shortages of basic foodstuffs and commodities', which helped push the official inflation rate to 36 per cent in 1986 and 60 per cent in 1987 (unofficially 100 per cent in both years).[75] Despite Asad's public insistence that the economy was in 'difficulties' rather than crisis, there was an obvious need for a change in economic policy even if only as an emergency measure. The development Plan drafted for 1986–90 was abandoned and steps were taken to alleviate the crisis. In addition to the continuation of such austerity measures as subsidy reductions, priority within the public sector was given to earners of foreign exchange, especially the oil industry. But now the desperate need for foreign exchange also required the mobilisation of the private sector. For example, agriculture was an important export earner and its failure to keep pace with population growth had also resulted in an increasing drain on foreign exchange for food imports. As early as February 1986 it was decreed that joint-stock companies (with minority state shareholding) could be established in agriculture and tourism, and they were given major privileges and freedoms.[76]

A more programmatic response to the crisis became evident in 1988 when the acquisition of foreign currency was given absolute priority by the government.[77] In the previous two years only minor and *ad hoc* reforms had been instituted in response to the crisis, such as changes in the (multiple-exchange-rate) foreign-exchange system to encourage private-sector exports.[78] (One likely reason for the lack of urgency was the hope that such changes would be rendered unnecessary by a revival in oil prices and/or by revenues from new oil fields that had been discovered earlier in the decade and had already begun to be exploited.[79]) But in 1988 the regime instituted a series of significant liberalising reforms, some of which went beyond an immediate concern with exports. The continuing concern with exports was still evident: export trade was deregulated, a more 'privileged' exporters' exchange rate (basically the same as the black-market rate) was adopted to further encourage private-sector exports, and state enterprises were made more self-financing as regards foreign exchange. However, the state monopoly on importing was also lifted in many areas, presumably in part to promote more efficient use of the limited funds available for imports. Furthermore, the government signalled a fundamental change in the official view of the role the private sector should play in the economy. Abandoning its usual practice of annually listing which industrial activities were permitted to the private sector, in 1988 the government listed only those which were reserved for the state sector – implying that all other industries were open to private enterprise. Such (indirectly) privatising inclinations, however slight or symbolic, provided some justification for Syrian business leaders' references to an economic *infitah*, of an opening up of the economy domestically as well as internationally.[80]

The regime's programme of economic reforms continued into the early 1990s. Measures favourable to the private sector continued to be implemented. For example, taxes on business profits were reduced from (albeit largely symbolic) 90 per cent and above levels, and the formation of wholly private joint-stock companies was allowed. Internationalisation continued, with the freeing up of foreign-exchange controls over commercial transactions being virtually completed by the end of 1992.[81] Perhaps the most important internationalising measure was the 1991 investment law which was aimed largely at attracting more foreign investment and granted generous terms to approved projects by Syrian or foreign investors. It was followed up by 'the creation of special industrial zones in several provinces to provide suitable locations for modern private and mixed-sector plants'.[82] Hundreds of new investment projects were soon approved but a sizeable amount of the new investment was coming from expatriate Syrians (and other rapidly exhaustible sources) and there was little of the hoped-for investment by large Western companies.[83]

By the mid-1990s the reform programme had run its course. The loss of momentum was evident in the deferring or abandoning of the more radical economic reforms being prepared or mooted in the early 1990s: no longer prohibiting private-sector banks, setting up a stock exchange, and establishing a fully convertible currency. The government now made it clear that there were no plans for banking reform, despite the problems that investors were having with the state banking system. At the end of 1994 there was still no stock exchange and a multiple-exchange-rate system was still being maintained. Other limits on the extent of economic reform were very evident. For example, although state economic planning had largely been abandoned, the investment and import licensing systems continued to provide the state with powerful controls over economic activity. Nor had there ever been any prospect of removing the legal restrictions on individual land ownership or of instituting a privatisation programme.[84]

The obvious limits to the economic reform programme revealed the political limits on their scope. Asad had always viewed economic policy as a secondary issue compared to such 'higher', directly political concerns as foreign policy and internal security.[85] And from the perspective of internal security – or rather political self-interest – he had always adopted a cautious attitude to economic policy, seeing high risks and avoiding such risky changes in policy. (The same caution was evident in his attempts to avoid stirring up ideological opposition by introducing only a 'corrective movement' in 1970–1 and by avoiding any ideological recognition of the change in economic approach in the 1980s.) He had 'never favoured abandoning unnecessarily any element of state control and the means of patronage such control implies'; nor had he ever favoured 'introducing or envisaging far-reaching changes that might be considered a challenge to parts of his political base'.[86] Asad's despotism sought not to challenge vested interests but to create or manipulate them.

Therefore Asad had limited the restructuring of some areas of the economy and had retained many of the economic controls, such as investment and import licensing, that had been used to build up patronage-based support from segments of the business class.[87] Moreover, Asad had long ago 'privatised' the regime's use of such economic patronage by allowing the regime's personnel to abuse their public powers in lucrative private arrangements with businessmen seeking their favour. Here he had already been using as a conscious strategy the process (seen later in China) of the loyalty of regime personnel being strengthened by their being allowed to indulge in corrupt practices. The senior personnel in the military, Party and security services as well as in the Ministries had been allowed through such means to acquire 'extravagant wealth' as 'a reward for political loyalty' and the 'better to control them'.[88] Moreover, as in China, there was a tendency for senior regime personnel to merge into the business class as they or their families became involved in business ventures; even the ordinary members of the officer corps and high-ranking civil servants had become agricultural entrepreneurs through investing in land.[89] Although such regime personnel would benefit from some of the economic reforms, they also had 'a residual fear' that their 'positions, control, and patronage' could be jeopardised by too far-reaching a reform programme, especially extensive market-isation.[90] Therefore they provided Asad with self-interestedly loyal backing for the limited economic reforms (which in contrast were viewed with wary suspicion by the socialist Baath Party and its pre-dominantly state-employee membership[91]) but they had no interest in an extensive reform programme.

Another political limit upon the extent of economic reform was the need to limit any restructuring of the state sector. As 'a key source of patronage-linked and politically necessary employment' it was never in danger of privatisation and was 'insulated' from the reform pro-gramme.[92] Despite the regime's declared intent to improve the effi-ciency of state enterprises, they were allowed to respond to the changing economic environment with increasing losses or deficits that in turn pushed up the state's budget deficit.[93] The regime's only response was a gradual reform by omission or attrition, somewhat similar to the Chinese reformers' outflanking strategy, as the state sector was allowed to shrink in size relative to the growing private sector.[94] Not only had the state's role in the economy shrunk but also the state enterprises' share of production, investment and employment was being reduced by their declining performance and by the growth of the private sector's more dynamic enterprises.[95] Eventually, in September 1994, a more positive or direct move was made to reform the state enterprises. A presidential legislative decree granted greater autonomy to state enterprises and put all relations between them and the government on a commercial basis.[96] But the caution displayed in the limits to this reform was not simply economic. Concerns about higher inflation and unemployment if the state enterprises were marketised was only part of the wider politically driven anxiety about the potential ramifications of reforming the state sector.[97] 'Whatever its flaws, the public sector still serves as a means of patronage and control on the one hand, and of social security on the other.'[98]

Agriculture, too, was insulated by its political importance from at least some aspects of economic reform. The agrarian middle class, 'the leading class in the countryside', was a 'strong power base' of Asad's regime and could therefore expect to see its position protected.[99] While the regime was willing to remove the state purchasing monopoly over several agricultural products and to increase considerably state procurement prices, it had 'no intention of openly reversing the land reform laws of the 1960s', whose limits on land ownership had shifted power in the countryside from the upper class to the middle class.[100] In any case, there was little need to look to large-scale individual ownership of land as a means of improving agricultural production. The initial marketising moves of the late 1980s had significantly improved both the production and supply of agricultural goods and had encouraged the regime to lift procurement prices to near world-market levels in the 1990s.[101]

The regime's limited set of economic reforms soon seemed to have been very successful in returning the country to the progress and prosperity of the 1970s.[102] The trade balance was back in surplus. After a $600 million deficit in 1988 it had been nearly $1.2 billion in surplus in 1989 and would go on to register a surplus of over $2 billion in 1990 and nearly $1 billion in 1991. Economic growth had revived. Annual economic growth would average some 8 per cent in the 1990–4 period – almost back to the levels of the booming mid-1970s. Inflation was down to officially little more than 19 per cent in 1990 and about 8 per cent in 1991–2. The growing private sector had increased its share of non-oil exports from 33 per cent to more than 70 per cent in 1987–92, while the corresponding increase in its share of imports, from 25 per cent to 64 per cent, was improving the availability of consumer goods and helping to create the 'sheen of prosperity' that was evident in Syrian cities and towns by 1994.[103]

On the other hand, there was little long-term foundation to the successes. The improvement in the trade balance had been largely due to the quadrupling of oil exports in 1986–91; they were once again contributing the high proportion of export earnings – as high as 70 per cent – that they had a decade earlier.[104] Another feature of the prosperous years of the 1970s, massive official aid from Arab Gulf states, had also reappeared. In 1990 such grants had reached their nadir of only $127 million but no less than $2.5 billion was received in the aftermath of Syria's joining the US-led coalition to free Kuwait from Iraqi occupation.[105] Moreover, the growth of non-oil exports was fragile. The impressive contribution to improving the trade balance that had been made by the surge of manufactured exports from the private sector was mainly due to a temporary debt–barter arrangement with the Soviet Union, to which Syria owed a large debt from arms purchases.[106] In fact in the late 1980s normal Syrian trade with friendly Soviet-block countries had run into difficulties and the government had begun subsidising trade with these countries to compensate for the much less generous prices they were now prepared to pay for Syrian exports.[107] Finally, the private sector's new dominance of importing was also accompanied by substantial increases in imports, which endangered the trade balance and in 1993 would help push it back to a $1 billion deficit.[108] Considering the raft of longer-term economic problems looming on the horizon,[109] there was reason for scepticism about just how successful the reforms had been.

However, it is likely that the average member of society and regime viewed the reform programme as a marked success. It was delivering the goods to most Syrians and in particular to a section of society who had no 'natural' liking for the regime – the business class. Here the regime's economic and political strategies seemed to be running in tandem, for in the 1980s–90s Asad's Baathist socialist regime, with its long-standing ties to the farmers and state employees, was now trying to win over the business class.[110] As the business class, including small traders and artisans, had grown in size to some 11 per cent of the total population, it had become a sizeable force numerically and was strategically concentrated in Damascus and the larger cities.[111] And the increasing representation of business interests in the Assembly, albeit in the form of 'independents', was indicative of the move to integrate the business class into the regime or at least to strengthen its loyalty to Asad as Syria's ruler. The regime had apparently already succeeded in securing the loyalty of the newer members of this class, 'particularly merchants and manufacturers who owed their existence to *infitah* policies or to valuable connections with leading civil servants and officers.'[112] In addition to this old-fashioned patronage-based support and the new *infitah* clientele, other sections of the business class also apparently viewed political stability as their highest priority or political demand (along with more economic and personal, not political, freedom).[113] The regime could not yet expect that the business class as a whole would 'try to defend it if it was about to fall', but at least 'this class no longer posed a threat to Asad and his leadership.'[114] The removal of any political threat from the business class was particularly significant because of its role in the only serious threat there had been to the stability of the regime. For in 1980 Asad had faced his stiffest test when massive anti-regime demonstrations were staged by the traditional business sector of Homs, Hama and Aleppo, providing evidence of widespread public sympathy for the Muslim Brotherhood's urban-guerrilla campaign to bring down Asad's 'godless' and 'corrupt' regime.[115] What is more, the fact that the Damascus business sector had not joined in these anti-regime demonstrations had certainly reduced the pressure on the regime and helped it to ride out the storm.[116] If the Syrian business class as a whole had been politically neutralised in the 1980s–90s, the regime had done much to secure the stability of its rule.

7 Baathist Iraq

POLITICAL STRUCTURE

Until almost the beginning of the 1980s the political structure of the Iraqi Baathist regime had displayed the same unorthodox feature – being headed by a military man – as its Syrian counterpart. But with the formal transfer of power from President (Field Marshal) al-Bakr to his deputy Saddam Hussein in 1979 the regime had completed its gradual shift from military rule to being an orthodox, party-state Baath regime. Although the Iraqi Baathists had come to power in July 1968 through a military coup, during the 1970s the civilian wing of the Party and regime had become more powerful than the once-dominant military wing. The gradual shift in power was largely because the military man who headed the regime and Party, al-Bakr, had allowed his young (born 1937) civilian protégé and trusted deputy, Saddam Hussein, to build up the civilian wing's control of the regime. (In fact al-Bakr had entrusted this young relative and fellow-townsman with the formal deputy leadership of the Party years before the 1968 coup and with the formal deputy leadership of the coup's RCC junta as early as 1969.) In particular, he had allowed Saddam to become the real ruler of Iraq several years before the shift in power was formally completed in July 1979 when al-Bakr retired and passed on his posts of President, RCC Chairman and Party General Secretary to his civilian deputy. However, one unorthodox feature was being replaced by another in 1979, for Saddam Hussein was also completing his move towards achieving a degree of personal rule within the now party-state Baathist regime. During the 1980s he would strengthen and display his personal rule in what would also be the most significant change in the regime's structure. Although this was a change in degree rather than in kind, he would be moving towards attaining a virtually monarchical degree of personal rule similar to that being achieved by Asad in Baathist Syria in a less flamboyant fashion.

The key post which Saddam Hussein acquired in 1979, President/RCC-Chairman, was part of the only unique element in the regime's political structure and would continue on into the 1980s and 1990s as the key post within the now party-state regime. In Baathist Iraq the post of state President was combined with that of Chairman of the

114

Revolutionary Command Council and the holder of this Presidency/ Chairmanship was elected by and from within the RCC – an organ which had begun life as the 1968 coup's military junta. The RCC was established after the Baath-led military coup in July 1968 as a typical military junta with supreme executive and legislative authority. Its supreme authority was confirmed by the 1970 provisional Constitution, which was still in force in the 1980s. The Constitution declared that the RCC was the supreme state body, having the authority to promulgate laws as well as decrees and to have the Council of Ministers implement its executive decisions. Although the RCC had by then acquired a largely civilian membership, it remained the supreme constitutional organ and retained an unusually extensive, junta-like range of powers. The President/Chairman exercised the RCC's powers in such executive areas as appointing the Council of Ministers and making appointments to senior military, civil service and judicial posts. Although not authorised to exercise unilaterally the RCC's legislative powers, the President/Chairman's role of signing its legislation and decrees at least gave him a form of legislative veto.[1]

In theory the other RCC members could 'constrain' a President but in reality this was unlikely to occur in what had become a Party-ised as well as civilianised body.[2] The 1970 Constitution required that all new members of the RCC had to be members of the Baath Party's Regional Command, and by the end of 1971 the membership of the two bodies was almost identical. Therefore in practice not only was the holder of the Party's leadership position of General Secretary guaranteed the post of President/Chairman, but also the Party leader would be as little constrained by members of the RCC as he was by the same people in their role as members of the Party Regional Command. Therefore considering the authority enjoyed by the Party (Regional) General Secretary within an increasingly hierarchical Baath Party, it was unlikely that al-Bakr and his successor Saddam Hussein would be constrained by other RCC/RC members. (Neither Saddam nor al-Bakr could be any more than Deputy to the General Secretary of the international National Baath Party because Aflaq held that largely ceremonial post until his death in 1989.) In fact the powers of Party (Regional) General Secretary that Saddam Hussein formally acquired in 1979 had already been wielded by him informally as al-Bakr's Deputy General Secretary, and he had already built up in Stalin-like fashion a centralised organisational control over his democratic-centralist party.[3] Similarly, Saddam had recently also begun to build up a personality cult as 'he endeavoured to change his image

from that of ruthless party man of the mid-1970s to one of meri-
torious and accessible popular leader'.[4] He had already laid the foundations for the position of personal rule that he would strengthen and
decorate in the 1980s.

Apart from its military past and transition to a personal-rule future,
the political structure was by 1980 quite close to the orthodox
Baathist model of a Leninist or Communist-style party-state regime.
For example, during the 1970s Saddam had transformed the military
into a Baathist 'ideological army' that was under strong Party
control.[5] There had been continual purging of unreliable officers and
by the end of the decade most officers and NCOs were reliable Party
members. They provided the raw material for the network of supervisory Party committees and units that were established within the
military alongside the Political Department and its array of indoctrinating 'morale officers' and of political commissars equipped with a
veto power over military commanders' orders. In fact one of the
major structural differences between the two Baathist regimes was the
strength and comprehensiveness of the Iraqi regime's institutional
control over the military. There was much less difference in the
strength of Party supervision of the civil service, where the Iraqi as
well as the Syrian regime used orthodox Leninist methods of strong
Party supervision.[6] However, an unusual feature of the Iraqi regime
was the role given to the Party's security service. Established by
Saddam Hussein in the mid-1960s, the Party's security service had
been transformed into the powerful *state* General Intelligence
(Mukhabarat) Department, which supervised other policing organs
as well as the military, Ministries and mass organisations, but it still
reported directly to the Party leadership and was still occasionally
referred to as Party Intelligence.[7]

However, as in the Syrian Baath regime an unorthodox and
important role was played within the political structure by religious/
ethnic/regional minorities – in the Iraqi case the (Arab) Sunni religious
minority and the Tikriti regional minority. In Iraq the Shiite branch of
Islam was the faith of over half of the population and the (Arab)
Sunni minority comprised no more than 20 per cent of the population.[8] (The Kurdish ethnic minority was predominantly Sunni.)
Within this minority there was in turn a powerful regional minority
– the inhabitants of the area around the town of Tikrit, to the
northwest of Baghdad. Like the Alawites in Syria, these Sunni and
Tikriti minorities had already acquired a disproportionately powerful
position in the military and the Baath Party well before the Baathist

regime had been established.[9] The Sunni Arabs' dominance of the officer corps was such that even after Saddam Hussein moved to reduce their obvious predominance by promoting Shiites to important posts (and even after the massive expansion of the army in the Iran–Iraq war), Sunnis comprised about 80 per cent of the officer corps.[10] The Tikritis' long-standing prominence within the officer corps was diluted by the expansion of the military in the 1970s and 1980s but they continued to be 'the main source of high and medium ranking army officers – an estimated 2000 or so'.[11] As for the Party, it was 'a virtual Sunni party' in the late 1960s, and Tikritis had acquired vastly disproportional influence, at first largely because of the strong (Tikriti) military presence in the Party leadership and later also because of the power of the most prominent civilian Tikriti, Saddam Hussein.[12]

The *changes* in political structure in the 1980s-90s were quite similar to those in Baathist Syria, notably in the inclusion of marginal democratisation as well as increasingly personalist rule. In 1980 the regime finally established the elected National Assembly legislature envisaged in the 1970 Constitution and in Baathist orthodoxy. (A National Patriotic/Progressive Front had been set up in the early 1970s to form a Baath-led alliance with other 'progressive' parties which included some moderate Kurdish parties, a few 'progressive' groups and, until 1979, the Communists.[13]) But legally there was to be only one list of candidates for the Assembly, which would be determined by prospective candidates' having their qualifications reviewed by an election commission. In practice only Baathists and independents committed to the principles of the 1968 revolution were approved by the commission. The National Assembly even in theory had only the restricted role of ratifying or rejecting the RCC's legislative proposals. In reality its two short sessions a year rubber-stamped proposed legislation but were allowed limited discussion of some issues and occasional criticism of individual Ministers. The next signs of purported democratisation emerged after the Iran–Iraq war, when Saddam announced that a multi-party democracy would be established and that a new Constitution would remove such long-standing provisional features as the RCC and would institute a popularly elected Presidency. (Early in 1989 work was officially begun on drafting a new Constitution, and a draft was approved by the Assembly in July 1990 but was pigeonholed when the Kuwaiti crisis began in August.) Much was also made of the fact that in the 1989 elections to the Assembly half of the seats were allocated to supposed 'independents'.[14]

The lack of any real democratisation was only a hollow victory for the Party, which was losing any significant role within this party-state regime. In 1981 the Party's supervision of the civil service was officially reduced to only a monitoring role. Directives specifying that Party members were accountable to their state superiors (rather than Party units or officials) ended officially the strong supervisory role over the civil service that had been enjoyed by the Party in the early 1970s. In fact during the Iran–Iraq war the Party became more an instrument than a director of the war effort, becoming in practice an extension of the military and the security services. The Party's militia, the Popular Army, was opened up to huge numbers of non-Baathists as it was expanded to eventually as many as a million members. More significantly, the Party itself was opened up to mass membership during the war, with membership encouraged and often obligatory. In addition to this loss of any claim to be an elite, the Party was losing any remaining autonomy as it became more obviously the instrument of Saddam's personal rule. The Ninth Party Congress in 1982 stacked the Regional Command with his ministerial or security service subordinates, his advisers, and his relatives, and the new Regional Command bestowed upon him the new title of 'imperative leader'.[15]

The most important change to the regime's structure was this increasing degree of personal rule by Saddam Hussein as he strengthened not only his leadership of the Party but also other bases of his personal position. The Presidency would not be constitutionally strengthened until 1990, when the President would be defined as the 'people's leader and symbol'. But during the Iran–Iraq war Saddam used the presidential role of Commander-in-Chief to increase his standing with the military and the general public. He adopted a 'hands on' approach to presidential command of the armed forces, which was symbolised by his constant wearing of military garb and use of the Field-Marshal military rank he had bestowed on himself after becoming President. The propaganda accompaniment was the glorification of his leading role in making key (successful) military decisions, the claims that (successful) military strategies were examples of his 'military genius', and the references to the army as 'the army of Saddam Hussein'.[16] A virtually personal 'army of Saddam Hussein' was in fact created *within* the military by the expansion of the presidential bodyguard unit, the Republican Guard, into an elite force of about 100 000 who formed the army's strategic reserve and offensive cutting edge. The Guard's bodyguard loyalty to the President was maintained during the expansion by a careful vetting of recruits.

Predictably most of them were drawn from the Tikriti region, as were recruits for the new force, Special Security, that took over the Guard's more narrowly bodyguard role.[17] However, although Tikrit would also continue to supply many of his Generals, as well as key Party, state and security-service officials, Saddam had already in the 1970s found many of the Tikriti elite to be too ambitious and insufficiently obedient for his liking.[18]

Such problems may have strengthened his increasingly obvious inclination to use family members in key posts – another aspect of the greater degree of personal rule evident in the 1980s. Since 1977 his cousin Adnan had held the post of Minister of Defence (and would continue to do so until a public falling-out in 1989 was followed by the Minister's mysterious death). But in the 1980s Saddam also used close relatives in key security posts and for other vital missions. Among these usefully employed family members were his cousins on his father's side (the Majids) and his half-brothers from his step-father's family (the Ibrahims). Saddam's elder son, Udai, would not acquire any similarly significant posts in his path to becoming the second most influential figure in the regime, but the younger son, Qusai, was eventually given the post of head of Special Security.[19] Such nepotism was one of the monarchical features which were becoming increasingly apparent, particularly in the extravagant personality cult.

The burgeoning personality cult was the most obvious indication of Saddam's personal rule. In the 1980s the most important element was the massive propaganda effort put into boosting his military prestige during the Iran–Iraq war. Another important and unusual component in the 1980s was the manner in which the elderly and pliant Aflaq was used by Saddam as a means of strengthening his own credentials as Baathist ideologist and to ensure that he was seen as the successor to Aflaq as the ultimate Baathist ideologue.[20] Otherwise the personality cult seemed to differ from the standard international form only in degree or extravagance. It involved omnipresent portraits, constant public and television appearances, comparison with great historical figures, supposed personal piety (culminating in the pilgrimage to Mecca), and grandiloquent titles – 'Sword of the Arabs', 'Knight of the Nation', 'Leader of the Victory' and the like.[21] However, two unusually monarchical aspects were the attempt to identify Saddam with all sectors of Iraqi society, and the 1986 decree which made the crime of insulting the President punishable by life imprisonment or the death penalty.[22] The monarchical aspect was also very evident in the new heights to which the personality cult was taken in the late 1980s. There was 'a flurry of speculations that Hussein was paving the way for the restoration of monarchical rule with himself as king and was grooming his eldest son, Udai, as his heir apparent'.[23] A more favourable attitude to monarchy was apparent in the official rehabilitation of Iraq's Hashemite monarchy of the 1930s to 1958 (along with continuing glorification of the ancient Mesopotamian monarchs), and Saddam was himself adopting a more monarchical image.[24] The image of the ascetic and modest socialist had been replaced by monarchical pomp and grandeur that culminated in his leading a commemorative victory procession riding a white horse and dressed in the garb of a Hashemite monarch.[25] In January 1990 he was made President for life.[26]

The military humiliation inflicted by the US-led coalition in early 1991 produced signs of a less monarchical and more democratic approach. The Tenth Party Congress of September 1991 boosted the Regional Command's status, so that in theory both it and the Congress could challenge the power of the President and the RCC.[27] In 1991, too, the existence of other parties was legalised, with the proviso that they were not based on region, religion, an atheistic ideology, or hostility to the Arabs.[28] However, such measures were only pressure-easing tokenism, just as the regime years earlier, under the political and economic pressure of the late 1980s, had made token democratising gestures, promised more democracy and toyed officially with the notion of allowing a multi-party system.[29] By 1994 Saddam had returned to a more openly monarchical approach. Not only was his elder son, Udai, apparently the *de facto* number-two figure in the regime, but also Saddam himself was displaying monarchical trappings, as when on the occasion of his 57th birthday in April 1994 he 'was shown on television on a gold-coloured throne modelled, it seemed, on that of ancient Babylon'.[30]

IDEOLOGY

The Iraqi regime's ideology had seen no significant deviations from Baathist orthodoxy by the 1980s. There had been no conscious watersheds like the Corrective Movement in Syrian Baathism, let alone any significant modifications of inherited orthodoxy – not even by the Baathist founding ideologist Aflaq in his new position as head of the new Iraqi-based international Baathist movement (see

Appendix II). The Political Report of the Eighth Regional Party Congress in 1974 has been regarded as an ideological landmark by Iraqi Baathists, similar in status to the pre-schism 1963 Muntalaqat and 1947 Party Constitution. But although the Report adopted a more socialist approach than Asad's Syrian regime and also placed greater emphasis on Leninist-style party leadership of state and society (rather than 'popular democracy' through people's assemblies/councils), this was little different in content from the quite leftist and Leninist orthodoxy established by the 1963 Muntalaqat.[31]

Of more importance were the developments in the area of Iraqi nationalism which foreshadowed significant shifts in official ideology in the 1980s. When the Iraqi Baathists seized power in 1968, they had no new ideas and initially concentrated on the traditional Baathist theme of Arab unity. However, near the end of the 1970s a degree of Iraqi nationalism became apparent, albeit in the form of Iraqi leadership within the Arab nation. In the aftermath of the 1978 Egypt–Israel Camp David Accord, the Iraqi leadership depicted Iraq as the focus of Arab hopes for the future, as the 'veteran knight' which was assuming the 'historic responsibility' of defending the dignity of the Arab nation.[32] From then on expressions of Iraq's leadership of the Arab world became quite frequent and were included in the new national anthem.[33] Moreover, one of the justifications offered to the Iraqi people for this leadership was Iraq's glorious (pre-Arab) ancient history – such as King Nebuchadnezzar's bringing the conquered Jews back in chains to Babylon.[34] This was in turn an expression of the 'Mesopotamian' theme in a form of non-Arab Iraqi nationalism that was being promoted by Saddam Hussein in the late 1970s.[35] In fact even years earlier he had been a strong supporter of cultural festivals that had stressed the continuous history of the Iraqi people (since ancient times) and of 'Iraqi man'.[36] With Saddam's accession to formal regime leadership and increasingly strong personal rule, the theme of Iraqi nationalism was destined to play a more official and prominent role in the regime's ideology.

However, the most important *change* in the ideology in the 1980s was the shift in Baathist doctrine from a belief in collective leadership to a new emphasis on individual leadership.[37] Now Iraqi Baathist ideologists, and even Aflaq, referred to a 'historic leader' or 'necessary leader' with the historic mission of carrying the nation forward.[38] In particular it was argued that the multi-ethnic and multi-religious Iraqi state needed a leader to provide a unifying symbol; as the leader himself proclaimed, 'Saddam must therefore be shared by all of them'.[39] He also emphasised the leader's direct link with the people, to the extent of claiming that he was using the people against his Party officials.[40]

In contrast to the effort made to justify individual rule, no attempt was made to provide an ideological justification for the liberalising changes in economic policy evident in the 1980s. Even the term *infitah* (economic opening up or 'open door') was rejected by Saddam in 1980 as a description of his economic reforms because of what he considered to be the term's rightist, reactionary connotations.[41] However, in the 1970s he had already identified himself with a pragmatic, populist and developmental view of socialism that presented it as a means of raising productivity and of constructive development that would be the 'road to happiness' and 'enable us to face the enemy'.[42] With such a wide, moderate and flexible view of socialism there was little need to offer any new ideological justification for the shift to economic liberalisation.

In any case, shifts in economic or other policies could readily be justified in terms of the general patriotic-national attitudes officially encouraged during the 1980–8 war with Iran. Thus the 1982 Party Congress argued that private sector activities were part of the national wealth and were no less important than those of the socialist sector. The triumph of Iraqis' national solidarity over any class or other divisions was a prominent propaganda theme in wartime Iraq, as was the threat to Great Iraq and to hearth and home posed by the Iranians. But the war was also portrayed as an Arab versus Persian clash, with Iraq as the leader–protector of the Arab nation.[43]

This was one of the changes in degree/intensity that occurred in the 1980s as developing or nascent themes of the late 1970s became prominent features of the regime's ideology. Obviously the war with Iran provided a real opportunity and need to strengthen Iraq's ideological as well as political claim to leadership of the Arab world. Now Baathist Iraq could claim to be no less a 'front-line' Arab state than its Syrian counterpart; it was defending the Arab world against the new Iranian/ Persian enemy as much as Syria was defending it against the old Israeli enemy.[44] Moreover, the massive Iraqi military build-up during this 1980–8 war, including ballistic missiles and chemical weapons, eventually provided a basis for also claiming leadership of the Arab world in the struggle against Israel – in fact Iraq seemed to have rectified the long-standing Arab–Israeli strategic imbalance which Asad had sought and failed to counter in the 1980s.[45]

However, in the 1980s the Arab-leadership form of nationalism was accompanied by a non-Arab form that was much more difficult to incorporate within Baathist orthodoxy. After Saddam became President, the Mesopotamian myth became official doctrine and was reflected in such things as the new names of provinces (Nineveh and Babylon), the currency and postage stamps, the names of military units, and even the preamble to legal codes, where the influence of Hammurabi's code was acknowledged.[46] There was also official backing for the Mesopotamian influence that was visible in painting, sculpture, architecture, theatre, poetry and, of course, public monuments and sculptures.[47] Great emphasis was placed on archaeology, archaeological exhibits and restorations, notably the massive restoration work at Babylon.[48] The Iraqi 'deviation' into parochial or local nationalism was much more pervasive at the symbolic and cultural level than the Syrian example (though there was no equivalent of the expansionist notion of Greater Syria).

The regime also developed to a distinctly unorthodox degree its late 1970s tendency to emphasise the regime's Islamic credentials. The Islamic emphasis involved not only stressing the apparent piety of the leadership but also increased state patronage of religion and continual references to Islamic themes.[49] While never producing an explicit revision of Baathist orthodoxy's absence of religious commitment, the emphasis on the regime's Islamic nature became almost a supplementary ideology. A striking symbol of this development was that after Aflaq's death in 1989 it was announced that shortly before he died he had converted from Christianity to Islam.[50]

In the lead-up to the 1991 Gulf war the regime not only portrayed Baathist Iraq as leading and defending the Arab nation against the US-led coalition but also yet 'more firmly embraced the language and imagery of Islam', such as in adding the Islamic 'God is great' to the Iraqi flag.[51] In fact in the 1990s the regime's propaganda message was 'more conspicuous for its Arab and Islamic (generally Arab-Islamic), than its Mesopotamian component'.[52] Nevertheless, as was seen in the chapter on defiance, Iraqi nationalism and the Iraqi Baathist revolutionary heritage were still used in ideological interpretations of the 1991 Gulf war and the subsequent Kurdish and Shiite uprisings. Moreover, the Tenth Party Congress held in September 1991 reconfirmed its loyalty to the Baath Party's principles and rejected any notion of introducing 'Western-style democracy'.[53]

ECONOMIC POLICY

By the 1980s oil-rich Iraq had a mixed economy that was dominated by the state to an even greater extent than in Baathist Syria, particularly in the areas of commerce and agriculture.[54] The Iraqi Baathists had inherited in 1986 an economy which had already seen left-wing military regimes institute a redistributive land reform and the nationalisation of banks and large businesses. The socialist Baath regime had gone one crucial step further than its predecessors when in 1972 it nationalised the Iraq Petroleum Company, which was owned by a group of Western oil companies and virtually monopolised the country's vital oil industry. With some 10 per cent of the world's oil reserves and the lowest production costs in the Middle East, Iraq was now well placed to take advantage of the massive increases in world oil prices that occurred in the remainder of the 1970s. The huge increase in oil revenues, which had reached $26 billion by 1980,[55] provided the funds and imports that rapidly built up state-owned industry and commerce as well as social services. (On the other hand Iraq was also of course becoming dependent on oil for nearly all its export earnings and for much of its public revenue.) A major state sector had also been created in agriculture through the state's retention of land confiscated in further land reforms in 1970 and 1975, which had supposedly been aimed at creating peasant cooperatives that would eventually develop into collective farms.[56]

The Iraqi invasion of Iran in September 1980 at first brought little change to the economy, for Saddam Hussein sought to insulate civilian Iraqis as much as possible from the effects of his decision to go to war. Most of the one-third increase in public spending was on imported consumer goods and other civilian commodities to guard against shortages, and on continuing with the ambitious 1981–5 $130 billion development plan. However, even before the Iranian counter-invasion in mid-1982 (which at least removed the political need to keep the war as painless as possible), the 'business as usual' economic approach had had to be abandoned as oil revenues and foreign-exchange reserves fell. There was a halt to all but war-related and high-priority development projects and soon the 1981–5 plan would be replaced by an annual plan.[57]

More significantly, there was also a shift away from the Baathist approach of favouring the state sector and tight state control of the economy. Although usually an economy is subjected to increased state control in wartime, the Iraqi regime would resort to a liberalising economic approach to adapt its already state-dominated economy to wartime requirements. At the Ninth Party Congress in 1982 the Baath Party officially committed itself to promoting the private sector, which was declared to be of equal importance with the socialist sector. The commitment was reiterated by Saddam Hussein in 1984 and 1986, and he reassured the private sector in 1987 that even after the war it would be required by 'our brand of socialism'.[58] More concretely, in the early 1980s the private sector was granted tax benefits, less restrictive investment licensing, low-interest loans to encourage investment, and improved access to foreign trade, with substantial increases in the private sector's share of importing and exporting.[59]

But the change in approach was most obvious in agriculture and can be traced back to before the war – to promises to increase agricultural production that had been made by Saddam soon after his succession to the Presidency.[60] The more favourable attitude to private farming was evident in the halving of the (still relatively small) number of collective farms in 1979–80. Within a few years hardly any collective farms remained and agricultural cooperatives, too, had halved in number and had become largely nominal institutions. Soon there was official acknowledgement that it was no longer obligatory for a farmer to belong to a cooperative, collective or state farm. The commitment to promoting private farming went so far as to permit the 1970s land reforms to be undermined from 1982 onwards by individuals and families who ignored in practice the official limits on the size of landholdings.[61] (A 1983 law also allowed anyone to lease any amount of agricultural land from the state for up to twenty years.) As for marketising, the new unofficial policy towards marketing was regularised after 1982 when farmers were formally freed from the state's purchasing monopoly. They were now officially allowed to sell their produce to other wholesalers and to licensed private-sector retailers, where they could more easily take advantage of the black market prices as well as the substantially increased official prices.[62]

The success of these economic reforms in agriculture and, from the early 1980s, in the urban private sector is difficult to judge because of the distorting effects of wartime conditions and of Iraq's dependence on its now declining oil revenues. The urban private sector apparently experienced accelerated and rapid growth in the early 1980s, but the massive increase in the contribution of the private sector to the country's exports was due to the decline in the public sector's oil export earnings.[63] In agriculture, on the other hand, the decline in production experienced by the traditional and the state sectors was likely due to wartime conditions rather than any failure of the reforms, for there were significant increases in the production of fodder crops, fruit, vegetables and poultry, all of which were produced by the capital-intensive private farming that was most affected by the regime's new measures.[64] The regime itself appears to have been convinced of the economic reforms' success, as it would move further down the liberalising path when facing a severe crisis later in the war.

By the mid-1980s there was such confidence in the Iraqi military's capacity to beat off Iranian attacks that the regime hoped to complete a development plan in 1986–90 that would accomplish some of the abandoned 1981–5 development goals.[65] But 1986 brought a severe military and economic crisis. The fall of the Fao peninsula guarding the approaches to the southern city of Basra was followed by significant Iranian gains on the central front, and there was a devastating fall in oil prices, from $28 to only $9 a barrel during the first seven months of 1986.[66] What is more, the country had already drawn heavily on its credit worthiness; its external debt (albeit including friendly loans from Arab Gulf states) approached $50 billion.[67]

In response to the 1986 crisis the regime adopted a much more extensive programme of economic reform. In a key speech in February 1987, Saddam Hussein declared that economic reform was needed in order to increase output, which would in turn conserve foreign exchange and allow more to be used to 'buy weapons and other equipment needed on the battle front'.[68] (One obvious example of the need to increase output was in agriculture, for the annual food import bill of $2–3 billion absorbed an onerous proportion of Iraq's depleted oil revenues of some $13 billion a year.[69]) By the end of 1987 a range of measures had been introduced that went far beyond the predictable encouraging of exports and sale of state farms and agricultural land. Among the new measures were the privatisation of many state enterprises, a reform of the state sector, and a 'freeing-up' of labour markets through such drastic measures as abolishing not only the labour law but also the General Federation of Trade Unions and the Iraqi citizen's state-guaranteed right to employment.[70] The privatisation programme was particularly notable. Hotels, department stores, petrol stations, dairies, bakeries, food-processing companies and other factories were offered for sale or long lease on generous credit terms.[71] Eventually, well over $2.5 billion worth of state-owned businesses, including 80 substantial state enterprises, were privatised in 1987–90.[72]

The July 1988 cease-fire with Iran did not halt the momentum of the economic reform programme. A key marketising move was made in August, when price controls were lifted on some foodstuffs as well as on a large range of consumer goods. Having already reduced subsidies to state enterprises, the regime also moved to reduce its subsidising of food prices and public services, including health care. In 1990 it was announced that a stock exchange would be set up in order to attract local savings and expatriate Iraqi funds into financing new and existing businesses. The stock exchange eventually emerged in 1992 and the state monopoly in banking was removed in 1993, when three private banks were established. By then the Iraqi regime had carried out a more extensive economic liberalisation than anything seen in Baathist Syria or elsewhere in the Arab world.[73]

The contrast with Syria, though, is not as marked as at first appears. Saddam Hussein may seem to have been a more economically enlightened despot than Asad and one more willing to take political risks by challenging vested interests and ideological opposition. For example, the privatisation programme did create a 'severe backlash' in sections of public opinion (such as state employees and the Party) that were still committed to the regime's socialist ideological heritage and/or had a vested interest in maintaining the *status quo*.[74] But there were limits to Iraq's economic liberalisation and they were probably as political as the limits to the Syrian economic reform programme – again the political agenda shaped the economic.

Saddam was no different from Asad in viewing economic policy as a secondary issue compared to national-security and internal-security concerns. Even after the war and the maturing of the economic reform programme, his regime continued to direct the economy towards the political goals of increasing Iraq's military power and reviving the development of prestigious heavy industry after the wartime deferrals in 1982 and 1986.[75] These goals required huge expenditures which, after the 1986 collapse in oil revenues, had to be found by cuts in other areas of state spending, such as food subsidies, and by redeploying the state's reduced resources through such means as the privatisation programme. While petrochemical plants and other prestigious heavy-industry projects were excluded from privatisation, capital and (indirectly) revenue were freed-up by relinquishing smaller enterprises that were in most cases loss-making burdens on the state budget.[76] The discarding of these enterprises thus left more resources available for military purposes and the development of heavy industry.[77]

Similarly, the political risks involved in Saddam's economic reform programme were reduced by shaping the reform process to cater to internal-security concerns (and political self-interest). The risky privatisation programme was used in Syrian fashion to reward and control regime personnel and in Chinese fashion to give them a vested interest. Many of the privatised state assets were taken over by 'individuals who were close to the regime', presumably high-ranking regime personnel or their family, friends or clients.[78] By allowing his senior regime personnel to establish these ties to the private sector – whether in person or through the medium of family, friends or clients – Saddam was strengthening their loyalty to his regime and was creating new vested interests in the maintaining of the reform process. In fact a vested interest in economic reform had been developing among some regime personnel since the reforms of the early 1980s. Party and state officials of high and medium rank were to be found among the new urban-based agricultural entrepreneurs, and many of those who had profited from the increased role of the urban private sector had belonged to the Party hierarchy.[79] But, as in Syria and China, these regime personnel had developed a vested interest in the economic reforms' not being extended so far as to undermine their privileged position in what was still a politicised market sector. They had little cause for concern. The regime's removal of price controls and reduction of subsidies represented only a partial marketisation of an economy that still operated under the influence of various state controls, and the comparatively unimpressive internationalisation had not abolished import licensing.[80]

As in Syria, the economic reforms also presumably strengthened the loyalty of the business class to the socialist Baath regime and its leader. The Iraqi regime's more favourable attitude towards the private sector earlier in the 1980s had apparently been eliciting a form of patronage-based support from entrepreneurs who had exploited the new opportunities and continued to depend upon good relations with the regime for their success. Agricultural contractors and new, urban-based agricultural entrepreneurs had exploited the new opportunities for private agriculture, and a 'burgeoning' group of commercial and industrial entrepreneurs had benefited from the new measures and attitudes that expressed the official encouragement of private enterprise.[81] (In addition, the regime may have elicited support from the wider business community by meeting such general needs as the 'guarantee of order' that the stable Baathist regime provided.[82]) On balance, the political risks involved in Saddam's more sweeping economic reform programme may not have been much higher than those involved in Asad's cautious and more limited programme.

The Iraqi reforms were certainly less successful than the Syrian in delivering the goods. Although the liberalisation of the late 1980s did ease the shortages of foodstuffs and other consumer goods, it was at the cost of large price increases.[83] Overall inflation rose to 25–40 per cent levels, well above the increases in wage and salary earners' incomes.[84] Saddam's reaction showed the limits of his economic enlightenment and of his willingness to face the political risks posed by a discontented society. He responded to the inflation problem in 1989 by sacking his Finance Minister and Agriculture Minister for incompetence and by approving a package of anti-inflationary measures that included a price freeze on all consumer goods and services emanating from the public sector, a freeze on all retail prices, and an increase in subsidies paid to agricultural producers.[85] By 1990, however, it was clear that this partial reversal of the reform programme had also failed to deliver the goods. A typical complaint was that the state stores suffered from shortages of basic foodstuffs or charged twice the official price for them, while the private traders were charging four to five times the official prices.[86]

Therefore at the beginning of the 1990s the regime was still unable to offer any relief to a population that had seen its standard of living decline to below 1975 levels and whose economic expectations had risen with the end of the debilitating war with Iran.[87] The country's oil revenues of $13 billion could not cover current expenditure, let alone pay for the extensive reconstruction required after a damaging war,[88] and there was little possibility of borrowing more funds. The size of Iraq's foreign debt ($80 billion), the cost of servicing the debt ($8 billion annually), and Iraq's poor record of repayment, 'made foreign banks and companies wary of extending any new loans.'[89] The prospect of any significant economic improvement was diminished still further by the regime's continuing waste of resources on ambitious military and industrial projects and on prestigious reconstruction projects so economically useless that it has been suggested they were used to disguise the country's cash-flow problem.[90]

Facing such obvious failure to meet the people's economic aspirations, Saddam took a huge gamble. For 'the failure of the 1989 measures to solve the deepening economic crisis seems to have persuaded the government to look southward for a solution – to Kuwait'.[91] Although not the only reason behind the move to seize oil-rich Kuwait, 'there can be little doubt that Iraq's multiple economic crises played a decisive, if not *the* decisive, role in the decision'.[92] Publicly and privately the regime was well aware of the prospective economic benefits arising from the conquest of Kuwait: an increase in oil revenue to $38 billion a year, control of Kuwait's investment assets in the West (estimated by Iraqis at $220 billion), and terrorising the other Gulf states into 'writing off' their wartime loans to Iraq.[93] After the invasion of Kuwait, though, economic policy would be driven largely by the huge problems arising from the United Nations' comprehensive economic sanctions and from their continuation after Iraq's expulsion from Kuwait. By 1994 the country had experienced years of shortages, rationing, massive inflation, the collapse of the currency's exchange value on the black market, and annual falls in output of 10 per cent or more. Tens of billions of dollars in prospective reparations had been added to the massive foreign debt and there still remained the task of reconstructing the country after a devastating bombing campaign. If successful economic reform, or any form of economic success, were ever explanations of political stability, they certainly were not in Saddam Hussein's Iraq in the 1990s.

8 Qadhafi's Libya

POLITICAL STRUCTURE

The political structure of the Libyan regime cannot be described by using some model of orthodoxy as a benchmark; the Libyan dictatorship is simply unique and bears no family resemblance to any other regime. For all its idiosyncrasies, though, in 1980 the regime was still basically a military regime. It had originated in a 1969 military coup or supposed 'revolution' that overthrew the monarchy and set up a regime emulating Nasser's regime in neighbouring Egypt, with a Revolutionary Command Council junta headed by the coup leader and now Commander-in-Chief, Colonel Qadhafi. In the later 1970s the new regime had been transformed into a unique example of military-party regime, where a unique party-like political movement (the revolutionary committees) dominated a unique system of supposedly direct participatory democracy. The military had in theory handed over power to this Jamahiriya (state of the masses) system in 1977, with the country being renamed the Socialist People's Libyan Arab Jamahiriya. But Colonel Qadhafi had established a degree of personal rule as 'Leader of the Revolution' and still dominated the regime.

The Jamahiriya system in theory devolved sovereignty to local Basic People's Congresses, incorporating every adult citizen, which met annually (each night for a week) to deliberate and vote on key issues. Although this was in theory a system of direct democracy, there was also a national General People's Congress to which the BPCs sent mandated delegates with their decisions on these key issues. As the agent of the BPCs the GPC's annual session not only voted on policies and regulations but also elected the equivalent of the country's government: an executive committee, the General People's Committee, of Secretaries who each headed the equivalent of a Ministry.[1]

In practice there were many aspects of the Jamahiriya system which fell short of democratic norms. In addition to the banning of political parties, there was the fact that the central authorities controlled the agenda of national issues to be decided by the BPCs and GPC – and the government had wide powers to interpret the general lines of policy approved by the BPC/GPCs. Furthermore, at BPC meetings some participants felt inhibited in speaking for fear of reprisals, there was no secret ballot, and in many cases decisions on policy issues were made by 'consensus', as interpreted by the meeting's chairman. Nevertheless, during the 1980s and 1990s the BPCs and GPC would prove to be much more than just a rubber-stamping legitimiser of Qadhafi's policies.[2]

The revolutionary-committees movement can be seen as fulfilling the role that an official party might have done if political parties had not been an ideological anathema. The committees had been set up in the late 1970s to cope with 'shortcomings' in the new Jamahiriya system. As well as combatting apathy and reactionaries (notably by preventing 'political opponents and traditional tribal forces asserting their interests within the BPCs'),[3] the revolutionary committees would ensure that the BPCs followed the revolutionary direction set by Qadhafi. He gave them the authority to supervise the BPCs and (by nominating and vetoing candidates) to organise their choice of local officials and of delegates to the GPC.[4] In addition to being a vanguard political movement, the committees performed such other roles as intelligence gathering and providing a paramilitary force whose military training and specialised military units made them a counterbalance to the regular military.[5] By the end of the 1970s they had also been given policing and quasi-judicial powers which 'included the right to arrest and detain, to hold revolutionary tribunals, and administer what is described as "revolutionary justice"'.[6]

The initial cadres of the revolutionary-committees movement were selected from activists within the BPCs or student organisations and were then sent off to training camps for not only political-ideological education but also military and intelligence training. These cadres in turn recruited new members (who would not be full members until having undergone similar training) and began to develop an organisational structure for the movement, with a headquarters and a vertical command structure that banned contacts with other committees. The movement's structure also became more extensive as revolutionary committees were established in workplaces, universities, the civil service, the police and even the military (where they acted as a political watchdog able to arrest officers they suspected of conspiracy). Yet this unique multi-role and pervasive organisation would remain a small elite of militants. Estimates of the size of membership range from just a few thousand to only 100 000, and even those based upon an assessment of the number of committees required for so many locations have produced estimates of from 20 000 to 60 000 out of a population of 3–4 million.[7]

By the 1980s the military – the original revolutionaries – had lost some of their prestige and influence to the new revolutionary political structures, as was symbolised by the abolition of the RCC junta when power was supposedly handed over to the new Jamahiriya system. The military remained an elite, privileged group but already there were indications, notably the introduction of revolutionary committees within the army, of the pressure they would come under during the 1980s as their leader protected his personal position at the head of the regime.

Qadhafi's degree of personal rule was a crucial feature of the political structure long before the 1980s. In fact in 1979 he had felt secure enough to resign from all official political posts and offices and concentrate upon the role of revolutionary ideologist and leader.[8] Despite his claims to be just an ordinary citizen, he continued to hold political centre stage through his personality cult and 'Brother Colonel's' other sources of political influence.[9] The most obvious source was the revolutionary-committees movement which he had set up and continued to direct. Its headquarters, the Central Coordinating Office, was virtually a branch of Qadhafi's personal staff, and he met with the several dozen leaders of the movement (the 'speakers' of the most powerful committees) on an almost weekly basis to plan the movement's activities.[10] But he had also retained his position as ultimate head of the military and, despite the continuing use of the title 'Colonel', had acquired the rank of army Field Marshal and its equivalent rank in other services.[11] Furthermore, he had already begun to use his tribe and family as an informal pillar of his regime, notably by increasingly entrusting his personal security to them.[12]

The 1980s–90s saw significant *changes* in the regime's political structure.[13] The main change experienced by the military was the further reduction in their political prominence and influence. Qadhafi feared and distrusted the military he had led to political power, as they remained the most likely source of any effective move to topple his personalist and populist form of military regime.[14] He allowed the officer corps to retain the personal privileges acquired in the 1970s, when they had been the regime's sole elite and power base, and he conferred new corporate benefits on the military through a programme of expansion and massive arms purchases.[15] But he also sought to guarantee loyalty by inserting revolutionary committees into the military and by using loyalists (such as members of the former RCC junta) and tribe or family members to hold key posts. Moreover, he adopted the practices of a) rotation, demotion or early retirement of commanders, b) fomenting mutual suspicions within the officer corps, and c) structural compartmentalisation to prevent the development of corporate political unity within the military.[16] Such interference in military life in turn increased the officers' list of political and corporate grievances, which already included the military interventions in Chad, the inefficiency within the military, and the regime's clear lack of trust in the loyalty of its armed forces.[17] (The regime had good cause for its official mistrust of the military, as they had been the source of most of the dozen or more attempts to overthrow Qadhafi that had been made since the mid-1970s.[18]) In the mid-1980s the military also saw its political rival, the revolutionary-committees movement, allowed by Qadhafi to launch an attack against the various material privileges enjoyed by the officer corps, and receive new powers of surveillance over the officer corps and the military arsenals.[19] Although this rival pillar of the regime would soon suffer a crippling setback, by the later 1980s the military was having to deal with a new threat. It arose from Qadhafi's newly strengthened commitment to his notion of replacing the military with a militia-like 'armed people' (as part of his wider project of actually dissolving or drastically pruning the whole state apparatus). Such a 'People's Army' was formally established in 1989 but the military would survive the threat of extinction and enter the 1990s as still the greatest latent threat to Qadhafi's rule, as was confirmed by the major coup attempt of October 1993.[20]

The most striking change in political structure was the rise and fall of the revolutionary-committees movement. In the early 1980s Qadhafi had occasionally criticised them for arrogance, power-grabbing, hypocrisy, corruption, not implementing his directives promptly, showing signs of becoming a political party, and wearing jeans and long hair.[21] Yet by the mid-1980s they had become so powerful that they were in practice, like a Communist regime party, 'the main executive authority in Libya'.[22] Qadhafi was reported to have elevated them to pre-eminence among the regime's organisations and bodies and to be using them to keep the other two pillars of his regime – the military and his tribe – under control.[23] But after the American air raid of April 1986 the revolutionary committees had lost ground in their rivalry with the military, and the revolutionary 'excesses' perpetrated by the committees in their repression of the regime's opponents had aroused the public's anger and anxiety.[24] Therefore it was understandable that the committees would suffer in the political liberalisation which Qadhafi incorporated into the purported 'revolution within the revolution' that he began in 1987 in response to rising public discontent. By 1988 the political liberalisation included not only Qadhafi's severe criticism of the revolutionary committees but also the actual removal of their security, judicial, paramilitary and even political-leadership roles – they would no longer control the BPCs.[25]

Yet despite the revolutionary committees' political eclipse and functional downgrading, sceptics wondered whether these apparently drastic changes would have much effect on the structure of power; the revolutionary committees remained 'a powerful watchdog over the army and the regular [central and local government] committees'.[26] In the 1990s they maintained a relatively low public profile but continued to have Qadhafi's support in what was officially their only role of indoctrination and mass mobilisation.[27]

Qadhafi consolidated the degree of personal rule he had acquired in the 1970s but otherwise there was little change in his position at the head of the political structure. He continued to hold only the unofficial public post of Leader of the Revolution and the military post of Supreme Commander of the Armed Forces with the army rank of Field Marshal (not the still publicly preferred 'Colonel'). He also remained the unofficial head of the revolutionary-committees movement and of his kinship/tribal body, whose increasing prominence and privileges were so typical of a personally ruled regime.[28] Qadhafi's tendency to rely on family and tribe for his personal security became much more evident as his life and regime continued to be endangered.[29] Young members of his Qadhadfa tribe were packed into his personal guard and into a Deterrent Battalion and other special army units tasked with putting down mutinies or coup attempts.[30] Qadhafi also entrusted key professional posts in the military, such as commanders of military districts and posts in military intelligence, to members of his family or tribe.[31] That his family and the Qadhadfa were becoming the informal third pillar of his regime, holding many of the key civilian as well as military posts, was resented by the other two pillars, especially the revolutionary committees.[32] In 1985 Qadhafi did rein in the Qadhadfa elite through the medium of the revolutionary committees.[33] But his tribe and family remained ultimately the most reliable pillar of his regime.

The continuation of his personality cult, despite Qadhafi's exhortations to desist, was most evident in the ubiquitous portraits to be found even on the country's stamps.[34] In the 1990s 'Gaddafi, variously referred to as the leader of world revolution, the international thinker, and pioneer of revolution of the masses, is pictured all over Libya in bedouin, civilian and military poses.'[35] As in many other personality cults, one of the strongest elements was the leader's role as ideologist – and in the Libyan case it may well have been the strongest. For it has been argued that at the heart of the personality cult lies the assertion that Qadhafi's Third Universal Theory 'provides the ultimate solution to the problems of humanity'.[36]

IDEOLOGY

By the 1980s the Libyan regime had developed an ideology that was as unique as its political structure. The most striking feature was its purportedly universal appeal. Qadhafi's Third Universal Theory, from its initial formulation in 1973, had been presented as an alternative to the other two universal theories: materialistic capitalism and atheist Communism. As the Theory was given detailed form in the three parts or volumes of *The Green Book* (published successively in 1975, 1977 and 1978), it maintained this self-confident universalism by titling the three parts in turn: 'The Solution of the Problem of Democracy', 'The Solution of the Economic Problem' and the more modest 'The Social Basis of the Third Universal Theory'.

The ideology's proposed solution to the problem of democracy involved first a rejection of all forms of representative democracy – a rejection embodied in Qadhafi's often-cited slogan 'representation is fraud' – which included a sweeping and vitriolic attack on political parties.[37] It went on to propose instead a system of direct participatory democracy operating through local Popular Congresses; this was the culmination of 'the journey of the masses in quest of democracy' – the true 'state of the masses' (Jamahiriya).[38]

The ideology's solution to the economic problem had overtones of Marxism not only in its references to 'exploitation of man by man' and other similarly Marxist terms but also in its attack on wage labour, with the abolition of the wage system presented as the ultimate solution of the economic problem.[39] However, this solution involved a unique form of socialism: 'privately-owned property to satisfy one's needs without exploitation' (some form of self-employment) and 'collective property in which the producers are partners in its production'.[40] The key notion was that of a workers' partnership in owning their factory or firm instead of being employed for wages by private or state owner – 'partners, not wage earners' was the most widely displayed slogan in Libya.[41]

The description of the social basis of the Third Universal Theory seemed to depart from the radicalism of the two earlier volumes/parts in depicting nationalism as *the* social factor and as the 'dynamic force behind history'.[42] Yet there was no attempt to specify or single out any particular nation, such as the Libyan or the Arab nation.[43] This is surprising in the light of Qadhafi's reputation for an almost quixotic attachment to the cause of (Pan-)Arab nationalism, as expressed in his many failed attempts at mergers with other Arab states and in his virulent opposition to Israel. Here the assessment of what was the regime's ideology must be expanded beyond the Third Universal Theory to include the survival of the Nasserist Arab nationalism which had inspired the original revolution and dominated its early years.

Another surprising omission from the Theory, and again presumably dictated by its claim to universalism, was the lack of any mention of Islam. The reference to 'green' in the title is the only Islamic connotation in *The Green Book*.[44] Religion receives very little attention or prominence in the book and is apparently accorded lower priority than national unity.[45] In the later 1970s Qadhafi had tried to defuse Islamic opposition to his ideology by claiming that his ideas were actually interpretations of the Koran. But several leading clergy declared that Qadhafi's attacks on wage labour and private property were incompatible with Islam. He responded by launching his populist 'Islamic Revolution' against clerical conservatism and claiming that the people were better qualified than the clergy to interpret the Koran and Islam. He acknowledged that his economic ideas conflicted with Islamic tradition but argued that they were in accordance with the Koran, that the Koran was the only source of religious authority, and that he and every citizen had the right to exercise independent judgement in interpreting the Koran. Qadhafi would seek to maintain his Islamic credentials by such moves as preaching televised sermons, but he still made no attempt to justify his ideology by specific references to the text or doctrines of the Koran.[46]

There were no major *changes* to the official ideology until the late 1980s. *The Green Book* continued to be the official ideological text, with one of the three television channels devoted entirely to its exposition, and the Third Universal Theory was still to be 'spread to the masses of every country'.[47] Qadhafi continued to proclaim the Islamic nature of such key doctrines as the 'state of the masses' (Jamahiriya) political system but the dispute with conservative clerics was not eased by such measures as the government's closing down of Libya's Koranic schools in 1986–7.[48] Nor was conservative opinion happy with the shift in Qadhafi's views on women's role. The social basis of the Third Universal Theory had adopted an 'equal but different' attitude with an emphasis on the childbearing/rearing role. But in the 1980s Qadhafi sought more equality for women, such as military training, despite arousing substantial opposition from a still patriarchal society.[49]

The major official change in the regime's ideology came late in the decade with the ideological recognition of the politically and economically liberalising 'revolution within the revolution' that Qadhafi began in 1987. Its key principles were enshrined in the 1988 Green Charter, known as the Great Green Charter of Human Rights or the International Green Document for Peace and Human Rights in the Era of the Masses.[50] Although largely a reformulation of the existing ideological message, the Charter also contained new principles not to be found in *The Green Book*. Among them were the independence of the judiciary and the right to legal counsel, the sacredness and protection of private property, and a condemnation of terrorism.[51] (Qadhafi declared that the new commitment to private property did not contradict or replace the 'partners not wage slaves' ideology.) The more right-wing approach was also evident in the 1990s, not just in Qadhafi's commitment to economic liberalisation that will be described in the next section but also in his greater support for established Islam. In 1993 he depicted himself as a proponent of Islamic law, calling for the implementation of its more draconian, corporal punishments and condemning the drinking of alcohol.[52] However, he also still condemned such 'reactionary movements' as the Muslim Brotherhood and he remained opposed to the veil and other patriarchal interpretations of Islam.[53]

ECONOMIC POLICY

When the military took power in 1969, they took control of an already quite oil-rich, state-controlled mixed economy that was almost entirely dependent upon oil for its export earnings.[54] Thanks to the new regime's shrewd manipulation of the competing foreign companies within Libya's oil industry and to the massive rise in world oil prices in 1973–4, the country's annual oil revenues more than quadrupled.[55] The regime had been able to provide the small Libyan population with a comprehensive package of health, education, welfare and housing benefits and to import an industrial sector of foreign-built plants (and a migrant labour force that would grow to several hundred thousand menial and skilled workers). In the later 1970s the regime also began to establish a socialist economy that would be dominated by the state to a greater degree than any of the other Middle Eastern regimes. It began the state takeover of all importing, finance, industry and agricultural land. The takeover became focused politically and ideologically on the 1978–9 'producers' revolution', which supposedly saw employees transform their firms into producers' partnerships – in theory run by these producers themselves but in practice controlled by the state.[56] However, the vital oil industry was not affected by this revolutionary upheaval (remaining in foreign majority-ownership) and the undisturbed flow of oil revenues continued to underpin the regime's economic, political and ideological 'revolutions' by providing Libyans with a per capita income of nearly $10 000 at the end of the 1970s.[57]

The 1980s saw a continuation of the recent statist momentum as the producers' revolution was now extended from industry to commerce. All except family-operated businesses were taken over, not only Western-style wholesale and retail operations but also the traditional market (*souk*) traders and merchants.[58] Qadhafi had been preparing for their replacement since 1978 with the opening of the first of a planned 165 huge state supermarkets.[59] The urban population was left almost completely dependent upon this new state distribution system of 'people's supermarkets', which was plagued by 'intermittent gluts and shortages'.[60] But public criticism in the local BPC meetings and in the 1983 GPC session led to the reopening of farmers' markets selling produce directly to the public and to more official tolerance of the black market.[61] It was a foretaste of the type of response this apparently despotic regime would make to much more serious economic (and political) problems in the late 1980s.

A marked downturn in oil prices and revenues was taking its toll on Libya by the mid-1980s. Oil prices had slipped back dramatically after the 1979 boom, reducing Libya's oil revenue from $22 billion to $10 billion by 1984 and the trade balance from an $8.2 billion surplus to a $2.6 billion deficit.[62] The state supermarkets were now constantly suffering from shortages as the supply of imported food and consumer goods fell, forcing the people to rely increasingly on the farmers' markets and black market.[63] The Transformation Plan for 1981–5 had seen its targeted annual economic growth of 9 per cent reduced in reality to only 3 per cent, and the secretaries of local and workplace executive committees were being threatened with dismissal for the new offence of failure to achieve production targets.[64] Qadhafi's short-term response to the crisis was to expel as many as 200 000 migrant workers, but he also now gave up any idea of eliminating all private trading and instead shifted attention to his new notions of economic independence and import substitution.[65]

The developing crisis of the mid-1980s, symbolised by the inability to produce a Development Plan for 1986–90, became a very acute crisis when the collapse in oil prices in 1986 virtually halved Libya's oil revenue.[66] The further cuts in imports created more shortages, which were exacerbated by the recent renewed banning of the farmers' markets, and black-market prices soared.[67] What has been termed 'wholesale patronage' (the use of massive public revenues to maintain the whole society as economic clients of the regime) now 'became increasingly difficult' and the ties of loyalty were strained.[68] In February 1987 the GPC strongly criticised the government's economic policies as well as the disastrous military intervention in Chad and the excesses of the revolutionary committees.[69] Clearly the regime was facing a potential political crisis on top of its immediate economic crisis.

On 27 March Qadhafi responded to the serious public discontent by announcing the economic and political liberalisation which he termed the 'revolution within the revolution'.[70] But there did not appear to be any revolutionary change in economic policy, and the regime sought to portray its new economic measures 'as following logically from its earlier policies'.[71] In particular, Qadhafi and the government were careful not to refer to the new economic policies as an *infitah* ('opening up' of the economy), for Qadhafi had several years earlier denounced the *infitah* occurring in Egypt and several other Arab states as being a sign of failure and a surrender to economic colonialism.[72] There was some validity in this rejection of comparisons with the more ambitious, sweeping and internationalising (especially as regards foreign investment) economic liberalisations carried out in Egypt and Tunisia.[73] The change in Libyan economic policy was aimed primarily at the quite narrow goal of 'giving Libyans more freedom to trade and to acquire a greater variety of goods'.[74] As economic reforms the Libyan measures would therefore involve a narrowly targeted marketisation and internationalisation aimed at the distribution sector. No longer would merchants and shopkeepers be called 'parasites' – Qadhafi actually praised the black marketeers who had eased the consumer shortages – and the regime's new economic approach would be that the private sector should be allowed to distribute the goods produced by the public sector.[75] In September 1988 this 'consumer *infitah*' or 'distribution-sector *infitah*' was completed by the reopening of the market traders' *souks* that had been closed in the early 1980s, the lifting of a number of the restrictions on retailing, and the abolition of the state monopoly on importing.[76]

The economic 'revolution' did have some effect outside the distribution sector. In agriculture the regime's new approach meant that officially the responsibility for marketing agricultural produce was shifted from the state to the farmers, which in practice meant the return (as in 1983) of the recently banned farmers' markets.[77] But there was no change to the principle that all land was owned collectively by all Libyans and could be used by individuals and families only to satisfy their needs (or to earn a livelihood). The only change to this usufructuary principle was that Qadhafi was now prepared to accept the notion of farmers employing non-family labourers – but as profit-sharing partners, not wage earners.[78]

In industry there seemed to be more radical change, with the apparent collectivisation of many state industries representing an at least partial privatisation of some of the state sector. But this was more a case of long-delayed implementation of the ideological principles which had supposedly motivated the producers' revolution of the late 1970s. Light industry saw most of its state-run enterprises turned over to their workers, which was what the producers' revolution of the late 1970s had presumably been meant to do. The only really new element was Qadhafi's notion that the producers' partnership arrangement embodied in his new slogan of *tashrukiyya* (self-management) could involve some partners' contributing capital rather than labour. Although this opened the way for a form of fuller privatisation, no enterprises were transferred to private entrepreneurs. Nor would any be transferred to foreign companies; internationalisation was confined to importing and did not seek foreign investment in any areas other than the oil industry.[79]

Therefore the changes in economic policy had constituted a distinctly limited programme of economic reform that sought to revive the people's standard of living by improving the distributive rather than the productive sector. Qadhafi did suggest that self-management would solve the problem of state-sector inefficiency, and the 140 firms turned over to self-management committees by August 1988 were theoretically (in practice only marginally) denied the state subsidies they had formerly enjoyed.[80] But non-oil production was of such minor importance compared to the oil industry that there was apparently little concern about inefficiency, low productivity, or such 'signs of serious structural deficiencies' as producing goods for which there was no international and too small a domestic market.[81]

The focus on distribution rather than production was a politically enlightened (self-interested) approach for an oil-rich despotism under economic and political pressure. For no reforms of the non-oil productive sector could be expected to have any significant effect on the export/public revenue situation in the short or medium term and they could be expected to involve major political risks. In addition to the recent evidence that society was in no mood to accept further economic pain, there was also evidence that key regime personnel, notably key military loyalists, would resist any policies threatening their vested interests – the most lucrative of which arose from the abuse of their political power in a non-marketised economy.[82] Moreover, Qadhafi would have difficulty in maintaining his ideological credibility if he too obviously abandoned the 'solution to the economic problem' proclaimed by his Third Universal Theory and expounded by the regime for almost a decade. In the short term, it was less politically risky to improve the distribution of the available (wholesale-patronage) resources than to make any economically, politically and ideologically disruptive effort to improve a part of the productive sector which contributed so little to those resources. As for the longer term, there was always the prospect of a revival in oil prices and in the resources available for wholesale patronage.

The success of the regime's limited economic reforms has to be judged – as in the case of Syria – in terms of these short-term political factors rather than in terms of how economically enlightened the policies were in the longer term. The standard, dismissive assessment is that they 'can hardly be called a genuine liberalization' and 'served as much as a chance to collect and hoard scarce goods as an opportunity to establish economic enterprises'.[83] But the greater availability of scarce goods was exactly the form of success sought and needed by the regime as it dealt with a potential political as well as very real economic crisis. As early as mid-1988 the practical effects of the reforms were visible. Private-sector shops were easing shortages of Western as well as Libyan goods not only in the big cities but also in the small towns and the villages.[84] The opening (or reopening) of opportunities in commerce would have also been likely to strengthen the loyalty of the beneficiaries of the new policy. However, there was also an underlying gamble involved in Qadhafi's approach – that the oil revenues would eventually improve. For Libya's young and rapidly growing population would require major increases in oil revenues to ensure that all Libyans would continue to enjoy the level of wholesale patronage to which they had now become accustomed. If the 1990s seemed to offer only the prospect of another decade of falling living standards, then presumably the regime would be in serious difficulty. The reform of the distributive sector was a 'one-off' measure that could buy time for an improvement in oil prices but provided no hope of longer-term improvement.

That oil prices failed to recover sufficiently in the later 1980s to alleviate the regime's longer-term political problem was reflected in its much more ambitious plans for economic reform in the 1990s. However, the plans for economic reform ran into the public opposition that this despotic regime had shown itself on previous occasions to be wary of confronting. In 1990 the government's Qadhafi-supported plan to cut public-sector employment and subsidies was rejected by the GPC, whose members actually put forward new demands for public spending.[85] The public's complacency and the regime's reluctance to force the issue seemed to be vindicated when oil revenues rose substantially in 1990–1, thanks to the Gulf crisis's effect on oil prices.[86] But by 1992 the economy was clearly in difficulties as oil revenues fell back again to almost the 1989 level, and there were restrictions on imports, rationing of basic commodities, an inflation rate of around 100 per cent, and delays in paying state salaries.[87] Libyan officials blamed the Lockerbie-bombing crisis for these economic woes, as the government's cash-flow problem was created partly by its financial manoeuvres to protect Libya's overseas assets and revenues from possible United Nations or Western punitive actions.[88]

The relatively light sanctions that were imposed by the United Nations in April 1992 did not seriously threaten the economy but provided the government with a justification for cuts in public spending and provided Qadhafi with new, more politically defensible justification for seeking a sweeping liberalisation of the economy.[89] The GPC was presented in June 1992 with radical proposals for restructuring the financial sector, including privatisation of banks, competition from foreign banks, and even the creation of a stock exchange.[90] Nothing came of these proposals, except that in September the GPC approved a law which allowed individuals to invest more freely in the private sector and to practise their professions independently.[91] In a 1993 speech to the GPC Qadhafi called for further economic liberalisation, such as reform of the exchange rate (with the prospect of establishing a convertible currency), the promotion of foreign investment, and the encouragement of tourism to reduce Libya's dependency on oil revenues.[92] However, once again the actual implementation of reform did not match the rhetoric. A new law permitting the establishment of privately owned banks was the only significant measure.[93] 'Gaddafi has repeatedly pledged economic liberalisation and the measures to be taken are visible to all. Very little has been done.'[94] In fact the GPC session in February 1994 saw a commitment to continuing with price controls, subsidising rationed goods, free education and health care, and the provision of essential needs for food, clothing and transport.[95] The country's oil industry could still provide Libyans with a per capita income of $6000 a year and a trade balance surplus of $1 billion.[96]

9 Khomeinist Iran

POLITICAL STRUCTURE

The political structure of the Iranian regime was by 1980 as unique as the Libyan and would experience more major changes in the 1980s than any of the other defiant dictatorships. Only (Grand Ayatollah) Khomeini's continuing personal theocratic or clerical rule over this predominantly Shiite Muslim country would provide an underlying stability, despite such outward dramatic changes as the establishing and discarding of the façade of IRP party-state dictatorship. The Khomeini-headed revolution that had replaced the Shah's monarchical regime in 1978–9 with an Islamic Republic would lead on to almost a decade of apparent instability in political structure. The Islamic Republic's democratic institutions were taken over by an apparent party-state dictatorship that ended in 1987 with the Islamic Republican Party's dissolution, revealing the underlying framework of clerical rule that in turn shifted from a personal to collective form in 1989 with the death of Khomeini. By then he had overseen the development of a unique form of modern clerical dictatorship that should be termed Khomeinist in recognition of its founder.

The Constitution of the new Islamic Republic, promulgated at the end of 1979, featured some marked changes from the Shah's secular monarchical regime. Most obvious were the republican elements, such as the replacement of the ruling monarch by an elected President as head of state and by a mixed presidential/parliamentary executive with a powerful Prime Minister as head of government. Together with an elected legislature, the Majles, that could veto ministerial appointments, this formed the constitutional basis for a democratic republic. The Islamic elements of the new republic were less obvious and more unusual. The Constitution specified that the rights to free speech, assembly and the like were conditional on their exercise not being harmful to Islam (and the Republic). New constitutional organs were granted important powers to protect the Islamic nature of the Republic: a Council of Guardians comprising six clergy and six laymen was to rule on whether bills passed by the Majles were congruent with Islam and therefore could become law; the Council was also to review (and if necessary reject) the Islamic suitability of candidates for election to such public offices as the Presidency and membership of the Majles; and the large Council of Experts was to choose the holder of the new and very powerful Islamic post of Supreme-Faqih/Rahbar.[1]

The post of Supreme Faqih (supreme religious judge) and Rahbar (leader) of the Islamic Republic was a unique and crucially important Islamic element in the Constitution. The holder of this post exercised the *velayat-e faqih* (the jurist's guardianship) as supreme religious judge and, according to the Constitution, was also to be the people's leader. The powers of the Faqih/Rahbar extended beyond such juristic areas as appointing leading judicial officials and half of the Council of Guardians; the Faqih/Rahbar was also the Commander-in-Chief of the armed forces and had the right to declare war and peace. Moreover, the Faqih/Rahbar could be removed only in extraordinary circumstances and only by the Council of Guardians. When Khomeini became the first holder of this powerful new constitutional post (which had been shaped with him in mind), it marked not only another major Islamic limitation on democratic institutions but also a clerical and Khomeinist future. By the end of 1979, even before he had acquired the constitutional powers of Faqih/Rahbar, Khomeini had already established a degree of personal rule and this would be consolidated and further developed during the 1980s to become the backbone of the Islamic Republic.[2]

The first marked structural *change* in the 1980s was the establishment of a party-state dictatorship by the Islamic Republican Party. Established by close followers of Khomeini, the IRP's three main ideological features were support for Khomeini, a leftist presentation of Khomeinist populism, and a return to Islamic principles in their totality.[3] In the early 1980s the IRP saw all other political parties (except the trusted Islamic Liberation Movement) eliminated or forced underground and the removal from office of the IRP's main rival among Khomeini's political following, the relatively secular President Bani-Sadr.[4] The Party outwardly had the typical structure of a modern regime party: a small, elitist membership, a network of hundreds of local branches, an executive Central Committee and a General Secretary.[5] The means of control also appeared quite typical of a party-state dictatorship. IRP members or sympathisers controlled the Presidency, the Cabinet of Ministers, the legislature, the provincial and, sometimes, the district and municipal levels of government.[6] However, the party-state dictatorship of the IRP was really only a façade for clerical rule and the Party's strength was based upon the support it received from not only its clerical members, who provided most of its leaders, but also much of the clergy as a whole.

As essentially the political agent of the clergy, the IRP could rely on the tacit or active support of most clerics, even though only a minority were actually IRP members.[7] (There were some 180 000 clergy, in the widest sense, in Iran at the beginning of the 1980s, about one for every two hundred lay people.[8]) Relations between the clerical/mosque network and the IRP were so close that IRP branches were often based on the local mosque and were often also headed by the local Friday Prayer Leader.[9] The clerical/mosque network was an unrivalled machine for mobilising electoral support (through such means as Friday Prayer Leaders' sermons and the patronage opportunities now available to the mosques) that guaranteed the IRP's electoral dominance as much as did the forceful methods used against rival parties.[10]

The clergy had acquired a dramatic degree of control over the state during the revolution. Politicised clergy dominated a) the purge committees and placement committees which supervised the dismissal and appointment of civil servants and military officers, b) the Islamic Societies set up in every Ministry and c) the Ideological-Political Bureaus established in the police and the military, where some 270 clerics 'served in the role of political commissars'.[11] The clergy also increased their hold on society by dominating the Islamic Societies that were established in work places and educational facilities to police the Islamic purity of society and to support the regime's ban on strikes and discouragement of labour militancy.[12]

What is more, the clergy exercised a degree of control over new public organisations that had been established during the revolution, notably the *komiteh* (revolutionary committee) guards and the Revolutionary Guards. By 1982 the network of tens of thousands of *komiteh* guards had been 'officially placed in charge of all police precincts' and were policing 'every street in every city'.[13] Their accompanying official subordination to the clergy (purportedly to 'prevent them straying from the path of virtue') only formalised the existing situation of clerical control of the guards at the grassroots level.[14] The Revolutionary Guards, otherwise known as the Islamic Revolutionary Guard Corps (or the Pasdaran), was officially established by Khomeini in 1979 as a security force, but developed into a paramilitary and then professionalised military force.[15] As with the Waffen-SS, the outbreak of a long and bitter war provided the Revolutionary Guards with the opportunity to expand in size and capability until they rivalled the state's regular forces. During the war with Iraq the Guards expanded in number to several hundred thousand members, acquired sophisticated weaponry, created naval and air force units, and became more militarily professional.[16] But they remained under clerical control from the top downwards. Khomeini was constitutionally the commander of the Guards and had devolved command onto senior political clerics, while other clerics were members of the Guards' internal Ideological-Political apparatus.[17]

The 1987 decision to dissolve the IRP brought an end to the appearance of party-state dictatorship and starkly revealed the underlying structure of clerical rule or, more accurately, personal clerical rule by the Ayatollah Khomeini. Although not as obvious as the establishment and then discarding of the IRP party-state structure, the consolidation and further development of his personal rule was a more important structural change. The formal post of Faqih/Rahbar of the Islamic Republic was complemented by an official personality cult and by genuine popular prestige as the 'Great Leader of the Revolution and Founder of the Islamic Republic'.[18] He also exercised a unique mixture of supreme political and religious authority that he had acquired during the revolution. His religious authority was illustrated by his appointment of the Friday Prayer Leaders of the major cities, who in turn appointed the Prayer Leaders of the town mosques.[19] His political authority was illustrated by his appointment of personal representatives – who considered themselves to be superior in authority to the official government – to supervise various Ministries, military institutions and even universities.[20]

An aspect of his political authority which had become very apparent in the 1980s was his 'hands-off' approach to day-to-day government and his tolerance of factionalism among those of his followers who sought to take on this task or influence its direction. Khomeini adopted not only an 'above-parties' stance (he did not link himself to the IRP in any formal or public sense) but also an 'above-factions' approach. Although he insisted on his supporters' maintaining the appearance of regime unity, he allowed factional politics to flourish – to the extent of deliberately keeping the factions competitive and intervening to protect a weaker faction from being politically eliminated by a stronger one.[21] The Speaker of the Majles declared that Khomeini wanted factions to adopt a 'critical stand' but not to 'clash' with or 'weaken each other'.[22] The above-factions approach contributed to Khomeini's apparent ambivalence or hesitation over some policy issues but it also held together a broad alliance of Khomeini followers which represented a wide range of viewpoints and 'revolved around loyalty to Khomeini and adhering to his guidelines'.[23] Such an approach further strengthened his personal position, as it 'kept his populist appeal intact and precluded the possibility of any one faction getting powerful enough to challenge him.'[24] But it may also have been based upon the realisation that 'ongoing factional infighting could potentially erupt into open warfare once he departed from the scene', and upon the hope that such fratricidal conflict within the regime might be avoided by preventing any of the factions becoming so powerful as to seem a threat to the others.[25] Certainly his tolerance of factionalism would have an enduring, posthumous influence upon the political development of the Islamic Republic.

The death of Khomeini in June 1989 brought the greatest structural change of the 1980s, as his personal rule was replaced by collective leadership headed by his close associates. President Khamenei took over the now vacant post of Faqih/Rahbar, and his post of President was in turn taken over by Rafsanjani, who until then had been Speaker of the Majles. The Presidency was strengthened by 1989 constitutional amendments that eliminated the post of Prime Minister in favour of making the President the head of government.[26] The post of Faqih/Rahbar remained in theory the most powerful one in the country, and was recognised in the 1989 constitutional amendments to be the source of the Republic's general policies.[27] But the post had lost much of its religious authority as Khamenei, like Rafsanjani, was only a middle-ranking cleric; the regime officially admitted that Khamenei lacked the theological qualifications of the many more senior clerics, such as the some 200 Ayatollahs and several Grand Ayatollahs.[28] Despite his quickly acquiring the rank of Ayatollah, the new Faqih's religious decrees were still not viewed as of any higher authority than those of Grand Ayatollahs.[29]

After the successful shift to collective leadership, the Islamic Republic's largely defunct democratic institutions gained a new prominence as they expressed not only factional divisions within the regime's extensive collective leadership but also popular disenchantment with the regime's performance. Factionalism within the regime had helped give independence and life to the Majles in the 1980s as a source of open and harsh criticism of the government by disgruntled factions.[30] Such factionalism was again on very public view in the 1992 Majles elections. In these supposedly non-party elections, in which 2050 candidates approved by the Council of

Guardians competed for 270 seats, there was virtually a two-faction or nascent two-party contest, with each faction publicising a list of the candidates that it endorsed.[31] The indications of public discontent that had been discernable in the Majles elections were more evident in the 1993 presidential election. President Rafsanjani, in competition with three other approved candidates, was re-elected with only two-thirds of the vote on a less than 60 per cent turn-out.[32]

But for all these signs of democratisation, especially the competition between two quasi-parties, the competition for power was going on *within* the regime's collective leadership. Although the competition and divisions within the leadership were being expressed in a very public fashion and through outwardly democratic institutions, there was no likelihood of power being extended to groups outside this clerically dominated collective leadership. However divided by factionalism, the collective leadership still ensured that the Islamic Republic and its political life would remain ultimately under clerical control. The clerical presence in the government and Majles had declined markedly in the late 1980s and early 1990s, from about 40 per cent to less than 20 per cent in the Majles and to only two Ministers in the government.[33] But the key posts continued to be held by the clergy, who continued 'to form the backbone of post-Khomeini Islamic Republican Iran'.[34] That the two factions contesting the 1992 elections based their campaigns upon two rival clerical associations was indicative of the manner in which the outwardly democratic institutions of the Islamic Republic still operated within a clerical strait-jacket.

IDEOLOGY

Just as Khomeini established a unique political structure, he also provided the regime with a unique set of official beliefs that has been termed Khomeinism. The uniqueness of Khomeinism arises from its combination of theological with ideological elements to produce a set of Islamic/ideological official beliefs. These beliefs will be analysed as the regime's 'ideology' in the broadest sense but will be covered separately, first the theological and then the more narrowly ideological.

The ideologically orthodox aspects of Khomeinism's 'Islamic revolution' were: the reintroduction of Islamic law, and with it the reintroduction of the traditional corporal punishments; the transfer of judicial authority to the clergy; the prohibition of usury in the sense of any interest-bearing loans; and the incorporation into the Constitution of various safeguards to maintain an Islamic dominance of state and society.[35] The patriarchal aspect of this Islamic revolution involved not only the reintroduction of patriarchal Islamic personal, family and criminal law, but also the legal imposition of the veil, the banning of coeducation, the imposition of various other forms of segregation, and the attentions of the new Office for Propagation of Virtues and Prevention of Sins.[36] However, Khomeini was not in favour of traditionalist extremism (he emphasised the need for technology and modern industry) and he proclaimed that it would be un-Islamic to deprive women of the vote – and some women would actually be elected to the Majles in the 1980s–90s.[37]

Khomeinism also contained some major reinterpretations of orthodox theology, the most politically significant being his interpretation of the Shiite Muslim doctrine relating to the *velayat-e faqih* (the jurist's guardianship).[38] When he published his new interpretation in 1970, Khomeini acknowledged that this principle of the jurist's guardianship had been 'distorted' over the centuries to refer only to the religious judges' protective guardianship over widows, orphans and other defenceless members of society.[39] He argued instead that the religious judges exercised such guardianship over all believers, who all needed the sacred Islamic law and the correct judicial interpretation of its content. He concluded that the religious judges possessed the same authority as had the Prophet himself and thus possessed a divine right to rule.[40] This theocratic argument was used by Khomeini in his attacks on monarchy as a form of government, and it also posed problems for any claims to authority by a democratic regime. Khomeini argued that an Islamic legislature, even if democratically elected, cannot legislate – the only source of law is the will of God – and can only set 'programmes of action' that are based upon Islamic law.[41] In contrast, the guardian jurist interpreting Islamic law was declaring the will of God. Here was the theological justification for the power bestowed on the new post of Supreme Faqih by the Islamic Republic, albeit at the cost of removing one of the most appealing elements, the rule of the people, from the populist aspect of Khomeinism.

The main element of the regime's ideology, as distinct from theology, was a populist message that was similar in many features to the populism seen in other Third World countries, notably in Latin America.[42] It was a radical or leftist populism that divided society into the two classes of the 'oppressors' and the 'oppressed' (*mostazafin*), the lower class of exploited and deprived urban and rural poor.[43] Khomeini had used this populist line of attack against the Shah in the 1970s, and its unique combination with or integration into the Islamic message can be seen in some of the Khomeini catch-phrases espoused by anti-Shah demonstrators: 'Islam belongs to the oppressed, not the oppressors', 'Islam represents the slum dwellers, not the palace dwellers', 'Islam will eliminate class differences'.[44] Where Iranian populism differed from forms of populism found in other Third World countries was not only in its Islam-linked lack of commitment to the rule of the people but also in its incorporation of an international perspective. The Constitution's commitment to 'strive for the total unity of all Muslims' was matched by its commitment to 'help the oppressed of the world struggle against their oppressors'.[45] Similarly, the seemingly theologically motivated labelling of the United States as the 'Great Satan' and of the Soviet Union as 'the Lesser Satan' was based at least as much on the populist charge that the two superpowers dominated the world at the expense of its dispossessed and exploited masses.[46]

The *changes* in the regime's ideology were less dramatic than those in political structure but were still significant. By the mid-1980s the socially divisive aspect of the populist ideology was being diluted. The term 'the oppressed' became a political label rather than a socioeconomic category or class, and as a political category it included any and all of the regime's supporters, even wealthy merchants. The emphasis shifted to harmony between middle and lower classes, and now Iran as a whole was referred to as an oppressed nation. However, the projection of the notion of 'the oppressed' on to the nation as a whole was also an indication of the increasing prominence of a new, nationalist element in the regime's ideology.[47]

The appearance of nationalism within the ideology was particularly notable because in the immediate aftermath of the revolution there had been marked opposition to Iranian nationalism. In part the post-revolutionary anti-nationalism was a theological attempt to remove all non-Islamic influences that might threaten the dominant role Islam was to have in Iranian society and state.[48] There was a downplaying of Persian culture and history, especially that of pre-Islamic Iran, and history was rewritten to the glorification of Muslims rather than Persians.[49] In part, too, this anti-nationalism was a political or ideological attack on what had been the ideological focus of the Pahlavi dynasty of Shahs: an emphasis on the pre-Islamic era of Iranian history and a glorification of the great monarchs of the ancient Persian empire.[50]

Khomeini's theological/ideological position on nationalism was to reject any form of chauvinism or over-attachment to non-Islamic aspects of history and culture but to accept a patriotic attachment to one's people and territory.[51] He would increasingly speak of 'the Iranian fatherland, the Iranian nation, the Iranian patriot, and the honourable people of Iran.'[52] The war with Iraq may have influenced him in this direction, as can be seen in his accompanying shift away from the theological notion of an Islamic world order that has no place for the territorial state.[53] Although the Iraqi invasion drew from him calls for the defence of Islam rather than of Iran, by 1982 he was advocating an end to Iran's hermit status and in 1984 called for Iran in effect to join the international state system.[54] In fact 'the imperative of the survival of the nation and regime, plus the strength of nationalism... led to a reemergence of cultural and political Iranianism.'[55]

The regime came to accept officially the notion of an Iranian nation and of an 'Iranian-Islamic' culture. Although even in the 1990s Islam remained the senior partner, this was a major change from when the new regime had been monolithically Islamic.[56] Furthermore, nationalism seemed to be influencing Islamic theological as well as populist ideological themes. By the later 1980s 'realists' were calling for priority to be given to carrying through the Islamic revolution at home, in the 'Islamic citadel', while even proponents of exporting the revolution had come to see this in terms of creating in Iran an Islamic country that would be 'a model for other deprived countries'.[57] At an official level, in the 1990s the regime at times referred to Iran's role in the development of Islamic civilisation and to Iran's status as the vanguard of the Islamic world – as the only nation to have established 'the government of God'.[58]

Finally, the most striking change in the regime's policies – the 1990s economic liberalisation – did not require any official theological/ideological change. Khomeini had never had much interest in economic policy,[59] but he was committed to Islamic law's traditional protection of private property and enterprise. Until his death and in his political testament Khomeini constantly reiterated his commitment to private property rights.[60] In the 1980s he advised Ministers 'to supervise rather than control the economy and to encourage entrepreneurs to do what they did best, such as importing goods and managing small factories'; he warned that 'the bazaar merchants should be treated as honourable partners rather than as untrustworthy outsiders'.[61] Even his concern for the poor, which was reflected in repeated urging that the government provide for their needs, was of a charitable-welfare rather than statist-redistributional nature, and he displayed what was virtually a liberal, trickle-down approach in his political testament when arguing that having the 'wheels of the economy' turned by free enterprise would produce social justice for all, especially the poor.[62] In his approach he seems much closer to the conservatives who opposed the statist government policies of the 1980s than to the populists who dominated the governments of that era.

It is true that in 1984 Khomeini publicly declared his support for the statist approach to economic policy but this was 'more likely to have reflected his overriding concern about the war with Iraq than a definitive jurisprudential statement in favour of statism.'[63] (He also balanced his support for the statist approach with a warning not to go too far in that direction and to let the people and the bazaar participate in the economy.[64]) When he was formally asked in 1988 for his advice on how the regime should proceed with the post-war rebuilding of the country, his reply included calls for 'appropriate' planning operating within Islamic precepts (implicitly the protection of private property and enterprise), more freedom of foreign trade, expanding exports, and support for technocratic expertise.[65] Therefore the reformists who pushed through economic liberalisation after his death were able to present the shift in economic approach as having been sanctioned by the Ayatollah Khomeini – and the earlier, statist approach as having been due to wartime needs that no longer existed.[66]

ECONOMIC POLICY

The Islamic Republic had inherited from the Shah's regime an oil-dependent mixed economy (which had seen annual oil revenues rise from less than $3 billion in 1972/3 to over $20 billion in 1976/7) with agriculture, commerce and much of industry in private ownership and relatively moderate state control of the economy.[67] The 1978–9 revolution had led to a sizeable part of the private sector being taken into public ownership.[68] All the banks and almost all the large and medium-sized industrial firms were taken over, and a National Iranian Industries Organisation was established to administer some 450 nationalised industries.[69] The onset of wartime conditions with the Iraqi invasion of September 1980 led to the *ad hoc* establishment of a range of interventionist state organisations and measures that covered not just rationing, consumer subsidies, price and wage controls but also importing and distribution of essential goods, domestic procurement and distribution, and the compulsory state purchase of agricultural produce.[70]

However, the statist momentum began to run into resistance in 1982–3 as opposition developed among the bazaar merchants and some elements of the civil service and the clergy.[71] The government's attempt to introduce a form of economic planning, the proposed First Development Plan, was blocked by deliberations in the Majles that delayed the Plan's approval until 1986 and reduced it to a set of qualitative generalities.[72] The government also found that its legislation to secure a state monopoly over foreign trade was vetoed by the Council of Guardians (in 1982 and again in 1984), and it had to be content with controlling foreign trade through such administrative controls as import licensing and allocation of foreign exchange.[73] But the clearest indication of conservative resistance to state intervention was provided by the failure to pass a land-reform law. Proposed land-redistributing legislation emerged from the Majles in 1982 in a much milder form that involved only the leasing of landowners' excess land to the poor, and even this revised bill was vetoed by the Council of Guardians as infringing property rights.[74] As was mentioned earlier, Khomeini had to intervene in 1984 to support the government's statist approach to dealing with wartime economic needs. But the upshot was that the 1982–8 governments of Prime Minister Moussavi presided over a directionless state-dominated economy that 'tended to bring out the worst' in both public and private sectors, such as the development of an array of inefficient, loss-making state enterprises.[75]

With the end of the Iran–Iraq war in 1988 came an end to not only the regime's justification for so much state control of the economy but also the regime's main excuse for its poor economic performance.[76] The economy had shrunk by nearly 16 per cent in the 1979–87 period and per capita (real) income had been almost halved in the decade since the revolution.[77] During the war Iran had spent only some 12 per cent of its annual GNP on military expenditure as compared to Iraq's over 50 per cent.[78] And unlike Baathist Iraq, the Iranian regime had not resorted to massive foreign borrowing to ease the economic pain of the war – Iran's foreign debt of about $12 billion was not much greater than its pre-revolutionary level.[79] However, Iran had certainly not fought the war 'on the cheap'. In addition to its much higher human casualties, Iran had suffered more physical devastation than Iraq and estimates of the total physical and other costs of the war went as high as $600 billion.[80] Furthermore, Iran had suffered major damage to its oil installations as well as suffering from the same collapse in oil prices that had crippled its Iraqi enemy's ability to fund the war and post-war reconstruction: in 1986 Iran's oil revenues fell to little more than $7 billion instead of the projected $18.5 billion.[81] Considering the raised expectations among the Iranian people that finally the revolution would be able to deliver on its populist promises of a better life for ordinary Iranians, especially the poor, the regime was facing a major political as well as economic crisis in the late 1980s.[82]

In response to the crisis, a programme of liberalising economic reforms would be put in place by a reformist coalition that dominated the collective leadership established after Khomeini's death in 1989. The main elements in the reformists' loose coalition were a) 'pragmatists' who believed economic success was required for the Islamic Republic's political success and b) religious conservatives whose orthodox commitment to Islamic law meant that they were supporters of private property and enterprise as well as Islamic social policies.[83] The keystone of the reformist coalition was the alliance between the new President, Rafsanjani, and the new Faqih/Rahbar, the Ayatollah Khamenei. President Rafsanjani was 'one of the clerics most interested in economics' and his long-standing pragmatic approach to economic questions had led him to favour technocratic competence, marketising reforms, privatisation, and an 'open door' welcoming of foreign investment and expertise.[84] The more conservative Khamenei was not as interested in economics and economic liberalisation but had become a supporter of using foreign expertise to help with reconstruction.[85] And he would join with Rafsanjani in publicly emphasising such themes as reconstruction, realism, expertise and competence, individual self-reliance, and even entrepreneurship.[86] The theme of post-war reconstruction was used by President Rafsanjani to win support for the largely technocratic composition of his Cabinet and to put what he called his 'extremist' opponents on the defensive.[87] But probably the main reason for the overwhelming support Rafsanjani would elicit in his election to the Presidency (with 95 per cent of the vote) and in securing unprecedentedly wide Majles approval of his Cabinet choices was the desire for unity and stability in the aftermath of Khomeini's death.[88]

The major divisions that existed within the collective leadership would become apparent as the reformist programme was put into effect. The implementation of economic reforms in Iran was politically similar to the Chinese case in being pushed through by a collective leadership that was divided over the issue of whether liberalisation was the 'enlightened' approach to economic policy. Although the Iranian reform coalition appears to have been in a more despotic position than the Chinese reformers had been, it also faced more fervent and open opposition within the collective leadership. The Iranian opposition to economic reform was more like the hostility shown by the defeated Chinese leftists than the qualified opposition to liberalisation shown by Chinese conservatives, who had supported the replacement of the leftist Hua Guofeng by the more pragmatic Deng Xiaoping and continued to recognise him as the regime's senior leader. Like the Chinese leftists, the opposition within the Iranian collective leadership had earlier implemented or supported the statist policies that the reformers were now seeking to dismantle. But in the Iranian case the main battle with the hardline opposition would be fought *after* rather than before the reform programme was under way.

The faction or coalition opposed to economic reform can be labelled the 'populists' because they emphasised the populist element of the regime's theological/ideological heritage, as in their arguments that Rafsanjani's economic reforms would harm the poor and 'put yet more money into the pockets of the "bloodsucking bazaar mafia"'.[89] (The core of the opposition to the reform programme were 'variously labelled by the press as hardliners, radicals or statists.'[90]) Although often displaying as much a statist as a populist economic perspective, they showed great concern about typically populist issues, such as consumer subsidies and charges for public services. The wider opposition to the reformers also included other groups or tendencies, notably the religiously ultra-orthodox traditionalists or 'fundamentalists', whose opposition to Western materialism made them hostile to internationalising the economy and to over-concern with material progress.[91]

Although, as was seen earlier, the economic reformers were on quite solid ground theologically/ideologically, the opposition to economic reform seemed to be based largely on ideological differences rather than on vested interests among regime personnel and society. A 'new privileged business elite' had emerged during the 1980s by exploiting informal links to state officials and influential clerics who controlled access to the lucrative business opportunities presented by such state-bestowed privileges as import licences, foreign exchange, and government contracts.[92] But neither this privileged group within the business class nor the regime personnel who had been in corrupt relations with them were in a strong position to oppose economic reforms that threatened their vested interests. The 'widespread bureaucratic shenanigans and public sector corruption' (extending down to petty bribe-taking by minor officials dealing with ordinary citizens) was too unpopular and contrary to Islamic values to allow such vested interests to be defended in the relatively public arena of Iranian politics.[93] The most dangerous opposition, presenting the greatest political risks to the reformers, would come from the fervour of ideological opposition.

The main vehicle for the economic reformers' 'rolling back' of the state's dominance of the economy was, somewhat paradoxically, a Five Year Plan. As a revised version of the Comprehensive National Reconstruction Plan which had been based upon Khomeini's formal advice about reconstruction, the Plan had an inherent authority and was formally approved by the Majles in January 1990 after several months of deliberation.[94] Although the Plan contained many familiar and non-controversial policies, the new approach was evident in such features as: the envisaged use of foreign loans and foreign joint-venture investment; the increase in prices and fees for public goods and services; the reduction in subsidies to loss-making state enterprises; and the actual privatisation of some industrial enterprises – soon 500–800 of them were earmarked for privatisation.[95] The Plan's first budget, the 'Rafsanjani budget' of 1990/91, also displayed the new approach by its commitment to the gradual elimination of all subsidies on consumer goods, to no longer absorbing the losses of state enterprises, to introducing more competition among producers, and to removing special interests' privileges.[96]

The Iranian economic reform programme was developing into the most comprehensive economic liberalisation yet seen in the Middle East. Marketisation would involve a reduction of price controls, permission for agricultural producers to sell some of their produce in free markets rather than to the state, and allowing non-essential imports to be sold on the free market.[97] Internationalisation would be furthered by the new policy of opening up importing to the private sector, which would involve removing licensing and other limits on importing and freeing up access to foreign exchange by legalising free-market foreign-exchange dealers.[98] Exporters, too, would be given a range of new incentives including being allowed to retain their foreign-exchange earnings and sell them at the market rate.[99] Although the system of multiple official exchange rates would only be simplified, not abandoned, in practice most non-official transactions were made at the market rate.[100] Privatisation would mean not just selling off mines, petrochemical plants, aluminium rolling mills, car factories and the like to the private sector but also selling off shares to the public, with the National Iranian Industries Organisation offering 28 million shares in its firms to the public in 1991/2 and planning to finish selling off all its shares in the following year.[101] The Teheran stock exchange would experience 'an extraordinary surge' and be trading shares in more companies at higher total values than it had in pre-revolutionary days.[102]

However, the criticism of the Plan's and budget's liberalising features by opponents within and outside the Majles marked the end of the 'honeymoon' period for the Rafsanjani government. From then on increasingly serious and open attacks were launched upon the reformist government, and the populists displayed their influence within the Majles in leading its March 1991 vote-of-no-confidence dismissal of the Health Minister.[103] (Some of the opposition had even launched an attack on the Khamenei element in the reform coalition in autumn 1990, and for a time in 1991 courted Ayatollah Montazeri, who had held the position of deputy/successor Faqih until only months before Khomeini's death.[104]) However, the opposition to the government was a 'loose and shifting coalition' and Rafsanjani was able to exploit this weakness and his own ability to put together supportive (if similarly loose and shifting) coalitions to protect his other Ministers and ensure the smooth passage of most government bills through the Majles.[105] The seemingly conclusive victory over the populists that he won in the 1992 Majles elections was the product of similarly skilful coalition-building and preparation from behind the scenes.

Rafsanjani had long ago chosen the April–May 1992 Majles elections as the principal arena in which he would deal with the populist challenge to his reformist government and to the direction in which he was taking the country.[106] His pro-government electoral coalition incorporated: sympathetic officials in the Interior Ministry, provincial governments and municipalities; mosques and their Prayer Leaders; the state media and sympathetic newspapers; the Association of Guilds and Bazaars; and a number of prominent Ayatollahs.[107] A pre-emptive strike was launched against the opposition by having a substantial number of opposition candidates disqualified by the conservative Council of Guardians, using its constitutional right to screen Majles candidates to ensure they had sufficient Islamic credentials.[108]

During the campaign the pro-government coalition kept up the pressure on the opposition by blaming the populists for the economic and social problems inherited from the 1980s, often using populist-style grievances and rhetoric in accusing 'extremist pseudo-clerics' of such misdeeds as allocating state contracts to their relatives and friends.[109] The pro-government coalition's campaign was based upon the Ruhaniyat association of clerics, which publicly endorsed the appropriate candidates, while the populists' campaign was based upon the rival Ruhaniyoun association of clerics, which similarly provided the public with a list of the candidates that it endorsed.[110] The pro-government Ruhaniyat advocated 'market-oriented reform', obedience to the leader (Khamenei) and support for Rafsanjani; the populist Ruhaniyoun argued against economic liberalisation, espoused such populist slogans as 'solving economic problems in favour of the deprived and disinherited' and also demanded that the Council of Experts' choice of Faqih/Rahbar require the voters' approval.[111] Therefore the pro-government candidates' landslide victory seemed a clear endorsement of the reformers and economic reform. Even their opponents recognised that the pro-government candidates' capture of over 70 per cent of the 270 Majles seats was only partly due to various electoral advantages and was mainly due to popular support, particularly in the larger cities.[112] The Ruhaniyoun's decision to suspend its activities seemed the ultimate admission of defeat and of acceptance that the reformers were riding a wave of popular support.[113]

However, the regime was having some problems in 'delivering the goods' to the public from its liberalising reforms, as was reflected in the voter turn-out of only some 60 per cent and the apparent lack of public interest in the election.[114] In the first three years of the Plan the economy grew at about 8 per cent a year, but inflation had soon exceeded the targeted 9 per cent, reaching nearly 20 per cent in 1991/2, increasing further in the following year and being projected to exceed 30 per cent in 1993/4.[115] Although domestic consumption had benefited from the more than doubling of imports, this had been at the cost of a more than doubling of foreign debt (to as much as $30 billion) and the onset of debt-repayment and foreign-exchange problems that would produce a currency crisis in 1993.[116] Nor did the foreign-exchange situation seem likely to improve in the near future. The windfall increase in oil revenue created by the Iraqi invasion of Kuwait had ended by early 1992 and had revealed again how dependent Iran still was upon the vagaries of the world oil market.[117] Non-oil exports still contributed only 6 per cent of the total, and attempts to attract foreign investors for joint-venture exporting were proving a dismal failure, despite a mid-1992 shift to more generous terms and the creation of two free-trade zones on islands in the Persian Gulf.[118]

Nevertheless, the government continued to implement economic reforms in 1993. In March–April there was further simplification of the exchange-rate system, a massive *de facto* devaluation, and the creation of a fully convertible currency.[119] But with a presidential election looming in June the government also seemed to be worried about the political risks that the reform programme entailed. Rafsanjani had already been stung into a vehement public declaration that he was not copying a Western economic model but maintaining 'a mixed, Islamic economy'; now there were proposals to slow down the pace of privatisation, re-establish some price controls and subsidies on consumer goods, and create a 'safety net' to cushion the impact of the reforms upon the poor.[120] Therefore it seems that anxiety about the political risks of opposition from society, not just from within the regime, was beginning to affect the economic reform programme.

The public's increasing discontent was evident in the presidential election results, especially when they are compared with those of the 1989 election.[121] Rafsanjani was re-elected on a turn-out of less than 58 per cent, down from 70 per cent, and with the support of only 63 per cent of these voters, compared to over 94 per cent in 1989.[122] Considering that Khamenei and other religious leaders had pronounced that voting was a religious duty, the low turn-out was in itself a sign of mass discontent.[123] The low turn-out may also have been partly due to the lack of any substantial policy differences between the four (approved) candidates.[124] But the runner-up candidate's slogan 'Less Luxury and More Austerity for Leaders' suggested that even such supporters of reform were discontented with the unexplained affluence, presumably born of corruption, that was 'increasingly setting the religious leadership apart from their less fortunate compatriots'.[125] The marketisation of the economy had not gone far enough to eliminate the opportunities for alliances between regime personnel abusing their powers for personal gain and businessmen seeking the competitive advantages and lucrative opportunities such alliances could still offer. Corruption 'flourished in the freed-up economy' and 'businessmen, importers, distributors and contractors with links to influential clerics and officials...amassed great wealth'.[126] Although in a sense new vested interests were being created

in maintaining (but not extending) the reform programme marketisation, their political significance was far outweighed by the
damaging effect on the loyalties of the wider society.

Encouraged by the decline in public support for the government,
the populists revived their Ruhaniyoun clerical association and indul-
ged in anti-Rafsanjani rhetoric, such as labelling him the 'American
President'.[127] More importantly, Rafsanjani's alliance with the conservatives was in some difficulties. Conservative newspapers and
Majles members had been warning Rafsanjani 'about rising popular
dissatisfaction concerning rampant corruption, inflation, profiteering
and exorbitant charges' and had urged him to emphasise social
justice.[128] When the President sought the necessary Majles approval
of the composition of his new Cabinet, the some 60-strong conservative faction refused to approve the reappointment of his Minister of
Economics and Finance, who 'had been the architect and executor of
the post-1989 economic reform strategy'.[129] Even Rafsanjani's alliance
with Khamenei seemed in doubt, as the Faqih seemed to be aligned
with the conservatives and in 1994 would publicly warn Rafsanjani
that any further austerity measures would endanger the regime.[130]

With inflation running out of control at an unofficial rate of at least
60 per cent and oil revenues having fallen to two-thirds of the 1992
level, there was good reason for Khamenei to be more concerned
about the survivability of the regime itself rather than the survival of
the reform coalition.[131] In fact 1994 saw the virtual abandonment, and
in fact partial reversal, of the reform programme. Not only did the
disgruntled Majles stall any further reforms but also the government
itself reimposed strict import controls that halved the import bill,
reintroduced a form of multiple exchange rate to protect state
and other official users of foreign exchange, and launched a
populist-style campaign against profiteering and hoarding.[132] An 'ever
more isolated' Rafsanjani had been rumoured to have tried to resign
three times but been told to soldier on for the good of the regime,
having become 'a useful fall guy'.[133]

Conclusion

Since the opening chapter's presentation of a *prima facie* explanation (the stabilising influence of defiance) for these eight dictatorships' stability, attention has been focused on other factors – changes in structure/ideology or economic policy – as potential alternative or supplementary explanations. However, it has to be concluded that none of these factors was sufficiently pronounced and prevalent within and among the eight regimes to be considered as an alternative to the 'defiance effect' explanation. The most that can be claimed for these factors is that two of the changes in structure/ideology may provide supplementary explanations, in the sense either of strengthening the defiance effect's stabilising influence or of providing a separate but lesser stabilising influence.

The defiant dictatorships' changes in political structure in the 1980–90s seem to have been in two opposing directions: a) some symbolic concessions to the democratic 'spirit of the age' and b) the strengthening of personal rule by an individual leader. The democratisation to be found among the eight regimes is clearly not significant or universal enough to offer even a supplementary explanation of their stability. The Vietnamese degree of democratisation was the most significant and least symbolic/manipulative, followed at some distance and in declining order of significance by the Syrian, Cuban, Chinese and Iraqi cases. The Iranian and Libyan regimes, though, saw no need for any further symbolic democratisation. The Islamic-revolutionary Iranian regime felt confident enough to change the shape of its impressive democratic façade from a (semi-competitive) multi-party to a one-party and then to a no-party/two-faction format; Qadhafi's Libya had already made a significant gesture towards democratisation in the 1970s in the form of an impressive façade of no-party direct democracy. Finally, the North Korean regime represents a straightforward case of continuing to reject any symbolic concessions to democratisation.

The North Korean regime was also in the forefront of these dictatorships' tendency to strengthen personal rule, with Korean personalism extending to actual hereditary succession of Kim Il Sung by his elder son, Kim Jong Il. Similarly, the Iraqi and Syrian cases showed a strengthening of the existing degree of personal rule enjoyed by Saddam Hussein and Asad, accompanied by hereditary overtones in terms of the role being given to the rulers' sons. The Cuban case differs in being a revival, if only in style, of Castro's highly personal rule of the 1960s and in the ruler's brother having long been recognised as his deputy/successor. A strengthening of an existing degree of personal rule is also evident in the Libyan and Iranian (until Khomeini's death in 1989) cases but without any hereditary aspect. The Chinese case is more unusual in seeing the rise of senior leader Deng Xiaoping culminate in his having a degree of personal rule bestowed upon him in his dotage. Finally, although the collegiate collective leadership of Vietnam seems an exception to this personalist tendency, the emphasis on the 'Uncle Ho' cult suggests an attempt to create a symbolic personal ruler out of the deceased founding leader. The personalist, almost monarchical tendency seems a universal feature that is evident in all eight of the defiant dictatorships, albeit in six of them only as the strengthening of an already existing degree of personal rule. However, there are obvious problems involved in accounting for why and how personalism could have a stabilising influence upon a dictatorship in a democratic age. Therefore it is difficult to view this factor as anything more than a potentially 'defiance-strengthening' supplementary explanation, for it is at least conceivable that the defiance effect is more easily focused on loyalty to an individual personality, as the symbolic embodiment of the regime, than to a 'faceless' collective leadership.

As for the changes in ideology, the most common feature was the new or renewed emphasis upon nationalism. Despite the contempt and suspicion that orthodox Communist ideology has for nationalism, it was given new or renewed emphasis by all four Communist regimes and in fact became the dominant element in the ideology of the Cuban and North Korean regimes. It is true that official nationalism was much less evident in China and Vietnam than in Cuba and North Korea, and that the encouragement of nationalism is less apparent in the Middle Eastern than in the Communist dictatorships. The rise of nationalism is evident in the Iranian and Iraqi regimes' ideologies, but neither the Syrian nor Libyan cases show an increased emphasis on nationalism. Nevertheless, it is possible that the encouragement of nationalism (if successful) contributed to regime stability in a separate supplementary fashion as well as in any possible 'defiance-strengthening' fashion, in the sense of increased national solidarity possibly producing a greater defiance effect.

The investigation of whether changes in economic policy, specifically the implementation of successful economic liberalisation, can provide a *prima facie* explanation for political stability was a complex and lengthy study. But the results can be briefly summarised. In the case of the Communist economies: China and Vietnam had quite extensive and successful restructuring (China's beginning in the late 1970s and Vietnam's in the late 1980s after a false start in 1985); Cuba opted for an alternative, leftist rather than liberalising economic reorientation (in the late 1980s) that was not very successful and was soon overwhelmed by an externally induced economic crisis that forced a resort to some *ad hoc*, limited economic reforms; and North Korea opted for the *status quo* but resorted (in the 1990s) to very narrow reforms aimed at coping with its externally induced crisis. As for the Middle Eastern, mixed economies, there was again a lack of uniformity. The Iraqi and Iranian regimes attempted major liberalising reforms (begun respectively in the late 1980s and early 1990s) that were not successful in 'delivering the goods' and in both cases suffered partial reversals – in the Iraqi case then being completely overwhelmed by an externally induced crisis that crippled the economy. The Syrian economy saw a less extensive but successful economic reform (begun in the late 1980s), and the Libyan economy saw a narrowly targeted but successful economic reform (in the late 1980s) and then a more extensive but stillborn reform programme.

Even leaving aside the lack of extensiveness and the late timing of many of these economic reform programmes, not all of them can be judged to have been successful – only the Chinese, the Vietnamese, the Syrian and the Libyan. Although a great deal of attention has been paid in preceding chapters to the economic factor as a possible explanation of stability, it is difficult to see how a coherent *prima facie* explanation can be advanced on the basis of these results.

Economic success may, though, provide an alternative to the defiance effect when the new democratic age loses the enthusiasm of youth and enters its somewhat disillusioned and cynical 'maturity'. In future years the defiance effect may be seen as having provided these dictatorships with a means of buying time to ride out the 1980s–90s wave of democratisation and lay the foundations for an economic prosperity that can take the place of defiance in a mature democratic age. The Chinese, Vietnamese and Syrian regimes already seem to be heading in this prosperity/stability direction and some of the other dictatorships may also make an attempt (or a further attempt) to do so. For defiance of external foes is an unreliable long-term basis for regime stability. Foes that present credible besieging threats or pressures cannot just be invented, and existing foes presumably will not be so obliging as to continue providing opportunities for defiance.

Appendix I: Communist Ideology, Economy and Political Structure – the Orthodox Model

ORTHODOX COMMUNIST IDEOLOGY

Communist ideology is so complex in its content and development that all that can be offered here is a cursory sketch of the most politically relevant features. The core of Communist regimes' ideology is the composite set of doctrines known as Marxism-Leninism. The contribution of the Marxist component to Communist ideological orthodoxy has been in two main areas, both of which have provided Communist regimes with a claim to legitimacy. First, Marxism espouses the proletariat's (working class's) revolutionary overthrow of capitalism and therefore has provided a basis for glorifying the 'revolutionary' origins of Communist regimes. (Marxism's emphasis on the class solidarity of the working class, as displayed in the ideal of 'proletarian internationalism', has also provided the basis for Communist ideology's opposition to racism and nationalism.) Secondly, Marxism has set the post-revolutionary goal of attaining a classless, communist society, where an abundant supply of goods and services will be distributed on the basis of 'to each according to his needs'. Marxism acknowledges that attaining communism will require more than just an anti-capitalist revolution; after the revolution there will have to be a transitional, 'socialist' stage of development during which the formerly capitalist economy is developed into the material basis for a communist society. No Communist regime has ever claimed to have completed the socialist stage of economic development (in the specifically Marxist sense of 'socialism' as distinct from the common and looser usage of the term). But the process of moving through socialism towards communism has been a claim to legitimacy that Marxism has offered to all Communist regimes.

The main contribution of Leninism to Communist ideology has been the legitimation or justification of rule (or 'leadership') by the Communist party over state and society. Marx had provided the notion of a post-revolutionary 'dictatorship of the proletariat' – rule by the proletariat as a class. But Lenin, as leader of the world's first Communist regime after the 1917 Russian revolutions, added the crucial doctrine of (dictatorial) *party* rule over state and society – 'leadership' by the Communist party as the 'vanguard of the proletariat'. Leninism also provided the principle of 'democratic centralism' as the basis for running a Communist party, and in its practical application this principle produced a centralised party with a façade of democracy. The

Leninist convention of collective leadership (implicitly by members of the party's central executive organs) apparently prevented such centralism from producing a personal dictatorship. But when Stalin became leader of the Soviet Union after Lenin's death in 1924, he used his administrative post of General Secretary of the now all-controlling Communist Party to establish just such a personal dictatorship in the 1930s. However, the most important contribution that 'Stalinism' made to Communist orthodoxy was in developing the orthodox model of a Communist economy.

ORTHODOX (STALINIST) COMMUNIST ECONOMIC MODEL

Stalin's first Five Year Plan (1928–32) for the socialist development of the Soviet economy established the orthodox economic model for later Communist regimes. The Plan completely restructured the economy by having the state take over ownership of all industry and commerce as well as finance and international trade. After this nationalisation or state-expropriation of the urban economy, it was operated as a command economy with Plan targets for annual and five-yearly production for various sectors and products of the economy. Plan-implementing directives were sent by the array of state economic Ministries (each administering a particular economic sector or industry) to the state-owned enterprises that operated as individually managed firms or factories. The new system removed virtually all traces of a market economy as well as of private enterprise, and the prices of goods and services were set not by market forces but by bureaucrats involved in the centralised administration of the planned economy. The economy had also lost much of its international aspect as state trading-arms took over all exporting and importing.

Agriculture was not taken into state ownership by Stalin's first Five Year Plan; only a small proportion of agricultural land was expropriated and transformed into state farms worked by wage-earners. But private farming was ended by the 'half-way house' of collectivising agriculture. Collectivisation replaced individual or household ownership of land with collective ownership (as a form of producer cooperative) of a very large farm by a large number of individuals/households, each of them receiving a share of the farm's returns in proportion to the quality and quantity of their work on the farm. (Collectively owned enterprises existed in the urban economy, too, but were much less prevalent than in agriculture.) The compulsory collectivisation of agriculture meant that the peasants were forced to transfer individual/household ownership of their land, animals and equipment to one of the thousands of new 'collective' (collectively owned) farms, upon which they would work at the direction of the elected farm management committee. The peasantry were also forced to relinquish control over marketing, as the collective farms had to sell their produce to the state at prices set centrally by the economic administrators. Furthermore, the collective farms were set annual 'production quotas' specifying the types and quantities of produce to be sold to the state. The only area of private/market sector activity was the small 'private plot' of land (less than an acre) allocated to each household belonging

to a collective farm. On this household plot the family could produce vegetables, fruit, eggs and other items not only for its own use but also for private
sale to urban consumers in the free farmers' markets operating in the local
towns.

The agricultural sector and consumer industries suffered from the Plan's
emphasis on heavy industry, which itself suffered from the demands placed
upon it as the vanguard of the drive for rapid economic growth. The pressure
on managers and workers was maintained by the use of material incentives
(notably the payment of bonuses linked to production achievements) which
increasingly overshadowed the use of such 'moral incentives' as applying
revolutionary fervour to attaining economic goals. As the Five Year Plan was
purportedly part of the socialist transition to communism, these material
incentives and the resulting inequalities were justified by the Marxist argument
that during this socialist transitional stage, workers would have to be
rewarded according to the quality and quantity of work they contributed to
society.

ORTHODOX COMMUNIST POLITICAL STRUCTURE

Although the key feature of an orthodox Communist regime's political
structure is the Leninist rule (or 'leadership') of the Party over the state, this
sketch of political structure will begin by first examining the structure of the
Party itself. The key feature of the Party's own structure is the triumph of the
centralist over the democratic element in the Leninist principle of democratic
centralism. In accordance with the democratic element, every four or five
years a Party Congress comprising elected delegates is held in order to decide
key policy questions and to elect an executive committee, the Central Committee, that will run the Party on the Congress's behalf. The very large,
several-hundred-member Central Committee usually meets no more than
twice a year and considers only key policy and political matters. The day-to-
day business of the Party is handled by the Central Committee's two small
subcommittees. These are the policy-making Political Bureau or Politburo
(the standard abbreviation developed in the Soviet Union) and the administrative Secretariat, which is composed of functionally specialised Secretaries
led by a General (or First) Secretary. As the Politburo and Secretariat are
elected by the Central Committee, the democratic element of democratic
centralism seems to have been maintained throughout the Party's pyramid
of institutions.

However, in practice the centralist element is dominant within the Party.
The elections for Party office amount to no more than voting for a single list
of candidates who have already been selected by higher executive and administrative organs. (Their 'nomenklatura', to use the original Russian term,
personnel powers allow these organs to make/approve appointments and
candidates for Party as well as public and state offices.) The Politburo is more
than an executive organ that deals with day-to-day policy making; unless
weakened by internal disputes, it provides the Party with authoritative and
often authoritarian leadership. Similarly, the Secretariat is more than just an

administrative organ. Not only are the General Secretary and usually several other Secretaries included within the Politburo, but also the General Secretary is normally the senior member of the Politburo and the leading figure in the Party.

That the Politburo always contains the state's Premier or Prime Minister, and usually several key Ministers, is indicative of the Politburo's other role – operating as the *de facto* government of the country. The Party's rule over the state is exemplified by the governing authority exercised by the Politburo (and ultimately the Central Committee) as the Party's executive organ. The state's executive organ, the Cabinet or Council of Ministers, is still the constitutionally recognised government but is left with only the authority to decide how to implement the general policies laid down by the Politburo (and the Central Committee).

The governing or 'leading' role of the Party extends beyond policy making by the Politburo; the Party also supervises the state's implementation of these policies. The supervision varies in strength from monitoring to vetoing to actually directing state activities. Historically and politically the first priority has been supervision of the military. Under Lenin, the first Communist regime soon developed a comprehensive system based upon a) the many individual Party members in the military, b) organised 'cells' and committees of Party members within military units, c) indoctrinating and monitoring 'political departments' within the military structure, and d) thousands of political commissars attached to military units and empowered to veto the orders of their unit's military commander, producing what was called 'dual command' of a unit by officer and commissar. However, by the mid-1920s the Communist regime had moved to the 'unity of command' system of leaving the officer, who was by now normally a Party member, in sole command of his unit. The new system can be viewed as the orthodox one, as when other Communist regimes were established after 1945 most of them copied the later rather than the original system.

However, the three Asian Communist regimes of China, North Korea and Vietnam developed supervisory systems with unorthodox features. Although unique to each regime, these features all involved the old-style vetoing commissar and/or a very powerful Party committee within the military unit. The three Asian regimes have also employed a small Party committee at the central level, similar to the Politburo and Secretariat, that specialises in military affairs. Known as the Central Military Party Committee in Vietnam, the Central Military Affairs Committee in North Korea, and the Military Affairs Committee (or Central Military Commission) in China, this committee has exercised varying powers from one country to another but there is sufficient uniformity for the existence of such a committee to be regarded as an orthodox variation from the norm.

The Party's supervision of the civilian state apparatus is almost as extensive and intensive as the supervision of the military. Although there are no equivalents of the political commissars and political departments, there are many Party members and units within the Ministries and other state organs (virtually all higher state officials being Party members). Furthermore, there is an extensive bureaucracy of supervising Party officials which at the central level is organised into specialised departments serving the Central Committee and directed by the Secretariat. Beneath the central level there are regional, district, city and local Party secretaries and officials exercising similar supervisory authority.

The Communist state institutions have few characteristically 'Communist' features. The parliaments are rubber-stamping legislatures that meet for only a few days once or twice a year. Moreover, although their members are 'elected' by the people, the voters are presented with a single list of candidates that have been directly or indirectly selected by the Party. A more distinctive feature is that in many Communist regimes the apparent head of state has in fact been the chairman of a collective head of state, usually known as the Council of State, which has also wielded some legislative powers between parliamentary sessions.

Finally, an orthodox feature which was not developed in the Soviet Union but has been found in many other Communist regimes is the presence of 'multi-partyism'. A few non-Communist parties are preserved as Communist-controlled puppet parties and are often joined with the Party in a coalition 'Front' organisation. The puppet parties are also allocated some places on the list of parliamentary candidates selected by the Front or by whatever other Party-controlled means are used to select the official candidates for parliament.

Appendix II: Baathist Ideology and Structure

INTRODUCTION

The movement called the Arab Socialist Baath ('Renaissance' or 'Rebirth') Party was from its inception an international movement, as its Pan-Arab nationalist ideology required in an era when the ethnic Arab nation was divided among many separate states, such as Syria, Iraq and Egypt. Therefore the overall Party was referred to as the 'National' Party in the sense of the (international) Arab nation, and the huge state-level 'branches' of the Party, such as the Syria and Iraq branches, were referred to as 'Regional' branches. The Regions had their own Regional Party Congresses and executive organs distinct from the (international) National Party Congress and executive organs.

A further complication was added when the Iraqi Baathists withdrew in 1966 from the Syrian-based National Party and in 1968 moved to regularise the situation by holding a Pan-Arab Baathist Congress in Iraq that elected a rival National Command executive in opposition to the Syrian-based original.[1] To give their rival organisation some credibility in its claim to be the 'sole legitimate Baath Party', the Iraqis invited Michel Aflaq, one of the two recognised founders of Baathism, to become their movement's National General Secretary and he was duly elected to that post at the founding Congress of the new, Iraqi-backed Baathist National Party.[2] Aflaq later moved to Baghdad, where he was given ceremonial precedence over President al-Bakr and Saddam Hussein and was visited by the Iraqi leadership for consultation with 'the Master'.[3] Therefore since 1968 Baathism has had two rival international parties claiming to be the sole legitimate National Party.

IDEOLOGY

Despite the splitting of Baathism into two separate movements in 1968, all Baathists seem to recognise the existence of a common core of ideology based upon two key ideological documents dating from 1947 and 1963. The first or oldest official Baathist ideological document was the Party Constitution, agreed upon at the first Party Congress in 1947.[4] The only other ideological statement that was ever formally approved by the Party before the 1968 schism was the Introduction to the Ideological Report of the Sixth National Party Congress in 1963. Titled 'Some Theoretical Points of Departure' (Ba'd al-muntalaqat an-nazariyya) and often referred to as the Muntalaqat, it became 'the main canonical source' of Baathism.[5] Its authority has never been challenged and appears to be as great with the Iraqi-based as with the Syrian-based Baathist movement.[6]

The 1947 Party Constitution was founded upon (Pan-)Arab nationalism, and its main aim was the uniting of all members of the Arab nation (defined loosely by language, culture or residence but implicitly not by religion) and to freeing the Arab nation from the bonds of colonialism. The political programme sought constitutional democracy, incorporating a parliament and an independent judiciary. The economic programme was only mildly socialist, with 'just' limits to be placed on the ownership of land and industry and with state control of domestic and foreign trade. The social policy was radical a) in its open espousal of sexual equality and its commitment to make women fit for equal citizenship, and b) its silence on the issue of Islam's role in Arab society – which would lead to Baathism's being condemned as a secular movement by its Islamic opponents.[7]

The Muntalaqat of 1963 had three sections, each one relating to a term within the Baath slogan: 'Unity, Freedom, Socialism'.[8] The section devoted to (Arab) unity contained few significant modifications of the 1947 Party Constitution doctrine. However, it acknowledged that simply merging existing Arab states was not the answer to achieving Arab unity. It also included Israel as one of the targets of the Arab foreign policy of removing colonialism and multi-national companies – Israel being identified as their lackey and agent.[9] The goal of freeing Palestine was included in the section on freedom, whose concern with freeing the Arab nation from colonial political and economic domination confirmed that Baathist 'freedom' is of the nationalist variety, not the liberal freedom of the individual.[10]

The freedom section also contained a major and politically very important change in the type of democracy sought by Baathism; now it is popular revolutionary democracy instead of parliamentary democracy. Popular revolutionary democracy would involve a pyramid of elected popular councils and an array of mass organisations, but these would be 'led' by the Baathist Party.[11] Such a Leninist-like approach was also evident in the requirement that this Baathist 'revolutionary vanguard' party should be organised along democratic centralist lines.[12]

In some ways the Muntalaqat was more Leninist than Lenin in openly calling for the Party to dominate the state administration and to use the military as an ideological instrument.[13] The Baathist concept of 'the ideological army' – educated in Baathist principles to be a barrier against all domestic and foreign enemies of (Arab) unity, freedom and socialism – would soon be viewed as one of Baathism's most important features.[14] The traditional distinctive social policy of espousing sexual equality and remaining silent about religion was maintained in the Muntalaqat.[15] But the section on socialism introduced some radical changes in economic policy.

The Marxist influence on economic policy was evident in the use of such terms as social 'contradiction', and in the denunciation of the 1947 economic programme as 'petty bourgeois' and as showing signs of 'reformism'.[16] The socialist transformation was to involve 'popular ownership of the main sectors of the economy', a planned economy and an agrarian revolution that would go beyond redistributive land reform and instead result in collective ownership – in the establishment of collective farms.[17] Combined with the new Leninist-style political programme, this economic programme would seem to constitute an almost Communist 'platform', despite the fact that neither Marxism nor Leninism was ever mentioned in the Muntalaqat.

POLITICAL STRUCTURE

It is on the basis of the Baath ideology that an orthodox model of a Baathist regime's political structure can be envisaged, admittedly one which in some aspects differs from the historical examples of Baathist regime. The political programme of the 1963 Muntalaqat sets forth a Leninist-style or Communist-style political structure: a leading party organised along democratic centralist lines; the party to have the political role of leading the pyramid of elected popular councils/assemblies; and the party to have the governing role of supervising the state apparatus, including an 'ideological' military. To this ideologically derived model can be added the unique Baathist feature of separate international 'National' and national 'Regional' party organs – Congresses, executives, Secretaries and the like.

Moreover, the Baathists had established by the 1960s a more than usually Leninist ideal of how elitist their Party should be. To maintain the ideal of a Party of 'ideologically disciplined militants', the Baathists opted for a greater than Communist level of screening, indoctrination, duration of candidate membership and proportion of candidate members.[18] For example, the Iraqi Baathists had a series of degrees of membership or stages to attaining full membership: sympathiser (two years), supporter (two to three years), candidate (year and a half), trainee member (one year), and then full (voting) member – producing a situation in which by the 1980s there were only 25 000 full members.[19]

Two other features which are suggested not by ideology but by the common experience of concrete examples of Baathist regime are a) the use of (Baath-controlled) multi-party 'Front' organisations to provide some non-Baath 'representation', and b) the tendency to develop personal rule. The first of these features copies the Communist orthodoxy and can be readily accommodated in the model of a Baathist regime. The second, however, the development of personal rule, is quite contrary to the implicit 'collective leadership' connotations of the Leninist and Baathist principle of democratic centralism. Furthermore, personal rule arose only because in Syria the original unstable collective leadership of the 1960s was ended by Asad's coup and because in Iraq al-Bakr was willing to permit Saddam Hussein's rise to power. Therefore this second feature clearly cannot be viewed as part of the Baathist orthodox model of political structure.

Finally, there is the striking incongruity of military rule over a Baathist regime. The Syrian Baathist regime, even before Asad's coup, was a military regime and so, too, was the Iraqi Baathist regime until Saddam Hussein finally took over from al-Bakr at the end of the 1970s. These were marked deviations from the ideology's prescription that a Baathist regime have a party-state, not military-party, structure. However, the Baathist military leaders themselves seem to have implicitly acknowledged that a party-state regime was the orthodox model of a Baathist regime. For the ideological norm of a party-state regime doubtless a) increased al-Bakr's and other Iraqi military men's willingness to allow the civilian Saddam Hussein to rise to power and also b) increased the Syrian military politicians' desire to present a civilian image of themselves and of their regimes.

Notes and References

ABBREVIATIONS

FEER	*Far Eastern Economic Review*
Keesing's	*Keesing's Contemporary Archives*
MER	*Middle East Review*

INTRODUCTION

1. The most famous description of the wave of democratisation locates its beginning in 1974, with the military's overthrow of the long-standing Portuguese dictatorship (Huntington, 1993, p.3). However, most of the prominent examples of democratisation that occurred in the 1970s were located in the West – notably Portugal, Spain and Greece – and can be seen as the ending of long-standing (Portugal and Spain) or incongruous (Greece) anomalies within the democratic Western world. The Communist world did not provide any examples of democratisation until the late 1980s, and the Third World was still showing setbacks for democracy in the middle and late 1970s. For instance, the most important example of stable democracy, India, was under threat from Mrs Gandhi's 1975–7 state of emergency; the only case of a true people's revolution, the Iranian revolution, opted in 1979 for a non-democratic Islamic Republic; and another long-standing (if less stable) example of Third World democracy, Turkey, was in major difficulties and would fall victim to military intervention in 1980. The late 1970s also saw the publication of important works on the breakdown of democratic regimes and on the new authoritarianism in Latin America (Linz, 1978; Collier, 1979). Not until 1986 was a series of works on 'transitions from authoritarian rule' published and not until 1989 a four-volume work on 'democracy in developing countries'.
2. Nor had they already converted themselves in previous decades, as the Mexican and Indonesian regimes had done, into purportedly democratised but in reality only semi-competitive multi-party regimes.
3. On the notion of the 'exceptionalism' of the Arab world in a democratic age and on the issue of Islam as a contributing factor see Salamé, 1994, especially pp. 1–2, 3–9; Waterbury, 1994, especially pp. 23, 31–2, 40–4; Leca, 1994; Hudson, 1991.
4. See the Preface to Diamond, 1989. However, the Islamic world has shown some examples of democratic regimes, albeit not very stable, in Turkey, Pakistan and Bangladesh. Furthermore, most countries within the Islamic world have made an attempt at democratisation even if only as a façade or resulting in failure and reversal.

175

5. The lack of full-scale liberalisation as well as the wide variation to be found among the Communist regimes is understandable in light of the immense burden of state-socialist ideology and bureaucratic vested interests of a state-owned/collectivist economy that must be overcome to push through economic liberalisation. It is hardly surprising that some Communist regimes might decide that economic liberalisation is simply not worth the political risks involved.

    As for the four Middle Eastern regimes, it is easier to find well-established explanations for their limited and less varying degree of economic liberalisation. For example, it can be argued that the section of society most likely to support economic liberalisation, the businessmen, are content with only a limited marketisation of the economy for the same self-interested reasons that they are content with only a limited political liberalisation that does not free and open up political 'markets'. (See Niblock, 1993, pp. 57–8; Waterbury, 1994, p. 27; Leca, 1990, p. 183.)

    From the regime's perspective, there has to be good reason to discard the state controls which are the basis for keeping the business community dependent upon the regime's favour. When it is also considered how many other vested interests, such as state employees, are opposed to any economic liberalisation, there have to be compelling reasons for a regime to attempt even a limited liberalising economic reform. (See Heydemann, 1992, pp. 15–16.)

6. The concluding analysis of the 1986 series of works on transitions from authoritarian rule declares that there is no predictable correlation between the (political) liberalisation of an authoritarian regime and its previous performance 'in meeting socioeconomic goals. Both relative success and relative failure have characterized these movements' of political 'opening' (O'Donnell and Schmitter, 1986, p. 20). Yet a contrast is then drawn between the 'failures' and the 'successes', in which it is mentioned in passing that the 'relatively successful' had 'hence' (implying a causal connection) 'encountered a less active and aggressive opposition' – that is, would be less likely to face stability-threatening behaviour from its society. It is also pointed out that one of the reasons for even successful regimes' opting for political liberalisation was the expectation of earning 'a nice bonus in the eyes of international public opinion' (ibid.). Where international public opinion may be more than just a bonus would be in a situation where the country faces an external threat of invasion and requires some degree of support from the West, notably the United States, which is more likely to be given to a democracy than to a dictatorship. This would explain the apparent anomalies of economically successful and externally defiant South Korea and Taiwan (defying respectively North Korea and China) joining the trend towards democratisation.

1 DEFIANCE AS A STABILISING INFLUENCE

1. Porter, 1993, p. 106. Salamé has argued that, especially in the Arab world (another case of its exceptionalism), military defeat can have the

effect of actually strengthening rather than weakening a dictatorship: 'To have defied the West will often compensate for the failure that may follow the attempt. The popularity of the challenge to the adversary often sustains the defiant regime even among the opprobrium of defeat' – though 'questioning' may arise later, 'at the moment when external pressure in fact seems to have relaxed' (Salamé, 1994, p. 17). He mentions the example of Saddam Hussein's survival after Iraq's disastrous 1991 defeat; another famous example would be Nasser's survival of Egypt's equally disastrous defeat in the June 1967 war with Israel, where the refusal to accept Nasser's resignation was possibly in itself depicted and seen as an act of national defiance of Israel and the West. The exceptionalism of the Arab world in this regard is not so obvious on closer examination. The example of Saddam Hussein will be dealt with later in the chapter, but the Nasser example seems a clear case of a lost but apparently defensive war leading to the occupation of a large part of the country's territory (the Sinai) by the enemy forces. Defiance of the foe in such a situation would be expected to produce a 'siege stability' in a regime in any region of the world. One real and once very important exception to the defiance factor, however, is that monarchical regimes seem to experience little if any siege stability in a long and disastrous war, as the Tsar and the Kaiser found in the First World War, nor do dictators who allow themselves to act as the apparent agents of monarchies in long and disastrous wars, as Mussolini found in the Second World War.

2. Bengelsdorf, 1994, p. 149; Smith, 1994, p. 97.
3. Whiting, 1995, p. 296.
4. Ibid.
5. Lam, 1995, p. 135.
6. Bearman, 1986, p. 283.
7. Legum, 1988–9, p. B480; *MER*, 1996, p. 68.
8. Hinnebusch, 1994, p. 112.
9. Hiro, 1989, p. 43; Milani, 1994, p. 180.
10. Karsh and Rautsi, 1991, pp. 147–8; Tripp, 1989, p. 60.
11. Tripp, 1989, p. 61. See Hiro, 1989, p. 45, on problems with Shiite troops.
12. Karsh and Rautsi, 1991, pp. 156–7.
13. Tripp, 1989, p. 72.
14. Ibid., p. 66.
15. Ibid., pp. 66, 72.
16. Ibid., p. 72.
17. Rugman, 1994.
18. Tripp, 1989, p. 72; Karsh and Rautsi, 1991, pp. 156–7.
19. Tripp, 1989, pp. 72–3.
20. al-Jabbar, 1994, pp. 99–101.
21. al-Khafaji, 1994, p. 29.
22. Rugman, 1994.
23. Hiro, 1989, p. 46; Bakhash, 1986, p. 233.
24. Bakhash, 1986, p, 236; Bakhash, 1993, p. 70; Hunter, 1992, p. 60; Ramazani, 1989, p. 209.

25. Ramazani, 1989, p. 209.
26. Bakhash, 1993, p. 70.
27. Bakhash, 1986, pp. 236–7.
28. Ibid., p. 237; Hunter, 1992, p. 59.
29. Hunter, 1992, p. 63.
30. Ibid., p. 71.
31. Bakhash, 1993, p. 76.
32. Ibid., p. 65.
33. Ibid., p. 83 n. 6.
34. Quoted by Calabrese, 1994, p. 36.
35. *Middle East*, Jan. 1994, p. 11; Reuters, 2 Nov. 1994. The threat from the US was seen in terms of not only its post-August 1990 political and military presence in the Gulf but also the West's 'cultural aggression' that sought to undermine the Islamic Republic by chipping away at its Islamic cultural foundations (Hashim, 1995, pp. 47, 45–6).
36. *Economist*, 23 July 1994, p. 39.
37. Reuters, 14 Apr. 1993.
38. Hinnebusch, 1993, p. 246.
39. Ma'oz, 1988, pp. 45, 104, xi.
40. Ibid., pp. 46, 177. See also p. 45.
41. Ibid., p. 180. See also pp. 146–8.
42. For this paragraph see Seale, 1988, pp. 335, 425; Ma'oz, 1988, pp. 179, 169.
43. Ma'oz, 1988, pp. xi, 182–3.
44. *Current History*, Feb. 1994, p. 86.
45. The lack of credibility for any claims of an Israeli threat was reflected in a temporary softening of Syria's stance in the August 1992 round of talks that may have been used to distract domestic public opinion from a build-up in discontent over the economic situation (Lawson, 1994, p. 146).
46. On the funding of the IRA and other such groups see Blundy and Lycett, 1988, Ch. 6, especially pp. 170–1.
47. Simons, 1993, p. 301; Bearman, 1986, p. 229.
48. Blundy and Lycett, 1988, p. 170; Harris, 1986, p. 100.
49. Blundy and Lycett, 1988, pp. 30, 29; Legum, 1985–6, p. B547.
50. Blundy and Lycett, 1988, pp. 28, 42.
51. For this paragraph see Simons, 1993, pp. 318–19; Legum, 1986–7; Deeb, 1990, pp. 178, 177; *Middle East*, March 1989, p. 6; Legum, 1988–9, p. B480.
52. Simons, 1993, pp. 62–3, 66.
53. Simons, 1993, pp. 60.
54. *MER*, 1996, p. 68; Vandewalle, 1995b, p. 235.
55. SarDesai, 1992, p. 135.
56. Pike, 1986, p. 74; Duiker, 1986, p. 103.
57. Thayer, 1994, p. 520.
58. Chanda, 1984, p. 32; Duiker, 1985, p. 104.
59. For this paragraph see Williams, 1992, p. 65; Vo Nhan Tri, 1990, pp. 99, 100; SarDesai, 1992, p. 131.
60. For this paragraph see Porter, 1993, pp. 206–10; Thayer, 1994, pp. 520, 522; Cima, 1989, p. 69; Goodman, 1995, p. 93; *FEER*, 17 Feb. 1994, p. 14.

61. Womack, 1992, p. 178.
62. Stern, 1993, p. 108.
63. Ibid., pp. 94–5.
64. Ibid., p. 108; Pike, 1991, p. 81.
65. Pike, 1991, p. 81.
66. Pike, 1994, p. 64.
67. Fahey, 1994, p. 347.
68. Thayer, 1994, pp. 524–5.
69. Macdonald, 1988, pp. 242–3.
70. Ibid., pp. 242–3, 248–9. These accusations of aggression were backed up by specific charges of US spy flights and South Korean military incursions (ibid., p. 243).
71. Clough, 1987, p. 53; Scalapino, 1992, pp. 56, 57.
72. Clough, 1987, p. 195.
73. Kihl, 1991, p. 44.
74. Smith, 1994, p. 112.
75. Kim, 1995, pp. 19–20.
76. Cardoso and Helwege, 1992, p. 18. The embargo was intensified to its 'definitive' form in 1962.
77. Dominguez, 1986, p. 129.
78. Cardoso and Helwege, 1992, p. 97; Liss, 1994, p. 64.
79. Duncan, 1993, p. 226.
80. Mesa-Lago, 1989, p. 103.
81. Dominguez, 1982, pp. 53–5; Mesa-Lago, 1989, p. 103.
82. Fitzgerald, 1989, p. 303.
83. Liss, 1994, p. 133.
84. Duncan, 1993, p. 223.
85. Cardoso and Helwege, 1992, p. 13; Bengelsdorf, 1994, p. 171.
86. Eckstein, 1994, p. 96.
87. Balfour, 1995, p. 171; Duncan, 1993, pp. 226, 225.
88. Shambaugh, 1991a, p. 247.
89. Levine, 1994, p. 79.
90. Wang, 1992, p. 221.
91. Lam, 1995, p. 139.
92. Shambaugh, 1991a, p. 273; Levine, 1994, p. 80.
93. Shambaugh, 1991a, p. 273; Lam, 1995, p. 140.
94. Whiting, 1995, p. 296; Lam, 1995, p. 195.
95. See Shambaugh, 1991b, on the intra-military campaign.
96. Levine, 1994, p. 80.
97. Ibid., pp. 80, 88.
98. Whiting, 1995, p. 306–9; Lam, 1995, p. 9.
99. Deng's approach required a relatively conciliatory stance towards the US over foreign policy issues (but not domestic policy matters) despite what was seen as a provocative stance by the US (e.g., Whiting, 1995, pp. 306, 309).
100. Lam, 1995, p. 175.
101. *FEER*, 9 Nov. 1995, p. 21.

2   COMMUNIST CHINA

1. Schram, 1988, p. 195.
2. Long, 1995, p. 55.
3. Ibid., p. 56; Lam, 1995, p. 326; Hamrin, 1992, p. 112.
4. To take one example of his authoritative position, in 1993 senior PLA commanders opposing in private the Dengist foreign policy line also made it clear that they would obey Deng's orders (Whiting, 1995, p. 310).
5. See Saich, 1992, pp. 1142–3, and Lam, 1995, pp. 36–9, on personality cult from 1992 onwards.
6. Bachman, 1995, p. 37.
7. 'Individual prestige and length of service to the Party are far more important than any formal position one might hold' (Saich, 1995, p. 50). The power of some of the elders was such that in the pyramid of policy making and coordination it was 'select elders' and members of the Politburo Standing Committee who occupied the level immediately beneath the paramount leader, collectively joined him in coordinating major policy decisions and in allocating policy responsibilities among themselves, and individually headed the informal interagency (incorporating relevant Party, ministerial and military officials) 'leadership groups' which 'oversaw each of the main policy sectors' – and had seen a dramatic increase in their role and number during the 1980s (Hamrin, 1992, pp. 100, 96; Halpern, 1992, pp. 129–30).
8. See Wang, 1992, p. 90; Saich, 1992, p. 1155.
9. Saich, 1992, pp. 1155.
10. Long, 1995, p. 55.
11. This was a newly created post that arose from the 1982 creation of a state Central Military Commission to command and supervise the military as a state organ – in similar fashion to the Party's own long-standing committee devoted to military affairs. In practice the Party and state military committees came to be viewed as a single generic entity, the Central Military Commission, with both committees' Chairmanships being held by Deng (see Wang, 1992, pp. 84, 173, 174; Pollack, 1992, p. 163).
12. Schram, 1988, p. 195.
13. Lam, 1995, pp. 209, 208.
14. Yeung, 1995, p. 166; Paltiel, 1995, p. 797.
15. Yeung, 1995, pp. 159–64.
16. Bickford, 1994, p. 461; Yeung, 1995, pp. 163–4.
17. Paltiel, 1995, p. 797 n. 57; *Economist*, 11 June 1994, p. 23.
18. See Yeung, 1995, p. 167, for a more pessimistic view.
19. Saich, 1992, p. 1150; Lam, 1995, p. 196. See also Lam, p. 197, on other apparent examples of new influence being given to the military.
20. Schram, 1988, pp. 185–6.
21. Saich, 1992, pp. 1147, 1144.
22. Lam, 1995, p. 247. 'Throughout 1993, the phenomenon of "cross leadership" also manifested itself at the regional level, with numerous cases of party secretaries doubling as heads of local governments or legislatures' (ibid.).

23. Ibid., pp. 308, 308–9.
24. Ibid., pp. 302, 309, on disappointment, and p. 304 on tighter Party controls, tightened in mid-1980s, on deputies.
25. On the CPPCC see ibid., pp. 296–7, 301, 302.
26. For this paragraph see Wang, 1992, p. 75; Saich, 1992, p. 1148 n. 29; Lam, 1995, pp. 303, 318, 319; Dearlove, 1995, pp. 122–4, 131; Blecher, 1995, p. 112.
27. For this paragraph see Brugger, 1989, p. 2; Schram, 1984, pp. 417–20; Wang, 1992, p. 59.
28. For this paragraph see Wang, 1992, pp. 58–9; Brugger, 1989, p. 4; Joseph, 1986, pp. 267–8; Joseph, 1985, pp. 254–5; Schram, 1984, pp. 432, 438, 441; Starr, 1984, p. 268.
29. Sullivan, 1988, pp. 216–17, 198–9.
30. Shambaugh, 1991b, p. 555.
31. Wang, 1992, p. 221.
32. See for example Jiang's 1991 speech quoted by Scalapino, 1992, p. 47.
33. Schram, 1988, pp. 185, 177–8.
34. For this paragraph see also Joseph, 1985, p. 254 n. 11; Joseph, 1986, p. 268 n. 10; Gold, 1989, p. 195.
35. *FEER*, 2 Oct. 1992, p. 10.
36. Saich, 1992, pp. 1143 n. 19, 1145.
37. Ibid., pp. 1142–3, 1143 n. 19.
38. Ibid., p. 1144; *FEER*, 1 Apr. 1993, p. 29.
39. *FEER*, 12 Nov. 1992, p. 23; Lam, 1995, pp. xii–xiii, 37– 40, 132; *FEER*, 25 Nov. 1993, pp. 14–15; *Economist*, 1 Oct. 1994.
40. Goldman, 1994, p. 330.
41. Scalapino, 1992, p. 46.
42. *FEER*, 9 Nov. 1995, p. 21.
43. Lam, 1995, p. 174.
44. *FEER*, 9 Nov. 1995, p. 21.
45. Ibid.
46. Scalapino, 1992, p. 47.
47. Shirk, 1993, p. 23.
48. Ibid., pp. 27–8.
49. Zhou, 1995, p. 146.
50. Ibid.; Brugger and Reglar, 1994, p. 52; Shirk, 1993, p. 35.
51. Shirk, 1993, p. 51.
52. Bachman, 1985, p. x; *Economist*, 22 Apr. 1995, p. 119.
53. Zhou, 1995, p. 147.
54. See Bachman, 1985, pp. 151–6, on Chen's economic views.
55. Shirk, 1993, p. 129. The ideological and vested-interest sources of opposition to reform did not always overlap. For example, Chen Yun favoured not only downplaying heavy industry in favour of consumption (that is, light industry and agriculture) but also seeking consolidation through merger and the like of unprofitable heavy industry enterprises in order to ease the centre's financial burden and to improve efficiency (ibid., p. 213).
56. Ibid., pp. 133, 132.
57. Brugger and Reglar, 1994, p. 62; Hsü, 1990, p. 181.

58. Wang, 1992, p. 259; Hsü, 1990, p. 172.
59. Watson, 1988, p. 7.
60. For this paragraph see ibid., pp. 7–8, 13, 14, 17, 23, 25.
61. Wang, 1992, p. 260; Hsü, 1990, p. 172.
62. Hsü, 1990, p. 172.
63. Brugger and Reglar, 1994, pp. 172–3.
64. Hsü, 1990, p. 174; Selden, 1993, p. 228.
65. Selden, 1993, p. 228.
66. Ibid., pp. 230, 232.
67. Blecher, 1995, pp. 112, 113, 116; Selden, 1993, pp. 228, 233, 235; Brugger and Reglar, 1994, pp. 84, 134, 136; *Economist*, 16 March, 1995, p. 21.
68. Shirk, 1993, p. 41.
69. Wang, 1992, p. 266; Hsü, 1990, p. 185.
70. Hsü, 1990, pp. 180–1; Gold, 1989, p. 197 table 1.
71. Gold, 1989, p. 198; Solinger, 1992, pp. 128–9.
72. Gold, 1989, p. 198; Solinger, 1992, p. 129.
73. Gold, 1989, pp. 195–8.
74. Ibid., p. 198; Solinger, 1992, p. 129.
75. Shirk, 1993, p. 43.
76. Ibid. This was double the proportion of a decade earlier and was thanks to a growth rate that was well over twice that of state-owned industries (ibid., p. 342).
77. Selden, 1993, pp. 229–30.
78. Blecher, 1995, p. 114.
79. Hsü, 1990, p. 172; Selden, 1993, p. 232.
80. Shirk, 1993, pp. 131, 130.
81. Ibid., pp. 206, 203.
82. Ibid., pp. 130, 197. See pp. 211, 218, 219, on how even many of the Plan-oriented heavy industries began selling and producing for the market sector.
83. Hsü, 1990, p.191.
84. Thoburn and Howell, 1995, p. 173.
85. Ibid., p. 172; Shirk, 1993, p. 48.
86. Shirk, 1993, p.48.
87. Ibid., p. 187.
88. Thoburn and Howell, 1995, pp. 176, 177; Shirk, 1993, p. 48.
89. Shirk, 1993, Ch. 9 and p. 149.
90. Ibid., pp. 149, 181, 183. As some three-quarters of provincial revenues were derived from such enterprise revenues, it is not surprising that provincial officials 'responded to the new incentives, promoting local industry like natural entrepreneurs' (ibid., p. 153).
91. Brugger and Reglar, 1994, p. 54.
92. Ibid., p. 58.
93. Joseph, 1985, p. 255; Schram, 1984, pp. 438–40.
94. For this paragraph see Chronicle and Documentation for October–December 1987 in *China Quarterly*, 113, March 1988, pp. 143–9.
95. Wang, 1992, p. 268.
96. Hsü, 1990, p. 188–9; Thoburn and Howell, 1995, p. 177.

97. Shirk, 1993, p. 17.
98. Benewick, 1995, p. 14.
99. Ibid., p. 17; Goldman, 1994, p. 316.
100. Goldman, 1994, p. 316.
101. Ibid.; Brugger and Reglar, 1994, p. 169.
102. Brugger and Reglar, 1994, p. 79.
103. Shambaugh, 1991b, p. 552.
104. Brugger and Reglar, 1994, p. 79.
105. Shirk, 1993, pp. 135 n. 7, 317. Some indirect support for such a view comes from the apparent lack of discontent shown in rural areas, which had not seen such recent increases in prosperity, and in fact it has been argued that the regime 'suppressed the protests with the passive support of most of China's villagers' (Blecher, 1995, p. 106).
106. Stavis, 1989, p. 238 table 1; Zhou, 1995, p. 152.
107. Stavis, 1989, pp. 248–9.
108. Goldman, 1994, p. 317.
109. Zhou, 1995, p. 152.
110. Ibid.; Brugger and Reglar, 1994, p. 78.
111. Goldman, 1994, p. 316.
112. Breslin, 1995, pp. 65–6; Zhou, 1995, p. 150; Shirk, 1993, pp. 300–1, 305–8.
113. Shirk, 1993, pp. 325–7; Stavis, p. 240, points out that as part of the preparation for the reform some administratively set prices were being adjusted upward and those for non-essential foods were raised by an average of more than 24 per cent. In 1985 there had been a market-isation of such non-essential foods as meat, fish, fruit and vegetables but in most cities local officials had imposed price controls to prevent discontent among residents (Shirk, 1993, 301–2).
114. Shirk, 1993, p. 18.
115. Ibid., pp. 143, 188.
116. Ibid., pp. 142–3, 188–9.
117. Goldman, 1994, p. 317; Shirk, 1993, p. 18.
118. Shirk, 1993, p. 184.
119. Ibid., p. 185, and p. 154 on inflation.
120. Brugger and Reglar, 1994, pp. 72–5; Stavis, 1989, p. 238 table 1; Hsü, 1990, p. 187.
121. Stavis, 1989, p. 244; Zhou, 1995, p. 152.
122. Lam, 1995, p. 8.
123. Brugger and Reglar, 1994, p. 80.
124. *FEER*, 25 Aug. 1994, p. 44.
125. Lam, 1995, p. 18.
126. Saich, 1992, p. 1151.
127. Soon some 70 companies were listed on the Shanghai and Shenzhen exchanges but local requests to establish more stock exchanges were refused by the Dengist policy makers of the mid-1990s (Prime, 1993, p. 260).
128. Bachman, 1994, p. 34.
129. For this paragraph see also *Economist*, 15 Jan. 1994, p. 29; *FEER*, 3 Mar. 1994, p. 53; Bachman, 1994, p. 35.

130. Bachman, 1995, p. 40.
131. Brugger and Reglar, 1994, p. 169.
132. Zhou, 1995, pp. 152–3; Saich, 1992, p. 1144.
133. *FEER*, 5 May 1994, p. 77–8.
134. Ibid.
135. Bachman, 1995, p. 41.
136. Ibid., pp. 40, 41.
137. Shirk, 1993, p. 288. See Hsü, 1990, p. 179 on the new autonomy in matters of production, pricing and wages delegated to managers in the early 1980s.
138. Solinger, 1992, p. 135; Wank, 1995, p. 161.
139. Bruun, 1995 p. 190; Saich, 1992, pp. 1159–60. Solinger, 1992, pp. 123–4 refers to such commercialised officials as being just as much 'entrepreneurs' as the businessmen dependent upon them.
140. Wank, 1995, pp. 160–5; Bruun, 1995, pp. 191–2, 194, 201, 203; Oi, 1989, pp. 230–1.
141. Wank, 1995, p. 171; Oi, 1989, p. 229.
142. Wank, 1995, p. 175; Lam, 1995, p. 256.
143. Bruun, 1995, pp. 200, 210.
144. Bachman, 1994, p. 36.
145. Brugger and Reglar, 1994, p. 86.
146. Breslin, 1995, pp. 68–9.
147. Ibid.; Brugger and Reglar, 1994, p. 86.
148. Brugger and Reglar, 1994, p. 134; Blecher, 1995, p. 116.
149. Blecher, 1995, pp. 116; Bachman, 1994, p. 36.
150. Blecher, 1995, p. 117.

3 COMMUNIST VIETNAM

1. Porter, 1993, p. 105. However, there had been one other death in office, six new members had been added and one was already on the way out because of his pro-Chinese sympathies.
2. Williams, 1992, p. 25; Vo Nhan Tri, 1990, p. 183.
3. For this paragraph see also Williams, 1992, pp. 25, 48; Porter, 1993, p. 107; Duiker, 1989, p. 245.
4. For this paragraph see Stern, 1993, pp. 176–7, 25; Williams, 1992, p. 28.
5. For this paragraph see Stern, 1993, pp. 176, 177; Porter, 1993, pp. 85–6 (on removing Politburo and CC Department 'guidance' to government and Ministries), 86–7 (on lower Party organs), 90 (on the Front's organisation of the process of nominating candidates for the National Assembly and People's Councils), 89 n. 110; Heng Hiang Khng, 1993, p. 355 (on the ratio of candidates to seats).
6. Porter, 1993, p. 75.
7. Ibid.
8. For this paragraph see also Stern, 1993, pp. 51, 75–6; Porter, 1993, p. 76.
9. Williams, 1992, p. 32; Stern, 1993, p. 79.

10. Cima, 1990, p. 93; Pike, 1991, p. 83.
11. Stern, 1993, pp. 79, 88–9, 174–5, 133; Joiner, 1990, p. 1056.
12. For this paragraph see Heng Hiang Khng, 1993, pp. 355, 354; Porter, 1993, p. 76.
13. For this paragraph see Pike, 1994, p. 67; *FEER*, 29 July 1993, p. 25; Fahey, 1994, pp. 346–7.
14. For this paragraph see Heng Hiang Khng, 1993, p. 354; Stern, 1993, p. 148, on military representation; Hebbel, 1993, p. 366.
15. Hebbel, 1993, p. 364.
16. For the rest of this paragraph see ibid., p. 366; Pike, 1986, pp. 168–71, 158–9, 166; *FEER*, 23 Dec. 1990, p. 40.
17. Boudarel, 1980, p. 137. See also Pike, 1994, p. 67.
18. Beresford, 1988, pp. 91, 92.
19. Boudarel, 1980, p. 137.
20. Duiker, 1980, p. 46.
21. For this paragraph see Duiker, 1989, pp. 82–3.
22. Ibid., p. 245.
23. Hebbel, 1993, pp. 369–70; *FEER*, 23 Dec. 1993, p. 40; Stern, 1993, p. 92; Beresford, 1988, p. 219 n. 12; Womack, 1992, p. 177.
24. *FEER*, 10 Feb. 1994, p. 15.
25. Pike, 1992, p. 77; *FEER*, 26 Oct. 1995, p. 52; Huynh, 1992, pp. 338, 342.
26. *FEER*, 10 Feb. 1994, p. 15.
27. Scalapino, 1992, p. 10.
28. McCarthy, 1990, p. 13; Stern, 1993, pp. 128–9; Elliott, 1993, pp. 68–70.
29. For this paragraph see McCarthy, 1990, p. 13.
30. Joiner, 1990, p. 1055.
31. Beresford, 1988, pp. 89, 105.
32. Ibid., p. 219 n. 12.
33. Ibid., p. 184.
34. Duiker, 1989, pp. 64–5, 46, 68.
35. For this paragraph see Vo Nhan Tri, 1990, pp. 81, 82, 92, 131; Duiker, 1989, pp. 78, 74, 77; Williams, 1992, p. 45.
36. Porter, 1993, pp. 120, 121.
37. Ibid., p. 121.
38. Ibid. See Vo Nhan Tri, 1990, p. 92, Duiker, 1989, pp. 74–5, and Williams, 1992, p. 44, on the envisaged reform: the use of incentives, efficiency-promoting price and wage setting, and more autonomy for local authorities and enterprises.
39. For this paragraph see also Porter, 1993, p. 121; Duiker, 1989, p. 78; Vo Nhan Tri, 1990, pp. 132–3. See Porter, 1993, pp. 121–2, on how central Party and state administrators finally organised sufficient consensus to implement the product contract system.
40. See Porter, 1993, pp. 119–20, on failures to implement collectivisation.
41. Wurfel, 1993, p. 26.
42. Porter, 1993, pp. 123–4.
43. Duiker, 1989, p. 249; Vo Nhan Tri, 1990, p. 143.
44. For this paragraph see also Vo Nhan Tri, 1990, pp. 162, 146–7; Duiker, 1989, p. 249; Porter, 1993, p. 124; Williams, 1992, p. 46.

45. For this paragraph see Vo Nhan Tri, 1990, pp. 165–6; Jeffries, 1993, p. 215; Wurfel, 1993, pp. 26, 28; Williams, 1987, p. 103; Williams, 1992, pp. 26, 49, 50, 46; Porter, 1993, p. 121.
46. Vo Nhan Tri, 1990, p. 167.
47. Ibid.
48. Womack, 1993, p. 282; Duiker, 1989, p. 245.
49. Vo Nhan Tri, 1990, p. 167; Stern, 1993, p. 82.
50. Jeffries, 1993, p. 215.
51. Williams, 1987, p. 103.
52. Vu Tuan Anh, 1995, pp. 28–9.
53. Le Cao Doan, 1995, pp. 119–20. For this paragraph see also Selden, 1993, pp. 241, 239; Le Cao Doan, 1995, pp. 117–18; Stern, 1993, p. 45.
54. Hoang and Hoang, 1995, p. 151. See also Reinhardt, 1993, p. 84, on rapid growth in numbers but only a few large companies.
55. Hoang and Hoang, 1995, p. 151.
56. Vo Dai Luoc, 1995, p. 71; de Vylder, 1995, p. 48; Hoang and Hoang, 1995, pp. 151 n. 1, 152.
57. McCarty, 1993, pp. 107–8.
58. Hoang and Hoang, 1995, p. 155.
59. de Vylder, 1995, p. 60; Vu Tuan Anh, 1995, p. 24.
60. de Vylder, 1995, p. 61.
61. For this paragraph see Cima, 1990, p. 92; McCarty, 1993, pp. 101–2; Vo Dai Luoc, 1995, pp. 79, 81, 82; de Vylder, 1995, pp. 61, 63.
62. de Vylder, 1995, p. 58. For this paragraph see also Cima, 1990, p. 92; Vo Nhan Tri, 1988, pp. 215, 216.
63. Porter, 1993, p. 211; Vo Nhan Tri, 1990, p. 224. By the end of 1987 the external debt was $8.6 billion, with over $6 billion in non-convertible currencies, mostly roubles (ibid.).
64. Vo Nhan Tri, 1990, p. 213.
65. Williams, 1992, p. 66; Porter, 1993, p. 213.
66. For this paragraph see Reinhardt, 1993, pp. 87, 88; Heng Hiang Khng, 1993, p. 358.
67. Heng Hiang Khng, 1993, p. 358.
68. Fahey, 1994, p. 348.
69. Reinhardt, 1993, p. 83.
70. Ibid.; Heng Hiang Khng, 1993, p. 358.
71. *FEER*, 3 Feb. 1994, p. 45.
72. For this paragraph see *FEER*, 1 July 1993, p. 64; *FEER*, 3 Feb. 1994, p. 26.
73. Williams, 1992, pp. 52–3; McCarty, 1993, pp. 101–2, 104.
74. Vo Dai Luoc, 1995, p. 79.
75. Heng Hiang Khng, 1993, p. 358. An estimate for 1993 is that no fewer than 7000 enterprises were the equivalent of insolvent (Fahey, 1994, p. 341).
76. *FEER*, 3 Feb. 1994, p. 45.
77. Ibid.
78. Ibid.; de Vylder, 1995, pp. 42, 49.
79. Vo Dai Luoc, 1995, pp. 79–80.
80. Fahey, 1994, p. 341.

81. de Vylder, 1995, pp. 40–1; McCarty, 1993, p. 133.
82. de Vylder, 1995, p. 39.
83. *Economist*, 5 Nov. 1994, p. 28; McCarty, 1993, pp. 131, 133. For this paragraph see also de Vylder, 1995, p. 68; McCarty, 1993, p. 133; Jeffries, 1993, p. 222.
84. The figures in this paragraph are taken from de Vylder, 1995, pp. 31, 65, 58; *FEER*, 29 July 1993, p. 29; Pike, 1994, p. 65.
85. *FEER*, 3 Feb. 1994, p. 45; *FEER*, 2 Sept. 1993, pp. 16–17.
86. Selden, 1993, p. 244.
87. de Vylder, 1995, p. 67; Fahey, 1994, p. 346; *FEER*, 4 Feb. 1993, p. 27.
88. Fahey, 1994, p. 344.
89. Goodman, 1996, p. 145.
90. Ibid.
91. Ibid.
92. Reinhardt, 1993, pp. 91–2, on Saigon area attracting 75 per cent of foreign investment and producing some 30 per cent of exports in 1991; Fahey, 1994, pp. 349–50, on highest average incomes in Mekong Delta, and northern and northern central Vietnam with lowest. However, McCarty, 1993, p. 132, points out that the coastal–inland distinction, as in the case of Haiphong and Da Nang province, had been growing rapidly since 1989.
93. McCarty, 1993, p. 132.

4 COMMUNIST NORTH KOREA

1. Tamaki, 1988, pp. 31, 32.
2. For this paragraph see also Lee, 1989, p. 166; *Vantage Point*, Apr. 1995, p. 42; North, 1992, p. 52; Scalapino, 1992, p. 53; Foster-Carter, 1987, p. 74.
3. Suh, 1988, pp. 271, 315; J. K. Park, 1979, p. 135; Tamaki, 1988, p. 33.
4. Suh, 1988, p. 271; Chung, 1986, p.28.
5. Suh, 1988, p. 271; Tamaki, 1988, p. 33; Chung, 1986, pp. 23, 24, 28.
6. Chung, 1986, p. 28; Suh, 1988, p.271.
7. Suh, 1988, p. 273.
8. *Vantage Point*, Oct. 1995, p. 3.
9. E.g., see Scalapino, 1972, pp. 661, 663, for 1970 situation.
10. Suh, 1988, p. 315.
11. Ibid., p. 316.
12. Yang, 1980, p. 161. See Foster-Carter, 1987, p. 77, and North, 1992, pp. 54–5, on protection from foreign sources.
13. For this paragraph see Clough, 1987, pp. 53–4; J. K. Park, 1979, pp. 138, 137 table IV.
14. For this paragraph see Suh, 1988, pp. 281–2; Rhee, 1987, p. 899.
15. Suh, 1988, p. 279.
16. Ibid., pp. 284–5; Okonogi, 1988, pp. 3,2.
17. Suh, 1988, pp. 287–8.
18. Ibid., pp. 287–9.

19. Koh, 1989, p. 42.
20. See J. K. Park, 1979, pp. 130–1, and Chung, 1986, p. 34, on the Secretariat.
21. For this paragraph see also Tamaki, 1988, p. 40; Kim, 1981, p. 113; Oh, 1990, p. 76; Merrill, 1993, p. 43.
22. For this paragraph see *Vantage Point*, Oct. 1995, p. 3; Lee, 1994, pp. 425, 440, 427; *Vantage Point*, Apr. 1995, pp. 41–3; J. K. Park, 1979, p. 133; Chung, 1986, p. 24; Kim, 1995, p. 16.
23. Lee, 1994, p. 427.
24. *Economist*, 21 Oct. 1995, p. 29.
25. Merrill, 1993, p. 44.
26. Ibid.; Suh, 1988, p. 286.
27. *FEER*, 23 Dec. 1993, p. 25.
28. McCarthy, 1994.
29. Ibid.; *South China Morning Post*, 27 Nov. 1994.
30. Okonogi, 1988, p. 8; Cotton, 1987, p. 90.
31. Okonogi, 1988, pp. 11–13.
32. For this paragraph see H-S. Park, 1979, p. 148; Rhee, 1987, pp. 892, 892 n. 20; Yang, 1987, pp. 528–30; Cumings, 1993, pp. 225–6.
33. Rhee, 1987, p. 890.
34. Ibid.
35. For this paragraph see Okonogi, 1988, pp. 1, 18; Cotton, 1987, pp. 88, 89; Park, 1982, pp. 548, 548 n. 4, 552–3; Smith, 1994, pp. 100–1.
36. For this paragraph see Yang, 1987, pp. 522–3, 517; Smith, 1994, pp. 99, 103–4; Macdonald, 1988, p. 250; Park, 1982, p. 556; Foster-Carter, 1987, pp. 66, 81.
37. For this paragraph see Tamaki, 1988, p. 31; Yang, 1987, pp. 518–19.
38. Park, 1982, p. 550.
39. For this paragraph see also Cotton, 1987, p. 89; Smith, 1994, p. 104; Park, 1982, pp. 549, 549 n. 5, 551.
40. Okonogi, 1988, p. 12.
41. For this paragraph see also Park, 1982, p. 551; Rhee, 1987, pp. 896 n. 29, 897, 894–5, 900; Okonogi, 1988, pp. 6–7; Koh, 1989, p. 40.
42. For this paragraph see Lee, 1994, p. 432; North, 1992, p. 59; Suh, 1988, p. 284.
43. Kim, 1995, p. 17.
44. Scalapino, 1992, p. 56.
45. Ibid., p. 57.
46. Kihl, 1991, pp. 43, 31.
47. For this paragraph see Clough, 1987, pp. 165, 90.
48. BBC Monitoring Service: Asia-Pacific, 12 Nov. 1994. 'Socialism is Science' was first published 1 Nov. and broadcast 7 Nov. 1994 by KCNA News Agency.
49. For this paragraph see also Macdonald, 1988, p. 32; Cumings, 1993, pp. 225, 220–1; Reuters, 5 Oct. 1994; BBC Monitoring Service: Asia-Pacific, 5 Oct. 1994, 16 Nov. 1994.
50. Clough, 1987, pp. 155–6.
51. Hwang, 1993, p. 44.
52. Clough, 1987, p. 156; Hwang, 1993, p. 48.

53. For this paragraph see Macdonald, 1988, p. 213; Clough, 1987, pp. 158–60; Jeffries, 1993, pp. 204, 200, 199; Foster-Carter, 1987, p. 70.
54. For this paragraph see Jeffries, 1993, p. 203; Suh, 1988, p. 297; Clough, 1987, pp. 164–6, 167; Foster-Carter, 1987, pp. 72–3, 71; Cotton, 1985, p. 153; Komaki, 1988, pp. 58–9.
55. Komaki, 1988, p. 59; Kim, 1993, pp. 865–6.
56. Lee, 1990, p. 26.
57. Rhee, 1991, p. 73.
58. Ibid., pp. 73–4.
59. Lee, 1990, pp. 32, 31.
60. Ibid., p. 31.
61. Ibid., pp. 25, 31–2, 33 n. 11.
62. Macdonald, 1988, p. 217.
63. Oh, 1990, p. 76; Jeong, 1992, p. 28.
64. Kim, 1993, p. 867; *FEER*, 9 Sept. 1993, p. 17.
65. For this paragraph see also Kim, 1993, p. 867; Rhee, 1992, pp. 58, 59; *FEER*, 9 Sept. 1993, p. 17.
66. Rhee, 1992, p. 58; *FEER*, 10 Feb. 1994, p.23.
67. Merrill, 1993, p. 47.
68. Rhee, 1992, p. 58.
69. Merrill, 1993, p. 47.
70. Lee, 1994, p. 424.
71. Kim, 1995, p. 25.
72. Lee, 1994, p. 424.
73. Merrill, 1993, p. 48.
74. *FEER*, 8 Sept. 1993, p.23; *FEER*, 19 Feb. 1994, p.24; Merrill, 1994, p. 16.
75. *FEER*, 4 Aug. 1994, p. 50.
76. Kim, 1993, p. 870; Merrill, 1993, pp. 49, 48; Jeffries, 1993, pp. 204–5; Kim, 1995, p. 26.
77. *Vantage Point*, March 1995, p. 19.
78. Kim, 1995, p. 25.
79. Merrill, 1994, p. 15.
80. Ibid., p. 16.
81. *FEER*, 10 Feb. 1994, p. 23; Merrill, 1994, p. 15.

5 COMMUNIST CUBA

1. Walker, 1993, p. 110.
2. Dominguez, 1986, p. 122.
3. For this paragraph see also Dominguez, 1982, pp. 20, 65, 66; Eckstein, 1994, p. 21.
4. Eckstein, 1994, pp. 19–20.
5. Azicri, 1988, p. 103.
6. Ibid., p. 112; Eckstein, 1994, pp. 22–3.
7. See Bengelsdorf, 1994, pp. 171–2; Lutjens, 1992, p. 64; Azicri, 1988, p. 100.

8. See Bengelsdorf, 1994, p. 145, on initiating each turning point and also such new schemes as reviving the construction micro- or mini-brigades. See ibid. and Eckstein, 1994, p. 114, on the marked increase in public appearances.
9. Balfour, 1990, p. 154, sees Rectification as not signalling 'a power shift within the regime' but 'a renewal of the populist style of the sixties in the service of a new social mobilization' – but he agrees that Castro 'almost certainly initiated' Rectification (ibid., p. 155).
10. Pérez-Stable, 1993, p. 72; Balfour, 1990, p. 154; Pérez-López, 1991, p. 41 n. 58.
11. Dominguez, 1982, p. 53; Azicri, 1988, pp. 89, 90 table 4.2, 96.
12. Gouré, 1989, pp. 587, 580, 582.
13. For this paragraph see also ibid., p. 589, 587–8; Baloyra, 1993, p. 54; Eckstein, 1994, p. 85.
14. Eckstein, 1994, pp. 102, 215.
15. For this paragraph see also Walker, 1993, p. 126; Dominguez, 1989, p. 48; *Economist*, 3 Sept. 1994, p. 42.
16. Pérez-López, 1991, p. 41, and see ibid., p. 41 n. 58, for example.
17. For this paragraph see also Dominguez, 1989, pp. 57–8; Lutjens, 1992, p. 62.
18. Pérez-Stable, 1993, pp. 77–8; Bengelsdorf, 1994, pp. 157, 169; Eckstein, 1994, p. 115; Reuters, 3 Jan. 1994; *Economist*, 5 Feb. 1994, p. 46.
19. For this paragraph see also Pérez-Stable, 1993, pp. 78–81; Bengelsdorf, 1994, pp. 170, 173; Eckstein, 1994, pp. 116, 117, 115.
20. Bengelsdorf, 1994, p. 145; Liss, 1994, p. 180.
21. *Independent*, 13 June 1992.
22. Reuters, 13 July 1992.
23. *Economist*, 3 Sept. 1994, p. 42; *Independent*, 2 Nov. 1994.
24. Liss, 1984, p. 268.
25. Liss, 1994, p. 35.
26. Balfour, 1990, p. 162. For this paragraph see also Liss, 1994, p. 34, 33; Kirk, 1980, p. 135, 136–9, 127; Balfour, 1990, p. 8 on Martí.
27. Liss, 1994, pp. 63–4.
28. Ibid., pp. 75, 79, on ideology; Eckstein, 1994, pp. 172–81.
29. Liss, 1984, p. 267.
30. Horowitz, 1975, p. 407; Gonzalez, 1974, pp. 93, 107, 153.
31. Guevara, 1971, p. 338.
32. Gonzalez, 1974, p. 133; Castro, 1971, pp. 362–3; Liss, 1984, p. 268.
33. Castro, 1971, p. 363.
34. For this paragraph see Liss, 1984, p. 262; Harris, 1992, p. 90; Castro, 1971, pp. 382, 368–9; Silverman, 1971, p. 17; Eckstein, 1994, p. 41; Fitzgerald, 1989, p. 306.
35. Balfour, 1995, p. 168.
36. Eckstein, 1994, p. 22; Bengelsdorf, 1994, p. 170.
37. Eckstein, 1994, p. 110, 111, 113, 114. See also Pérez-Stable, 1993, p. 77, on the Party's claim to the mantle of 120 years of struggle for Cuban independence and claims that only the present leadership could live up to that heritage.
38. Bengelsdorf, 1994, p. 170.

39. Pérez-Stable, 1993, p. 80.
40. Eckstein, 1994, p. 115.
41. Ibid., pp. 202–3.
42. Ibid., p. 114; Bengelsdorf, 1994, pp. 135, 153, 138.
43. Baloyra, 1993, p. 51; Balfour, 1990, pp. 136–7.
44. Balfour, 1990, p. 137.
45. Zimbalist and Eckstein, 1989, p. 135; Pérez-López, 1992, p. 114. This figure is for Gross Social Product, not GNP.
46. Zimbalist, 1989, p. 74; Jeffries, 1993, p. 179.
47. Jeffries, 1993, p. 179.
48. Zimbalist, 1989, pp. 72, 71, on slow development of work norms. See also Pérez-López, 1992, p. 115 n. 2.
49. Zimbalist, 1989, pp. 72-3; Pérez-López, 1991, p. 38; Jeffries, 1993, p. 38. A limited degree of marketisation was introduced through the encouragement of supplementary non- or above-plan (quota) production/sales by the enterprises and through encouragement of the increasing amount of direct contracting of production/sales between enterprises (Zimbalist, 1989, p. 74).
50. Dominguez, 1986, p. 120.
51. For this paragraph see also Zimbalist and Eckstein, 1989, pp. 135–6; Pérez-López, 1991, pp. 114, 125. Despite efforts at diversification, sugar still contributed over 75 per cent of all export earnings in 1983–4, as compared to over 86 per cent in 1975–9 (Zimbalist and Eckstein, 1989, pp. 135, 136).
52. Baloyra, 1993, p. 53.
53. For this paragraph see also Dominguez, 1986, p. 121; Pérez-López, 1992, p. 114; Baloyra, 1993, p. 53; Jeffries, 1993, p. 184; Zimbalist, 1989, p. 73; Pérez-López, 1991, p. 40.
54. Balfour, 1990, pp. 116–17. For the rest of this paragraph see Dominguez, 1986, pp. 119, 120–1; Betancourt, 1989, p. 834.
55. Eckstein, 1994, p. 72.
56. Ibid.; Pérez-López, 1992, p. 120.
57. Petras and Morley, 1992, p. 18. In 1983 Cuba had already had to reschedule debt payments (Jeffries, 1993, p. 188).
58. Jeffries, 1993, p. 189. Cuba had had no dealings with the IMF since the early 1960s. Nor did the future prospects look bright, and in fact in 1986–8 only one third of the 1984 level of hard currency would be available (Zimbalist, 1989, p. 78). See Pérez-López, 1992, p. 114, on the trade imbalance and the external sector's problems.
59. Baloyra, 1993, p. 53; Pérez-Stable, 1993, p. 84 n. 6.
60. For this paragraph see also Pérez-Stable, 1993, p. 84 n. 6; Jeffries, 1993, p. 186; Pérez-Stable, 1989, pp. 140, 142–3; Baloyra, 1993, p. 53; Fitzgerald, 1989, p. 305; Zimbalist, 1989, p. 75. See also Eckstein, 1994, pp. 73–4, on costs to state of farmers' markets; Zimbalist, 1989, p. 84, on the disruptive – economically and socially/ideologically – effects of the farmers' markets; Eckstein, 1994, p. 74, on worker manipulation of the 'system'; Pérez-López, 1992, p. 115, on public meetings which revealed management corruption, cronyism and fraud. In fact corruption had 'apparently reached epidemic proportions in Cuba' (Fitzgerald, 1989, p. 291).

61. Pérez-López, 1992, p. 115.
62. Pérez-Stable, 1993, p. 84 n. 6.
63. Lutjens, 1992, p. 62.
64. Fitzgerald, 1989, p. 307.
65. Ibid.; Mesa-Lago, 1989, p. 117, on mini-brigades; Eckstein, 1994, p. 63, on community voluntary labour; Zimbalist, 1989, p. 86, on how commitments to worker participation were only partially and unevenly met.
66. Petras and Morley, 1992, pp. 20–2; Fitzgerald, 1989, p. 306.
67. Balfour, 1990, p. 159; Cardoso and Helwege, 1992, pp. 9, 44.
68. Fitzgerald, 1989, p. 305.
69. Ibid.
70. Eckstein, 1994, pp. 75, 76, 72; Petras and Morley, 1992, pp. 17–18.
71. Zimbalist, 1989, p. 91 n. 32, and see also ibid., p. 76. Eckstein also sees it as a response to low-paid workers voting with their feet and moving to less arduous work (Eckstein, 1994, p. 76).
72. Eckstein, 1994, p. 75, 76; Petras and Morley, 1992, p. 16; Fitzgerald, 1989, p. 305; Zimbalist, 1989, p. 91 n. 32. And moralistic egalitarianism may have been part of the political price to pay to win popular acceptance of the austerity measures (Petras and Morley, 1992, p. 17).
73. Petras and Morley, 1992, p.20; Jenkins, 1992, p. 143; Zimbalist, 1989, p. 25; Eckstein, 1994, p. 73.
74. Harris, 1992, p. 91.
75. Petras and Morley, 1992, pp. 16, 21; Fitzgerald, 1989, p. 309.
76. Bengelsdorf, 1994, p. 142; Pérez-López, 1992, p. 116.
77. Pérez-López, 1992, p. 116; Eckstein, 1994, pp. 79–80, 223 table 3.1.
78. Eckstein, 1994, pp. 89–93; Balfour, 1995, p. 163.
79. Jeffries, 1993, p. 190.
80. Eckstein, 1994, p. 126.
81. Balfour, 1995, p. 163.
82. Eckstein, 1994, p. 96; Pérez-López, 1992, p. 124; Jeffries, 1993, p. 187; Cardoso and Helwege, 1992, p. 6. See Eckstein, 1994, p. 27, on the abandoning of Five Year Plans.
83. *Economist*, 19 Nov. 1994, p. 45. There had been two unofficial visits by a senior IMF official.
84. Balfour, 1995, p. 166.
85. Ibid. For this paragraph see also ibid., pp. 163, 164.
86. Eckstein, 1994, p. 111. For this paragraph see also Pérez-López, 1992, p. 124; Cardoso and Helwege, 1992, p. 80; Eckstein, 1994, pp. 96–102, 112–13; Bengelsdorf, 1994, p. 168.
87. For this paragraph see Eckstein, 1994, pp. 103, 104, 108–9, 110, 148; Cardoso and Helwege, 1992, p. 76.
88. See ibid., pp. 104, 108–9; *Economist*, 4 Dec. 1993, p. 74. The opening-up of self-employment opportunities involved over a hundred occupations and soon had attracted as much as 4 per cent of the work force, on official figures (*Observer*, 10 April 1994).
89. *Economist*, 25 June 1994, p. 41.
90. *Economist*, 19 Nov. 1994, p. 45; *Guardian*, 2 Oct. 1994; Balfour, 1995, p. 164.

91. *Economist*, 13 Aug. 1994, p. 42; *Economist*, 3 Sept. 1994, p. 41.
92. *Economist*, 13 Aug. 1994, p. 42.

6 BAATHIST SYRIA

1. For descriptions of his rule as personal see Seale, 1988, p. 178; Ma'oz, 1988, p.50; as a 'virtual presidential monarchy', Hinnebusch, 1994, p. 98.
2. For this paragraph see Ma'oz, 1988, pp. 50–1; Hinnebusch, 1994, p. 104.
3. Ma'oz, 1988, p. 50. Articles 103, 109 of the Constitution.
4. Ma'oz, 1988, p. 61.
5. Sadowski, 1988, p. 179.
6. Ma'oz, 1988, pp. 49, 57 on retirements.
7. Seale, 1988, p. 181; Perthes, 1995, p. 151, on his remaining the highest-ranking officer in the 1990s.
8. Dawisha, 1978, p. 355; Ma'oz, 1988, p. 60; Pipes, 1990, p. 134. The ideology indoctrinated into the military, however, has 'been reduced to a particularly intensive cult around the President' (Perthes, 1995, p. 151).
9. Hinnebusch, 1990, pp. 175, 190–1; Ma'oz, 1988, p. 49; Perthes, 1995, p. 170.
10. Ma'oz, 1988, pp. 69, 70. See Hinnebusch, 1990, pp. 166–7, and Perthes, 1995, p. 155, on the Party's much more centralist and hierarchical than democratic organisational structure.
11. Hinnebusch, 1990, pp. 167–8; Seale, 1988, p. 174.
12. Perthes, 1995, p. 154.
13. Ibid., pp. 156, 217.
14. Dawisha, 1978, pp. 352, 346; Ma'oz, 1988, p. 96.
15. Ma'oz, 1988, pp. 69, 183.
16. Pipes, 1990, p. 159; Batutu, 1981, p. 331.
17. Batutu, 1981, pp. 342–3, for reasons; Ma'oz, 1988, pp. 62, 65; Pipes, 1990, p. 184.
18. van Dam, 1979, pp. 32–3, on Baathist attraction to minorities.
19. Ma'oz, 1988, p. 52; Pipes, 1990, p. 184.
20. Ma'oz, 1988, p. 56. Perthes identifies four 'most important' security services, of which three were headed by military men (Perthes, 1995, p. 193 n. 44).
21. For this paragraph see Batutu, 1981, pp. 332, 331; Sadowski, 1988, p. 165.
22. For this paragraph see Ma'oz, 1988, p. 61; Bahout, 1994, p. 77; Kienle, 1994b, p. 130.
23. Hinnebusch, 1994, p. 105; Perthes, 1994, pp. 66–7.
24. It expanded to over 500 000 full and candidate members by 1984 and about a million by 1992, as compared to some 200 000 in 1977, and there was also a significant liberalisation of access to full membership (Hinnebusch, 1990, p. 179; Perthes, 1995, p. 155).
25. Roberts, 1987, p. 79; Seale, 1988, pp. 175–6. See also Dawisha, 1978, p. 334; and Perthes, 1995, pp. 162–3, also includes the Movement of Socialist Unionists.

26. Rabinovich, 1993, p. 20; Perthes, 1995, p. 168.
27. Rabinovich, 1993, p. 20. 'There is considerable confusion about the actual composition of the NPF' and it is 'more or less a matter of speculation', with some authorities not mentioning these three additions (Lobmeyer, 1994, p. 162 n. 2).
28. Perthes, 1995, p. 169.
29. Ibid., p. 168; Lobmeyer, 1994, p. 163 n. 9.
30. *Middle East*, Oct. 1994, p. 18; Perthes, 1995, p. 169.
31. Rabinovich, 1993, pp. 19–20; Lawson, 1994, p. 145.
32. Perthes, 1995, pp. 169, 170.
33. Ibid., pp. 222–3. Several millionaire deputies proved 'quite outspoken' and sometimes joined with other businessmen deputies as a block to promote their common interests (Lawson, 1994, p. 145; Hinnebusch, 1993, p. 255).
34. Hinnebusch, 1990, pp. 147, 149, on presidential monarchy.
35. Seale, 1988, pp. 339, 340.
36. Lobmeyer, 1994, p. 83; Ma'oz, 1988, p. 43.
37. Perthes, 1995, p. 268.
38. *Middle East*, March 1994, pp. 12, 13; Pipes, 1990, p. 176; Perthes, 1995, p. 268.
39. Perthes, 1995, pp. 268–9.
40. For this paragraph see *Middle East*, Oct. 1994, pp. 18–19; *Economist*, 7 Jan. 1995, p. 37; Perthes, 1995, p. 269.
41. Ma'oz, 1988, p. 73.
42. Hinnebusch, 1990, p. 1.
43. Roberts, 1987, p. 106.
44. Hinnebusch, 1986, p. 84.
45. Ma'oz, 1988, p. 79.
46. Ibid., p. 74.
47. Seale, 1988, p. 350.
48. Ibid., p. 460.
49. Pipes, 1990, p. 13, and p. 16 on extent.
50. Seale, 1988, pp. 349, 350. See also Ma'oz, 1988, p. 114, on Syrian references to Palestine's being part of southern Syria.
51. Roberts, 1987, pp. 13, 15; Seale, 1988, p. 349, on implicit use.
52. Seale, 1988, p. 349.
53. Roberts, 1987, p. 15; Ma'oz, 1988, p. 113; Pipes, 1990, p. 141.
54. Seale, 1988, p. 350.
55. It is also significant that claims to the effect that Asad was seeking to attain an ideological goal of Greater Syria tend to come from his opponents. See Pipes, 1990, pp. 142–7, for a catalogue of such claims.
56. Ma'oz, 1988, p. 114; Pipes, 1990, p. 147.
57. Seale, 1994, p. ix.
58. Perthes, 1994, p. 55.
59. Hinnebusch, 1994, p. 107.
60. Sukkar, 1994, p. 31.
61. Ibid.
62. Hinnebusch, 1994, pp. 103–4.
63. Sukkar, 1994, p. 33.

64. Hinnebusch, 1994, p. 109. See also Hinnebusch, 1993, p. 254.
65. See Perthes, 1994, p. 67, on media and regime representatives use of 'pluralism'.
66. Ibid., pp. 67–8.
67. Hopwood, 1988, p. 106; Perthes, 1995, p. 84. The maximum allowable land holdings of 120 hectares irrigated or 400 hectares non-irrigated land affected only the truly large landownwers (ibid., p. 88).
68. Syria was the least oil-based and least wealthy of the four Middle Eastern defiant dictatorships.
69. Devlin, 1983, p. 86.
70. Perthes, 1995, pp. 25, 24.
71. Firro, 1986, pp. 50–2.
72. For this paragraph see also Perthes, 1995, pp. 29, 46–7; Perthes, 1994, p. 55; Heydemann, 1992, pp. 25, 26.
73. Perthes, 1995, pp. 29–30. Although Syria's (non-Soviet) long-term foreign debt of about $3 billion was not excessive in debt-servicing terms, the country stopped repayments on its World Bank loans and did not resume payments until 1992 (Sukkar, 1994, p. 39).
74. Hopwood, 1988, p. 113; Sukkar, 1994, p. 28.
75. Ma'oz, 1988, p. 194; Sukkar, 1994, p. 28; Seale, 1988, p. 451.
76. For this paragraph see Perthes, 1995, pp. 45, 48; Perthes, 1994, p. 62; Heydemann, 1992, pp. 28–9.
77. Perthes, 1994, p. 57.
78. Ibid., p. 56.
79. Sukkar, 1994, p. 36. See also Perthes, 1995, p. 25.
80. For this paragraph see also Perthes, 1994, pp. 58, 57, 59, 60, 55; Sukkar, 1994, p. 33; Kienle, 1994a, p. 5.
81. For this paragraph see Sukkar, 1994, pp. 37, 33; Perthes, 1994, pp. 60, 58, 59.
82. Lawson, 1994, p. 150.
83. For this paragraph see also ibid., pp. 145, 150; Perthes, 1994, p. 60; Perthes, 1995, p. 60; *MER*, 1995, p. 111; *MER*, 1996, p. 115.
84. For this paragraph see Perthes, 1995, p. 58, 61; Perthes, 1994, pp. 63, 62; Pölling, 1994, p. 22; *MER*, 1995, p. 111; *MER*, 1996, p. 116.
85. Perthes, 1995, pp. 229, 218.
86. Ibid., p. 229.
87. Ibid., 112. See Sadowski, 1988, p. 169, on the lack of separation between politics and economics in Syria and his argument that what would be seen in the West as patronage and corruption is normatively accepted by most Syrians.
88. Seale, 1988, p. 456. See also Ma'oz, 1988, p. 194.
89. Kienle, 1994b, p. 119; Perthes, 1995, p. 115.
90. Kienle, 1994b, p. 119; Perthes, 1995, p. 231.
91. Perthes, 1995, p. 231.
92. See Hinnebusch, 1994, p. 106, Perthes, 1994, p. 64, and Perthes, 1995, p. 66, on privatisation. See Heydemann, 1992, pp. 30–1, on public sector reform.
93. Heydemann, 1992, p. 31; Sukkar, 1994, p. 35.
94. Sukkar, 1994, p. 41.

95. Sukkar, 1994, p. 41; Perthes, 1995, pp. 59, 61; Lawson, 1994, p. 151.
96. *MER*, 1996, p. 116.
97. Ibid.
98. Perthes, 1994, p. 63.
99. Perthes, 1995, p. 91. See Sadowski, 1988, pp. 172–3, on the close ties between the regime and the rural middle class.
100. Perthes, 1994, p. 59, 57; Perthes, 1995, p. 57, 91.
101. Perthes, 1995, p. 57; Sukkar, 1994, p. 35.
102. The statistics in this paragraph are taken from *MER*, 1995, p. 110; Sukkar, 1994, pp. 36, 37; *MER*, 1996, p. 115.
103. Sukkar, 1994, p. 37; *Economist*, 7 Jan. 1995, p. 38.
104. Perthes, 1994, p. 62; Sukkar, 1994, pp. 36–7.
105. Perthes, 1994, p. 62; Sukkar, 1994, p. 37.
106. Perthes, 1995, p. 62.
107. Lawson, 1994, p. 150.
108. *MER*, 1996, p. 115.
109. See Kienle, 1994b, pp. 120–2, 125–7, on these problems.
110. Hinnebusch, 1993, pp. 255, 254; Hinnebusch, 1994, p. 104.
111. Perthes, 1995, p. 101.
112. Ibid., p. 104.
113. Hinnebusch, 1993, pp. 254–5; Lobmeyer, 1994, p. 80; Hinnebusch, 1994, p. 108; Perthes, 1995, p. 104.
114. Perthes, 1995, p. 104.
115. Sadowski, 1988, p. 177; Seale, 1988, p. 325.
116. Seale, 1988, p. 326; Sadowski, 1988, p. 177.

7 BAATHIST IRAQ

1. For this paragraph see Helms, 1984, p. 89; Hooglund, 1989, pp. 179, 178, 182, 181; Farouk-Sluglett and Sluglett, 1987, pp. 114–15, 163.
2. Helms, 1984, p. 90. See Hooglund, 1981, p. 178, and Farouk-Sluglett and Sluglett, 1987, p. 136, on Party-isation.
3. See Khadduri, 1978, p. 41, on the Party's centralising emphasis upon discipline and obedience to avoid factionalism and splits. On Saddam's use of Stalin-like purges of threats within the Party in the early 1970s and immediately after taking over from al-Bakr, see Karsh and Rautsi, 1991, pp. 50–2, 118; Marr, 1985, p. 230.
4. Dawisha, 1986, p.23; Marr, 1985, p. 229.
5. On the Party control of the military see Abbas, 1986, pp. 216, 222, 217; Farouk-Sluglett and Sluglett, 1987, pp. 206, 207; Sciolino, 1991, pp. 83, 99; Khadduri, 1978, p. 38; Baram, 1993, p. 35; Karsh and Rautsi, 1991, p. 190, depicts the vetoing commissars as operating only at battalion level and above.
6. Farouk-Sluglett and Sluglett, 1987, p. 183; Khadduri, 1978, pp. 38, 42; Helms, 1984, p. 91.
7. al-Khalil, 1989, pp. 15, 36, 40, 5, 14.
8. Karsh and Rautsi, 1991, p. 38.

9. See Sciolino, 1991, pp. 56, 57, and Karsh and Rautsi, 1991, p. 38, for Tikritis' military dominance.
10. al-Jabbar, 1994, p. 102; Heller, 1994, p. 45.
11. al-Jabbar, 1994, p. 113.
12. Karsh and Rautsi, 1991, p. 38.
13. Hooglund, 1989, pp. 192–5; Heine, 1993, p. 44.
14. For this paragraph see also Hooglund, 1989, pp. 181, 182; Baram, 1993, p. 32; Karsh and Rautsi, 1991, pp. 197–8; *MER*, 1991–2, p. 68.
15. For this paragraph see al-Jaza'iri, 1994, pp. 44, 43; Karsh and Rautsi, 1991, p. 190; Tripp, 1989, pp. 63, 62.
16. For this paragraph see al-Jaza'iri, 1994, p. 44; Tripp, 1989, p. 70.
17. Tripp, 1989, p. 77 n. 18; Baram, 1993, pp. 34–5.
18. Sciolino, 1991, p. 99; al-Jabbar, 1994, p. 113; Farouk-Sluglett and Sluglett, 1987, p. 179.
19. For this paragraph see Karsh and Rautsi, 1991, pp. 183, 180–2; al-Khafaji, 1994, p. 29.
20. Karsh and Rautsi, 1991, p. 19; Helms, 1984, p. 105.
21. Sciolino, 1991, pp. 65–6, 50, 68. See ibid., p. 64, Baram, 1991, p. 116, and Dawisha, 1986, p. 29, on piety/pilgrimage.
22. Sciolino, 1991, pp. 65–6, 68.
23. Karsh and Rautsi, 1991, p. 196.
24. Ibid.
25. Ibid.; Sciolino, 1991, pp. 183–4. The ceremony was the August 1989 inauguration of the massive Victory Arches commemorating Iraq's victory over Iran.
26. *MER*, 1991/92, p. 68.
27. Baram, 1993, pp. 32, 33.
28. Heine, 1993, p. 43.
29. Baram, 1994, pp. 7, 29 n. 10. See also Karsh and Rautsi, 1991, pp. 197–8.
30. *Economist*, 12 Nov. 1994, p. 53.
31. For this paragraph see Farouk-Sluglett and Sluglett, 1986, pp. 102, 103, 104; Stork, 1982, p. 41; al-Jaza'iri, 1994, p. 39; Khadduri, 1978, pp. 44, 36–7.
32. Baram, 1991, p. 107.
33. Ibid., p. 109.
34. Ibid., p. 108.
35. Ibid., p. 116.
36. Ibid., pp. 60, 57.
37. al-Jaza'iri, 1994, p. 44; Khadduri, 1978, p. 47, on former commitment to collective leadership.
38. al-Jaza'iri, 1994, p. 47.
39. Ibid., p. 46.
40. Tripp, 1989, pp. 62–3.
41. Springborg, 1986, p. 34 n. 1.
42. See Farouk-Sluglett and Sluglett, 1986, p. 104; Stork, 1982, pp. 40–1, on populist and developmental view.
43. For this paragraph see Alnasrawi, 1994, p. 74; Baram, 1991, p. 139; Tripp, 1989, p. 61.

44. Baram, 1991, p. 140. See also Farouk-Sluglett and Sluglett, 1987, p. 261, on the regime's constant references to the Iranian threat to the Arab nation.
45. Baram, 1991, p. 109.
46. Ibid., pp. 61, 64, 66.
47. Ibid., pp. 73, 75, 76, 81-2, Ch. 8.
48. Ibid., pp. 43, 45, Ch. 4.
49. Dawisha, 1986, p. 29.
50. Baram, 1991, p. 137; Sciolino, 1991, p. 64.
51. Sciolino, 1991, p. 65.
52. Baram, 1991, p. 116.
53. Reuters, 6 Oct. 1992.
54. Leca, 1990, p. 180.
55. Karsh and Rautsi, 1991, p. 90.
56. Farouk-Sluglett and Sluglett, 1987, pp. 244-5; Springborg, 1986, p. 36.
57. For this paragraph see Karsh and Rautsi, 1991, pp. 153, 156; Crusoe, 1986, pp. 34, 40.
58. For this paragraph see Alnasrawi, 1994, p. 74; Crusoe, 1986, pp. 46-7.
59. Farouk-Sluglett and Sluglett, 1987, pp. 242, 246; Springborg, 1986, pp. 50-1. He points out that the increased private sector share of imports is even more significant when it is considered that the economy was ostensibly on a war footing.
60. Springborg, 1986, pp. 35, 36.
61. Ibid., p. 37. In practice the limits on size of landholding were 'no longer strictly enforced' and 'consolidation' had been occurring as families recombined their maximum holdings and purchased or rented more land (ibid.).
62. For the rest of this paragraph see ibid., pp. 36, 38, 40-1, 37; Crusoe, 1986, p. 46.
63. Farouk-Sluglett and Sluglett, 1987, p. 265; Springborg, 1986, pp. 49, 50.
64. Farouk-Sluglett and Sluglett, 1987, p. 245; Springborg, 1986, pp. 42-3.
65. Crusoe, 1986, p. 53.
66. Karsh and Rautsi, 1991, p. 171; Niblock, 1993, p. 78.
67. Niblock, 1993, p. 78.
68. Ibid.
69. Baram, 1994, p. 8; Karsh and Rautsi, 1991, p. 202.
70. Niblock, 1993, p. 79.
71. Ibid., pp. 79-80.
72. Ibid.; *Keesing's*, p. 38838, on state enterprises; *MER*, 1991/92, p. 68, on $2.5 billion by Jan. 1990.
73. For this paragraph see Alnasrawi, 1994, p. 75; Niblock, 1993, pp. 80, 81; *Keesing's*, p. 38838; *MER*, 1996, p. 39.
74. Karsh and Rautsi, 1991, p. 202.
75. Niblock, 1993, p. 82, on the 1988 plans for petrochemicals, steel and aluminium industries.
76. Ibid., p. 81.
77. Ibid.
78. Ibid., p. 83.
79. Springborg, 1986, p. 44; Tripp, 1989, p. 64.

80. Karsh and Rautsi, 1991, p.197.
81. See Springborg, 1986, pp. 34, 43–6; Tripp, 1989, pp. 64, 65.
82. Tripp, 1989, p. 65.
83. Ibid., p. 64.
84. Baram, 1994, p. 8.
85. Alnasrawi, 1994, p. 75. See also Niblock, 1993, p. 82, and Karsh and Rautsi, 1991, p. 202.
86. Baram, 1994, p. 8.
87. Alnasrawi, 1994, p. 77, on GDP per capita decline; Karsh and Rautsi, 1991, p. 202, on high expectations; Baram, 1994, p. 7, on crisis of expectations by 1990.
88. Karsh and Rautsi, 1991, p. 202.
89. Baram, 1994, p. 6; Karsh and Rautsi, 1991, p. 202.
90. Baram, 1994, p. 7.
91. Alnasrawi, 1994, p. 76.
92. Ibid., p. 77.
93. Ibid., p. 78; Baram, 1994, p. 12.

8 QADHAFI'S LIBYA

1. For this paragraph see Davis, 1987, pp. 169–70, 90, 173; Bearman, 1986, pp. 152, 154.
2. For this paragraph see Bearman, 1986, p. 155; Davis, 1987, pp. 90–1, 170, 22, 23, 173.
3. Bearman, 1986, pp. 188–9; Mattes, 1995, pp. 90–1.
4. Bearman, 1986, pp. 188–9; Harris, 1986, p. 65; Mattes, 1995, p. 100; Djaziri, 1995, pp. 192–3; El Fathaly and Palmer, 1995, p. 164.
5. Mattes, 1995, p. 101; El Fathaly and Palmer, 1995, p. 165. The latter point out that many committee members were not allowed to bear arms and so did not constitute a militia (ibid., pp. 169).
6. Bearman, 1986, p. 189.
7. For this paragraph see ibid., pp. 188–90; Harris, 1986, p. 66; Blundy and Lycett, 1988, p. 148; Anderson, 1987, pp. 67, 65; Mattes, 1995, pp. 95, 99. See Anderson, 1987, p. 65, Mattes, 1995, p. 96, and El Fathaly and Palmer, 1995, p. 167, on membership numbers.
8. Wright, 1982, p. 278.
9. Ibid.
10. Bearman, 1986, p. 190; Mattes, 1995, p. 96.
    See also Djaziri, 1995, pp. 192, 193, on committees as communicators from and to their political prophet.
11. Legum, 1984–5, p. B44.
12. Wright, 1982, p. 187.
13. There were only relatively minor additions, as in 1986–8 several new minor institutions were set up: a Follow-up Committee to check that GPC decisions were implemented by the state apparatus; a similar Accountability Bureau; a Supervisory Apparatus to ensure government decisions were implemented; and a Secretariat for Mass Mobilization

and Revolutionary Guidance (abolished in 1990) to ginger up the Jamahiriya (Legum, 1986–7, p. B535, 1988–9, p. B482, and 1987–8, p. B513).

14. Wright, 1982, p. 279; Cooley, 1983, p. 281; Anderson, 1987, pp. 66–7.
15. See Wright, 1982, p. 279, Harris, 1986, p. 73, and Davis, 1987, pp. 219–21, on privileges. On expansion and arms purchases see Legum, 1984–5, p. B49, and 1985–6, p. B541.
16. Harris, 1986, p'. 73; El Fathaly and Palmer, 1995, p. 173.
17. See Cooley, 1983, p. 282, and Deeb, 1990, pp. 150–1, on discontent over foreign interventions, and Harris, 1986, pp. 73, 72, on inefficiencies and distrust.
18. Harris, 1986, p. 72; Anderson, 1987, p. 67.
19. Blundy and Lycett, 1988, pp. 244–5; Bearman, 1986, pp. 292–3; Legum, 1986–7, p. B536.
20. For this paragraph see Bearman, 1986, pp. 239, 240; Legum, 1988–9, p. B485; Deeb, 1990, p. 151; *Middle East*, March 1989, p.7; Anderson, 1995, p. 233.
21. Bearman, 1986, p. 190; Harris, 1986, p. 71; El Fathaly and Palmer, 1995, p. 168; Mattes, 1995, pp. 106–7.
22. Legum, 1984–5, p. B44.
23. Legum, 1986–7, p. B536.
24. Mattes, 1995, p. 107.
25. Vandewalle, 1995a, pp. 34–5; Mattes, 1995, pp. 105–7; Vandewalle, 1991, p. 221; Deeb, 1990, p. 151.
26. Legum, 1988–9, p. B482.
27. Mattes, 1995, pp. 105, 108, 109.
28. For this paragraph see Legum, 1986–7, p. B537, 1988–9, p. B482, 1984–5, p. B44, and 1987–8, p. B537; *Middle East*, March 1989, p. 6; Djaziri, 1995, p. 189.
29. Harris, 1986, p. 72.
30. Cooley, 1983, p. 282; Legum, 1986–7, p. B536.
31. Harris, 1986, p. 72; Blundy and Lycett, 1988, p. 147; Bearman, 1986, p. 190; Anderson, 1987, pp. 66–7.
32. Harris, 1986, p. 72; Blundy and Lycett, 1988, p. 243.
33. Blundy and Lycett, 1988, p. 244; Anderson, 1987, p. 67.
34. Blundy and Lycett, 1988, pp. 31–2.
35. Reuters, 11 Dec. 1990.
36. Bearman, 1986, p. 284.
37. Qaddafi, 1987, chapter/section on 'The Party'.
38. Ibid., p. 33.
39. Ibid., pp. 57–60, 73, 75, 76.
40. Ibid., p. 74.
41. Cooley, 1983, p. 145.
42. Qaddafi, 1987, pp. 98, 99, and see also pp. 81, 82.
43. Davis, 1987, p. 214, asks 'which nation does he mean – Arab or Libyan?'
44. Cooley, 1983, p. 148, and Davis, 1987, p. 50, agree that Islam is never mentioned.
45. Qaddafi, 1987, p. 84.

46. For this paragraph see Wright, 1982, pp. 195, 144; Bearman, 1986, pp. 162, 163; Davis, 1987, pp. 57, 58.
47. Legum, 1987–8, p. B517.
48. Legum, 1986–7, pp. B536, B535.
49. Qaddafi, 1987, p. 112; Cooley, 1983, pp. 151, 153; Bearman, 1986, p. 243. The 1984 law relating to marriage still formally allowed polygamy (Djaziri, 1995, p. 195).
50. Vandewalle, 1991, p. 224; Deeb, 1990, p. 152. On its deficiencies and peculiarities as a human rights document see Mayer, 1995, pp. 123–4, and Vandewalle, 1995a, pp. 35–6.
51. Vandewalle, 1991, p. 225; Deeb, 1990, p. 152.
52. *Keesing's*, pp. 39438, 39888; Mayer, 1995, pp. 131–2.
53. Mayer, 1995, p. 132.
54. Vandewalle, 1995b, p. 207.
55. Wright, 1982, p. 251.
56. Bearman, 1986, pp. 191, 193. He points out that the producers' partnerships were greatly constrained by the direct and indirect effects of tight state control of the economy (ibid., p. 193).
57. Vandewalle, 1995b, p. 207.
58. Bearman, 1986, p. 195.
59. Davis, 1987, pp. 39, 237 n. 27.
60. Wright, 1982, p. 265.
61. Bearman, 1986, p. 269; Legum, 1984–5, p. B44.
62. Bearman, 1986, p. 265.
63. Ibid., p. 269.
64. Ibid., p. 266; Legum, 1985–6, p. B538.
65. Legum, 1985–6, p. B538, and 1984–5, p. B43.
66. Legum, 1986–7, pp. B548, B550.
67. Ibid., p. B549.
68. Vandewalle, 1991, p. 230.
69. Ibid., p. 221. The failure of the state supermarket system was not compensated for by the 'illegal but unofficially tolerated black market' because 'the average Libyan discovered that most available goods were beyond his or her purchasing power' – shortages of consumer goods were common in most cities (ibid., pp. 229–30).
70. Ibid., p. 221.
71. Ibid., p. 226.
72. Ibid., p. 225.
73. Ibid., p. 231.
74. Deeb, 1990, p. 151.
75. Ibid., p. 150.
76. Vandewalle, 1991, p. 226. He uses the term 'consumer infitah' to describe the changes (ibid., p. 231).
77. Deeb, 1990, pp. 150, 149.
78. For this paragraph see also ibid., p. 150.
79. For this paragraph see Vandewalle, 1995b, p. 213; Deeb, 1990, p. 150; Vandewalle, 1991, pp. 226.
80. Deeb, 1990, p. 150; Vandewalle, 1991, p. 226; Vandewalle, 1995b, p. 214.
81. Vandewalle, 1991, p. 228.

82. See Vandewalle, 1995b, p. 216.
83. Ibid.; Anderson, 1995, pp. 230–1.
84. Deeb, 1990, p. 150.
85. *Keesing's*, p. 37333.
86. Reuters, 12 June 1991.
87. *Middle East*, 1 Aug. 1992; Reuters, 2 Dec. 1992.
88. Reuters, 2 Dec. 1992.
89. *MER*, 1995, p. 63; *MER*, 1996, p. 68.
90. *Middle East*, 1 Aug. 1992.
91. *Keesing's*, p. 39119.
92. *Keesing's*, p. 39488.
93. *MER*, 1995, p. 63.
94. *Middle East*, Dec. 1993, p. 17.
95. BBC Monitoring Service: Middle East, 3 Feb. 1994.
96. *MER*, 1996, p. 68.

9 KHOMEINIST IRAN

1. For this paragraph see Milani, 1994, p. 156, 159.
2. For this paragraph see Abrahamian, 1993, p. 134; Milani, 1994, pp. 156–8.
3. Abrahamian, 1993, p. 73; Omid, 1994, pp. 71-2.
4. Milani, 1994, p. 193. On the removal of Bani-Sadr see Bakhash,1986, Ch. 6.
5. Kamrava, 1992, p. 90; Bakhash, 1986, p. 244; Omid, 1994, p. 71.
6. Bakhash, 1986, p. 255.
7. Entessar, 1992, p. 225.
8. Savory, 1988, p. 361.
9. Bakhash, 1986, p. 244.
10. Omid, 1994, pp. 94, 104; Kamrava, 1992, p. 90; Milani, 1994, p. 181.
11. Bakhash, 1986, pp. 226, 228, 243; Omid, 1994, pp. 94, 104.
12. Omid, 1994, pp. 157, 80–1.
13. Ibid., pp. 107, 100.
14. Ibid., p. 107; Bakhash, 1986, p. 59.
15. Bakhash, 1986, p. 63.
16. Omid, 1994, pp. 111–12; Calabrese, 1994, p. 41.
17. Bakhash, 1986, pp. 84, 63; Omid, 1994, p. 118.
18. Abrahamian, 1993, pp. 134, 89; Kamrava, 1992, p. 93.
19. Bakhash, 1986, pp. 241, 244; Kamrava, 1992, pp. 86–7.
20. Bakhash, 1986, pp. 241, 246.
21. Sarabi, 1994, p. 90; Milani, 1994, p. 199.
22. Akhavi, 1987, p. 184.
23. Sarabi, 1994, p. 90.
24. Milani, 1994, p. 199.
25. Kamrava, 1992, p. 112.
26. Ehteshami, 1995, pp. 37, 46.
27. Ibid., p. 49; Milani, 1994, p. 222.
28. Ibid., p. 223; Abrahamian, 1993, p. 134; Ehteshami, 1995, pp. 47, 53.

29. Sarabi, 1994, p. 91 n. 3.
30. Milani, 1994, p. 199.
31. Sarabi, 1994, pp. 100, 103.
32. *Middle East*, July 1993, pp. 13, 15; Ehteshami, 1995, p. 68.
33. Ehteshami, pp. 62 table 6, 69–70.
34. Ibid., p. 47.
35. Milani, 1994, pp. 200, 201, 158, 159, 156; Amuzegar, 1993, pp. 109, 117, 107, on banking.
36. Milani, 1994, pp. 202, 203; Omid, 1994, p. 182.
37. Abrahamian, 1993, pp. 58, 16, 33–4; Sarabi, 1994, p. 104.
38. See Hunter, 1992, pp. 19, 20, on this theory of guardianship being an innovation in Shiite doctrine.
39. Abrahamian, 1993, p. 25.
40. See ibid., pp. 24–5, on Khomeini's argument.
41. Hunter, 1992, p. 21.
42. See Abrahamian, 1993, pp. 37–8.
43. Ibid., p. 47.
44. Ibid., p. 31.
45. Ibid., p. 36. The new Constitution declared that Muslims formed 'a single nation', that the new Republic would seek the merging of all Muslim peoples, and 'strive for political, economic, and cultural unity of the Islamic world' (quoted by Calabrese, 1994, p. 27).
46. Ramazani, 1986, pp. 21–2.
47. For this paragraph see Abrahamian, 1993, pp. 51–3.
48. Hunter, 1992, p. 92.
49. Savory, 1988, p. 358; Omid, 1994, p. 157.
50. Hunter, 1992, p. 98. The most famous example of this had been the last Shah's extravagant celebration of the 2500th anniversary of the ancient Persian Empire, but his father had been playing the nationalist card in the 1920s–30s by such means as selecting the name of the country's pre-Islamic language, Pahlavi, to be his dynastic family name, changing the country's own name from Persia to Iran as part of emphasising its Aryan heritage and seeking to glorify Iran's pre-Islamic past (Milani, 1994, p. 33; Kamrava, 1992, pp. 53–4).
51. Hunter, 1992, p. 92.
52. Abrahamian, 1993, p. 15.
53. Ramazani, 1986, p. 25.
54. Ibid.; Ramazani, 1989, p. 212.
55. Hunter, 1992, p. 13.
56. Ibid., p. 95.
57. Ramazani, 1989, p. 213.
58. Hunter, 1992, p. 12; Ramazani, 1986, p. 20.
59. Bakhash, 1986, p. 242.
60. Abrahamian, 1993, pp. 39–42, 58.
61. Ibid., p. 56. See also Ehteshami, 1995, pp. 92, 95.
62. Bakhash, 1986, p. 242; Abrahamian, 1993, p. 42.
63. Calabrese, 1994, p. 30.
64. Ibid.
65. Amuzegar, 1993, p. 128.

66. Ibid., p. 319; Ehteshami, 1995, p. 101.
67. Ehteshami, 1995, pp. 80, 81.
68. Bakhash, 1986, p. 180; Amuzegar, 1993, p. 197.
69. Amuzegar, 1993, pp. 197, 199.
70. Ibid., pp. 46, 79.
71. Bakhash, 1986, p. 184.
72. Amuzegar, 1993, pp. 126–8.
73. Ibid., pp. 142–3; Bakhash, 1986, p. 193.
74. Bakhash, 1986, pp. 202, 210.
75. Ehteshami, 1995, pp. 98, 93.
76. Amuzegar, 1993, p. 305.
77. Ehteshami, 1995, p. 83.
78. Entessar, 1992, p. 222.
79. Amuzegar, 1993, pp. 161, 99.
80. Ibid., p. 276.
81. Ehteshami, 1995, p. 93.
82. In fact the Moussavi government had already taken steps in this direction in late 1988 and early 1989, with the beginning of what was intended to be a comprehensive privatisation programme and the approval of some foreign borrowing (ibid., pp. 97, 98).
83. Amuzegar, 1993, pp. 47–8; Bakhash, 1993, p. 72.
84. Sarabi, 1994, p. 91.
85. Calabrese, 1994, p. 31.
86. Abrahamian, 1993, p. 138.
87. Ehteshami, 1991, pp. 151, 154; Milani, 1994, p. 231.
88. Ehteshami, 1991, p. 151.
89. Abrahamian, 1993, p. 142.
90. Amuzegar, 1993, p. 48.
91. Ibid., p. 47.
92. Bakhash, 1986, p. 185.
93. Amuzegar, 1993, p. 284.
94. Ibid., pp. 128–9.
95. Ibid., pp. 129–33, 135; Hunter, 1992, p. 81; Ehteshami, 1995, p. 107.
96. Amuzegar, 1993, pp. 89–90.
97. Ibid., p. 80.
98. Ehteshami, 1995, p. 109; Amuzegar, 1993, p. 145; Hunter, 1992, p. 83.
99. Ehteshami, 1995, pp. 109, 110; Amuzegar, 1993, pp. 164–5.
100. Hunter, 1992, p. 83.
101. Ehteshami, 1995, pp. 107, 105; Amuzegar, 1993, p. 122.
102. Amuzegar, 1993, pp. 122, 120; Ehteshami, 1995, p. 106.
103. Sarabi, 1994, p. 93.
104. Bakhash, 1993, pp. 74–5; Hunter, 1992, p. 27; Sarabi, 1994, p. 92. See Ehteshami, 1995, pp. 31–3 on Montazeri being pushed out of this position in March 1989.
105. Bakhash, 1993, pp. 71–2; Sarabi, 1994, pp. 92–3.
106. Sarabi, 1994, p. 93.
107. Ibid., pp. 99, 100; Abrahamian, 1993, p. 137.
108. Sarabi, 1994, pp 96–7.
109. Abrahamian, 1993, p. 137.

110. Sarabi, 1994, pp. 89, 94, 99–100.
111. Ibid., pp. 94, 100.
112. Ibid., p. 105.
113. *Middle East*, Jan. 1994, p. 10.
114. Sarabi, 1994, p. 103, 102.
115. Amuzegar, 1993, pp. 135, 76, 77, 136.
116. Ibid., p. 161; Ehteshami, 1995, p. 117.
117. Amuzegar, 1993, pp. 236, 240.
118. Ibid., pp. 159, 168; Milani, 1994, p. 168; Ehteshami, 1995, pp. 111, 117.
119. Amuzegar, 1993, p. 167; Ehteshami, 1995, p. 108.
120. Amuzegar, 1993, pp. 137, 167.
121. Ehteshami, 1995, p. 68.
122. *Middle East*, July 1993, pp. 13, 15.
123. Ibid., p. 15.
124. Ehteshami, 1995, p. 68.
125. *Middle East*, July 1993, p. 14.
126. Amuzegar, 1993, p. 137; Bakhash, 1993, p. 80.
127. *Middle East*, Jan. 1994, p. 10.
128. Sarabi, 1994, p. 106; Ehteshami, 1995, p. 62.
129. *Middle East*, Jan. 1994, p. 10; Ehteshami, 1995, pp. 63–4.
130. *Economist*, 16 July 1994, p. 37.
131. Ibid.; *Economist*, 25 June 1994, p. 43.
132. *Economist*, 16 July 1994, p. 37; 25 June 1994, pp. 42–3.
133. *Economist*, 25 June 1994, p. 44.

APPENDIX II

1. Marr, 1985, p. 208.
2. Farouk-Sluglett and Sluglett, 1986, p. 102; Marr, 1985, p. 208.
3. al-Jaza'iri, 1994, p. 32.
4. Roberts, 1987, p. 63.
5. Rabinovich, 1972, p. 81; Roberts, 1987, p. 66. On the relationship between it and the 1947 Party Constitution see ibid.
6. Ibid.
7. Hopwood, 1988, pp. 171, 88; Roberts, 1987, p. 64.
8. Roberts, 1987, p. 67.
9. Ibid., pp. 68–9.
10. Ibid., p. 69.
11. Ibid., pp. 69–70; Rabinovich, 1972, p. 90.
12. Rabinovich, 1972, p. 90.
13. Roberts, 1987, p. 70.
14. van Dam, 1979, pp. 114–15.
15. Roberts, 1987, p. 70.
16. Rabinovich, 1972, pp. 87–8; Roberts, 1987, pp. 70–1.
17. Roberts, 1987, p. 71; Rabinovich, 1972, p. 89.
18. Hinnebusch, 1990, pp. 178, 179.
19. Helms, 1984, p.87.

Bibliography

Abbas, A. 1986. 'The Iraqi Armed Forces, Past and Present', in CARDRI, *Saddam's Iraq: Revolution or Reaction?* London.

Abrahamian, E. 1993. *Khomeinism.* London.

Akhavi, S. 1987. Spring. 'Elite Factionalism in the Islamic Republic of Iran', *The Middle East Journal*, 41, 2.

al-Jabbar, F. 'A. 1994. 'Why the Intifada Failed', in F. Hazelton (ed. for CARDRI), *Iraq since the Gulf War: Prospects for Democracy.* London and New Jersey.

al-Jaza'iri, Z. 1994. 'Ba'thist Ideology and Practice', in F. Hazelton (ed. for CARDRI), *Iraq since the Gulf War: Prospects for Democracy.* London and New Jersey.

al-Khafaji, I. 1994. 'State Terror and the Degradation of Politics', in F. Hazelton (ed. for CARDRI), *Iraq since the Gulf War: Prospects for Democracy.* London and New Jersey.

al-Khalil, S. 1989. *Republic of Fear: Saddam's Iraq.* London.

al-Sharqi, A. 1982. 'The Emancipation of Iraqi Women', in T. Niblock (ed.), *Iraq: The Contemporary State.* London.

Alnasrawi, A. 1994. 'Economic Devastation, Underdevelopment and Outlook', in F. Hazelton (ed. for CARDRI), *Iraq since the Gulf War: Prospects for Democracy.* London and New Jersey.

Amuzegar, J. 1993. *Iran's Economy under the Islamic Republic.* London and New York.

Anderson, L. 1987. February. 'Libya's Qaddafi: Still in Command?', *Current History*, 86, 517.

Anderson, L. 1995. 'Qadhafi's Legacy: An Evaluation of a Political Experiment', in D. Vandewalle (ed.), *Qadhafi's Libya, 1969–1994.* Basingstoke and London.

Azicri, M. 1988. *Cuba: Politics, Economics and Society.* London and New York.

Bachman, D. M. 1985. *Chen Yun and the Chinese Political System.* Berkeley.

Bachman, D. 1994. January. 'China in 1993: Dissolution, Frenzy, and/or Breakthrough?', *Asian Survey*, XXXIV, 1.

Bachman, D. 1995. January. 'China in 1994: Marking Time, Making Money', *Asian Survey*, XXXV, 1.

Bahout, J. 1994. 'The Syrian Business Community, its Politics and Prospects', in E. Kienle (ed.), *Contemporary Syria: Liberalization between Cold War and Cold Peace.* London.

Bakhash, S. 1986. *The Reign of the Ayatollahs: Iran and the Islamic Revolution.* London.

Bakhash, S. 1993. 'Iranian Politics Since the Gulf War', in R. B. Satloff (ed.), *The Politics of Change in the Middle East.* Boulder.

Balfour, S. 1990. *Profiles in Power: Castro.* London and New York.

Balfour, S. 1995. *Profiles in Power: Castro*, 2nd edn. London and New York.

Baloyra, E. A. 1993. 'Socialist Transitions and Prospects for Change in Cuba', in E. A. Baloyra and J. A. Morris (eds), *Conflict and Change in Cuba*. Albuquerque.

Baram, A. 1991. *Culture, History and Ideology in the Formation of Ba'thist Iraq, 1968–89*. New York.

Baram, A. 1993. 'The Future of Ba'thist Iraq: Power Structure, Challenges, and Prospects', in R. B. Satloff (ed.), *The Politics of Change in the Middle East*. Boulder.

Baram, A. 1994. 'The Iraqi Invasion of Kuwait: Decision- making in Baghdad', in A. Baram and B. Rubin (eds), *Iraq's Road to War*. Basingstoke.

Batutu, H. 1981. Summer. 'Some Observations on the Social Roots of Syria's Ruling, Military Group and the Causes for Its Dominance', *Middle East Journal*, 35, 3.

Bearman, J. 1986. *Qadhafi's Libya*. London.

Benewick, R. 1995. 'The Tiananmen Crackdown and Its Legacy', in R. Benewick and P. Wingrove, (eds), *China in the 1990s*. Basingstoke.

Bengelsdorf, C. 1994. *The Problem of Democracy in Cuba: Between Vision and Reality*. New York and Oxford.

Beresford, M. 1988. *Vietnam: Politics, Economics and Society*. London and New York.

Betancourt, E. 1989. 'Cuban Leadership After Castro', in I. L. Horowitz (ed.), *Cuban Communism*, 7th edn. New Brunswick, NJ.

Bickford, T. J. 1994. May. 'The Chinese Military and Its Business Operations: The PLA as Entrepreneur', *Asian Survey*, 34, 5.

Blecher, M. 1995. 'Collectivism, Contractualism and Crisis in the Chinese Countryside', in R. Benewick and P. Wingrove (eds), *China in the 1990s*. Basingstoke.

Blundy, D., and Lycett, A. 1988. *Qaddafi and the Libyan Revolution*. London.

Boudarel, G. 1980. 'Influences and Idiosyncrasies in the Line and Practice of the Vietnam Communist Party', in W. S. Turley (ed.), *Vietnamese Communism in Comparative Perspective*. Boulder.

Breslin, S. 1995. 'Centre and Province in China', in R. Benewick and P. Wingrove (eds), *China in the 1990s*. Basingstoke.

Brocheux, P. 1980. 'Vietnamese Communism and the Peasants: Analogy and Originality in Vietnamese Experience', in W. S. Turley (ed.), *Vietnamese Communism in Comparative Perspective*. Boulder.

Brugger, B. 1989. 'Ideology, Legitimacy and Marxist Theory in Contemporary China', in J. Y. S. Cheng (ed.), *China: Modernization in the 1980s*. Hong Kong and Sydney.

Brugger, B., and Reglar, S. 1994. *Politics, Economy and Society in Contemporary China*. Basingstoke.

Bruun, O. 1995. 'Political Hierarchy and Private Entrepreneurship in a Chinese Neighborhood', in A. G. Walder (ed.), *The Waning of the Communist State: Economic Origins of Political Decline in China and Hungary*. Berkeley, Los Angeles and London.

Calabrese, J. 1994. *Revolutionary Horizons: Regional Foreign Policy in Post-Khomeini Iran*. New York.

Cardoso, E., and Helwege, A. 1992. *Cuba after Communism*. Cambridge, Mass. and London.

Castro, F. 1971. 'To Create Wealth with Social Conscience', in B. Silverman (ed.), *Man and Socialism in Cuba: The Great Debate*. New York.

Chanda, N. 1984. January. 'Vietnam in 1983: Keeping Ideology Alive', *Asian Survey*, XXIV, 1.

Chung, C-W. 1986. 'The Evolution of Political Institutions in North Korea', in R. A. Scalapino *et al.* (eds), *Asian Political Institutionalization*. Berkeley.

Cima, R. J. 1989. January. 'Vietnam in 1988: The Brink of Renewal', *Asian Survey*, XXIX, 1.

Cima, R. J. 1990. January. 'Vietnam in 1989: Initiating the Post-Cambodia Period', *Asian Survey*, XXX, 1.

Clough, R. N. 1987. *Embattled Korea: The Rivalry for International Support*. Boulder and London.

Collier, D., (ed.). 1979. *The New Authoritarianism in Latin America*. Princeton.

Cooley, J. K. 1983. *Libyan Sandstorm*. London.

Cotton, J. 1985. June. 'Asymmetry on the Korean Peninsula: Pyongyang and the North-South Dialogue of 1984', *The Journal of Communist Studies*, 1, 2.

Cotton, J. 1987. December. 'Ideology and the Legitimation Crisis in North Korea', *Journal of Communist Studies*, 3, 4.

Crusoe, J. 1986. 'Economic Outlook: Guns and Butter, Phase Two?', in F. W. Axelgard (ed.), *Iraq in Transition: A Political, Economic, and Strategic Perspective*. Boulder.

Cumings, B. 1993. 'The Corporate State in North Korea', in H. Koo (ed.), *State and Society in Contemporary Korea*. Ithaca and London.

Davis, J. 1987. *Libyan Politics: Tribe and Revolution*. London.

Dawisha, A. I. 1978. Summer. 'Syria under Asad, 1970–78: The Centres of Power', *Government and Opposition*, 13, 3.

Dawisha, A. 1986. 'The Politics of War: Presidential Centrality, Party Power, Political Opposition', in F. W. Axelgard (ed.), *Iraq in Transition: A Political, Economic, and Strategic Perspective*. Boulder.

de Vylder, S. 1995. 'State and Market in Vietnam: Some Issues for an Economy in Transition', in I. Nørlund *et al.*, *Vietnam in a Changing World*. Richmond, England.

Dearlove, J. 1995. 'Village Politics', in R. Benewick and P. Wingrove (eds), *China in the 1990s*. Basingstoke.

Deeb, M-J. 1990. April. 'New Thinking in Libya', *Current History*, 89, 546.

Devlin, J. F. 1983. *Syria: Modern State in an Ancient Land*. Boulder.

Diamond, L., *et al.* (eds). 1989. *Democracy in Developing Countries*. Boulder.

Djaziri, M. 1995. 'Creating a New State: Libya's Political Institutions' in D. Vandewalle (ed.), *Qadhafi's Libya: 1969–1994*. Basingstoke and London.

Dominguez, J. I. 1982. 'Revolutionary Politics: The New Demands for Orderliness', in J. I. Dominguez (ed.), *Cuba: Internal and International Affairs*. Beverly Hills, London and New Delhi.

Dominguez, J. I. 1986. Fall. 'Cuba in the 1980s', *Foreign Affairs*, 65, 1.

Dominguez, J. I. 1989. December. 'The Cuban Armed Forces, the Party and Society in Wartime and during Rectification 1986–88', *The Journal of Communist Studies*, 5, 4.

Duiker, W. J. 1980. 'Vietnamese Revolutionary Doctrine in Comparative Perspective', in W. S. Turley (ed.), *Vietnamese Communism in Comparative Perspective*. Boulder.

Duiker, W. J. 1985. January. 'Vietnam in 1984: Between Ideology and Prag-matism', *Asian Survey*, XXV, 1.
Duiker, W. J. 1986. January. 'Vietnam in 1985: Searching for Solutions', *Asian Survey*, XXVI, 1.
Duiker, W. J. 1989. *Vietnam Since the Fall of Saigon*, updated ed. Athens, Ohio.
Duncan, W. R. 1993. 'Cuba–U.S. Relations and Political Contradictions in Cuba', in E. A. Baloyra and J. A. Morris (eds), *Conflict and Change in Cuba*. Albuquerque.
Eckstein, S. E. 1994. *Back from the Future: Cuba under Castro*. Princeton.
Ehteshami, A. 1991. 'After Khomeini: the Structure of Power in the Iranian Second Republic', *Political Studies*, XXXIX.
Ehteshami, A. 1995. *After Khomeini: The Iranian Second Republic*. London.
El Fathaly, O. I., and Palmer, M. 1995. 'Institutional Development in Qad-hafi's Libya', in D. Vandewalle (ed.), *Qadhafi's Libya, 1969–1994*. Basingstoke and London.
Elliott, D. W. P. 1993. 'Dilemmas of Reform in Vietnam', in W. S. Turley and M. Selden (eds), *Reinventing Vietnamese Socialism: Doi Moi in Comparative Perspective*. Boulder, San Francisco and Oxford.
Entessar, N. 1992. 'The Challenge of Political Reconstruction in Iran', in C. Bina and H. Zangeneh (eds), *Modern Capitalism and Islamic Ideology in Iran*. New York.
Fahey, S. 1994. 'Vietnam: "Pivotal Year"?', *Southeast Asian Affairs 1994*. Singapore.
Farouk-Sluglett, M., and Sluglett, P. 1986. 'Iraqi Ba'thism: Nationalism, Socialism and National Socialism', in CARDRI, *Saddam's Iraq: Revolution or Reaction?* London.
Farouk-Sluglett, M., and Sluglett, P. 1987. *Iraq Since 1958: From Revolution to Dictatorship*. London.
Firro, K. 1986. 'The Syrian Economy under the Assad Regime', in M. Maoz and A. Yaniv (eds), *Syria Under Assad: Domestic Constraints and Regional Risks*. London.
Fitzgerald, F. T. 1989. 'The Reform of the Cuban Economy, 1976–86: Orga-nisation, Incentives and Patterns of Behaviour', *Journal of Latin American Studies*, 21.
Foster-Carter, A. 1987. December. 'North Korea: The End of the Beginning', *The Journal of Communist Studies*, 3, 4.
Gold, T. B. 1989. Summer/Autumn. 'Urban Private Business in China', *Studies in Comparative Communism*, XXII, 2/3.
Goldman, M. 1994. *Sowing the Seeds of Democracy in China: Political Reform in the Deng Xiaoping Era*. Cambridge, Mass., and London.
Gonzalez, E. 1974. *Cuba under Castro: The Limits of Charisma*. Boston.
Goodman, A. E. 1995. January. 'Vietnam in 1994: With Peace at Hand', *Asian Survey*, XXXV, 1.
Goodman, A. E. 1996. Spring. 'Vietnam in 1995: It Was a Very Good Year', *Washington Quarterly*, 19, 2.
Gouré, L. 1989. '"War of all the People": Cuba's Military Doctrines', in I. L. Horowitz (ed.), *Cuban Communism*, 7th edn. New Brunswick, NJ.
Guevara, E. C. 1971. 'Man and Socialism in Cuba', in B. Silverman (ed.), *Man and Socialism in Cuba: The Great Debate*. New York.

Halpern, N. P. 1992. 'Information Flows and Policy Coordination in the Chinese Bureaucracy', in K. G. Lieberthal and D. M. Lampton (eds), *Bureaucracy, Politics, and Decision Making in Post-Mao China*. Berkeley, Los Angeles and Oxford.

Hamrin, C. L. 1992. 'The Party Leadership System', in K. G. Lieberthal and D. M. Lampton (eds), *Bureaucracy, Politics, and Decision Making in Post-Mao China*. Berkeley, Los Angeles and Oxford.

Harris, L. C. 1986. *Libya: Qadhafi's Revolution and the Modern State*. Boulder.

Harris, R. L. 1992. 'Bureaucracy Versus Democracy in Contemporary Cuba: An Assessment of Thirty Years of Organizational Development', in S. Halebsky and J. M. Kirk (eds), *Cuba in Transition: Crisis and Transformation*. Boulder, San Francisco and Oxford.

Hashim, A. 1995. *The Crisis of the Iranian State: Domestic, Foreign and Security Policies in Post-Khomeini Iran*. London.

Hazelton, F. (ed. for CARDRI). 1994. *Iraq since the Gulf War: Prospects for Democracy*. London and New Jersey.

Hebbel, H. C. 1993. 'The Vietnamese Military's Changing Role', *Southeast Asian Affairs 1993*. Singapore.

Heine, P. 1993. 'Political Parties, Institutions and Administrative Structures', in D. Hopwood *et al.* (eds), *Iraq: Power and Society*. Reading.

Heller, M. A. 1994. 'Iraq's Army: Military Weakness, Political Utility', in A. Baram and B. Rubin (eds), *Iraq's Road to War*. Basingstoke.

Helms, C. M. 1984. *Iraq: Eastern Flank of the Arab World*. Washington, DC.

Heng Hiang Khng, R. 1993. 'Vietnam 1992: Economic Growth and Political Caution', *Southeast Asian Affairs 1993*. Singapore.

Heydemann, S. 1992. 'The Political Logic of Economic Rationality: Selective Stabilization in Syria', in H. Barkey (ed.), *The Politics of Economic Reform in the Middle East*. New York.

Hinnebusch, R. A. 1986. 'Syria under the Ba'th: Social Ideology, Policy, and Practice', in L. O. Michalak and J. W. Salacuse (eds), *Social Legislation in the Contemporary Middle East*. Berkeley.

Hinnebusch, R. A. 1990. *Authoritarian Power and State Formation in Ba'thist Syria: Army, Party, and Peasant*. Boulder, San Francisco and Oxford.

Hinnebusch, R. A. 1993. Spring. 'State and Civil Society in Syria', *Middle East Journal*, 47, 2.

Hinnebusch, R. A. 1994. 'Liberalization in Syria: the Struggle of Economic and Political Rationality', in E. Kienle (ed.), *Contemporary Syria: Liberalization between Cold War and Cold Peace*. London.

Hiro, D. 1989. *The Longest War: The Iran–Iraq Military Conflict*. London.

Hoang Kim Giao and Hoang Vu Cuong. 1995. 'Vietnam's Private Economy in the Process of Renovation', in I. Nørlund *et al.*, *Vietnam in a Changing World*. Richmond, England.

Hooglund, E. 1989. 'Government and Politics', in H. C. Metz (ed.), *Iraq: A Country Study*. Washington, DC.

Hopwood, D. 1988. *Syria 1945–1986: Politics and Society*. London.

Horowitz, I. L. 1975. August. 'Military Origins of the Cuban Revolution', *Armed Forces and Soiety*, 1, 4.

Hsü, I. C. Y. 1990. *China Without Mao: The Search for a New Order.* New York and Oxford.

Hudson, M. C. 1991. Summer. 'After the Gulf War: Prospects for Democratization in the Arab World', *Middle East Journal*, 45, 3.

Hunter, S. T. 1992. *Iran after Khomeini.* New York.

Huntington, S. P. 1993. *The Third Wave: Democratization in the Late Twentieth Century.* Norman and London.

Huynh, F. C. H. 1992. 'Vietnam 1991: Still in Transition', *Southeast Asian Affairs 1992.* Singapore.

Hwang, E-G. 1993. *The Korean Economies: A Comparison of North and South.* Oxford.

Jeffries, I. 1993. *Socialist Economies and the Transition to the Market: A Guide.* London and New York.

Jenkins, G. 1992. 'Beyond Basic Needs: Cuba's Search for Stable Development in the 1990s', in S. Halebsky and J. M. Kirk (eds), *Cuba in Transition: Crisis and Transformation.* Boulder, San Francisco and Oxford.

Jeong, K-Y. 1992. Spring. 'The North Korean Economy: Structure, Performance and International Comparison', *Korea and World Affairs*, 16, 1.

Joiner, C. A. 1990. November. 'The Vietnam Communist Party Strives to Maintain the "Only Force"', *Asian Survey*, XXX, 11.

Joseph, W. A. 1985. September. 'The Dilemmas of Political Reform in China', *Current History*, 84, 503.

Joseph, W. A. 1986. September. 'China's Modernization of Mao', *Current History*, 85, 512.

Kamrava, M. 1992. *The Political History of Modern Iran: From Tribalism to Theocracy.* Westport.

Karsh, E., and Rautsi, I. 1991. *Saddam Hussein: A Political Biography.* London.

Khadduri, M. 1978. *Socialist Iraq: A Study in Iraqi Politics Since 1968.* Washington, DC.

Kienle, E. 1994a. 'Introduction', in E. Kienle (ed.), *Contemporary Syria: Liberalization between Cold War and Cold Peace.* London.

Kienle, E. 1994b. 'The Return of Politics? Scenario for Syria's Second *Infitah*', in E. Kienle (ed.), *Contemporary Syria: Liberalization between Cold War and Cold Peace.* London.

Kihl, Y. W. 1991. Fall. 'North Korea's Foreign Relations: Diplomacy of Promotive Adaptation', *Journal of Northeast Asian Studies*, X, 3.

Kim, S. 1993. September. 'Recent Economic Policies of North Korea: Analysis and Recommendations', *Asian Survey*, XXXIII, 9.

Kim, S. S. 1995. January. 'North Korea in 1994: Brinkmanship, Breakdown, and Breakthrough', *Asian Survey*, XXXV, 1.

Kim, Y. C. 1981. January. 'North Korea in 1980: The Son Also Rises', *Asian Survey*, XXI, 1.

Kirk, J. M. 1980. 'From "Inadaptado Sublime" to "Líder Revolucionario": Some Further Thoughts on the Presentation of José Martí', *Latin American Research Review*, 15, 3.

Koh, B. C. 1989. January. 'North Korea in 1988: The Fortieth Anniversary', *Asian Survey*, XXIX, 1.

Komaki, T. 1988. 'Current Status and Prospects of the North Korean Economy', in M. Okongi (ed.), *North Korea at the Crossroads*. Tokyo.

Lam, W. W-L. 1995. *China after Deng Xiaoping: The Power Struggle in Beijing since Tiananmen*. Singapore and New York.

Lawson, F. H. 1994. 'Domestic Pressures and the Peace Process: Fillip or Hindrance?', in E. Kienle (ed.), *Contemporary Syria: Liberalization between Cold War and Cold Peace*. London.

Le Cao Doan. 1995. 'Agricultural Reforms in Vietnam in the 1980s', in I. Nørlund et al., *Vietnam in a Changing World*. Richmond, England.

Leca, J. 1990. 'Social Structure and Political Stability: Comparative Evidence from the Algerian, Syrian and Iraqi Cases', in G. Luciani (ed.), *The Arab State*. London.

Leca, J. 1994. 'Democratization in the Arab World: uncertainty, vulnerability and legitimacy. A tentative conceptualization and some hypotheses', in G. Salamé (ed.), *Democracy Without Democrats?: The Renewal of Politics in the Muslim World*. London and New York.

Lee, C. 1990. Fall. 'An Analysis of North Korea's Economic Development with Special Reference to Agriculture', *Journal of Northeast Asian Studies*, IX, 3.

Lee, D-B. 1994. Fall. 'Kim Jong-Il's North Korea: Its Limitations and Prospects', *Korea and World Affairs*, 18, 3.

Lee, S-H. 1989. *Party-Military Relations in North Korea: A Comparative Analysis*. Seoul.

Legum, C. (ed.). 1984–5. *Africa Contemporary Record*, xvii. New York and London.

Legum, C. (ed.). 1985–6. *Africa Contemporary Record*, xviii. New York and London.

Legum, C. (ed.). 1986–7. *Africa Contemporary Record*, xix. New York and London.

Legum, C. (ed.). 1987–8. *Africa Contemporary Record*, xx. New York and London.

Legum, C. (ed.). 1988–9. *Africa Contemporary Record*, xxi. New York and London.

Levine, S. I. 1994. 'Sino-American Relations: Testing the Limits of Discord', in S. S. Kim (ed.), *China and the World: Chinese Foreign Relations in the Post-Cold War Era*. Boulder, San Francisco and Oxford.

Linz, J., and Stepan, A. 1978. *The Breakdown of Democratic Regimes*. Baltimore.

Liss, S. B. 1984. *Marxist Thought in Latin America*. Berkeley.

Liss, S. B. 1994. *Fidel!: Castro's Political and Social Thought*. Boulder, San Francisco and Oxford.

Lobmeyer, H. G. 1994. 'The Syrian Opposition at the End of the Asad Era', in E. Kienle (ed.), *Contemporary Syria: Liberalization between Cold War and Cold Peace*. London.

Long, S. 1995. 'Leadership Politics since 1989', in R. Benewick and P. Wingrove (eds), *China in the 1990s*. Basingstoke.

Lutjens, S. L. 1992. 'Democracy and Socialist Cuba',in S. Halebsky and J. M. Kirk (eds), *Cuba in Transition: Crisis and Transformation*. Boulder, San Francisco and Oxford.

Ma'oz, M. 1988. *Asad The Sphinx of Damascus: A Political Biography*. New York.

Macdonald, D. S. 1988. *The Koreans: Contemporary Politics and Society*. Boulder and London.

Marr, P. 1985. *The Modern History of Iraq*. Boulder.

Mattes, H. 1995. 'The Rise and Fall of the Revolutionary Committees', in D. Vandewalle (ed.), *Qadhafi's Libya, 1969–1994*. Basingstoke and London.

Mayer, A. E. 1995. 'In Search of Sacred Law: The Meandering Course of Qadhafi's Legal Policy', in D. Vandewalle (ed.), *Qadhafi's Libya, 1969–1994*. Basingstoke and London.

McCarthy, T. 1990. 4 August. *The Independent*.

McCarthy, T. 1994. 20 November. *Independent on Sunday*.

McCarty, A. 1993. 'Industrial Renovation in Vietnam, 1986–91', in M. Than and J. L. H. Tan (eds), *Vietnam's Dilemmas and Options: The Challenge of Economic Transition in the 1990s*. Singapore.

Merrill, J. 1993. January. 'North Korea in 1992: Steering Away from the Shoals', *Asian Survey*, XXXIII, 1.

Merrill, J. 1994. January. 'North Korea in 1993: In the Eye of the Storm', *Asian Survey*, XXXIV, 1.

Mesa-Lago, C. 1989. December. 'Cuba's Economic Counter-Reform *Rectificacion*: Causes, Policies and Effects', *The Journal of Communist Studies*, 5, 4.

Milani, M. M. 1994. *The Making of Iran's Islamic Revolution*, 2nd edn. Boulder.

Niblock, T. 1993. 'International and Domestic Factors in the Economic Liberalization Process in Arab Countries', in T. Niblock and E. Murphy (eds), *Economic and Political Liberalization in the Middle East*. London.

North, T. 1992. Spring. 'The Kim Jong-Il Succession Problem in the Context of the North Korean Political Structure', *Korea and World Affairs*, 16, 1.

O'Donnell, G., and Schmitter, P. C. 1986. *Transitions from Authoritarian Rule: Tentative Conclusions about Uncertain Democracies*. Baltimore and London.

Oh, K. D. 1990. January. 'North Korea in 1989: Touched by Winds of Change?', *Asian Survey*, XXX, 1.

Oi, J. C. 1989. Summer/Autumn. 'Market Reforms and Corruption in Rural China', *Studies in Comparative Communism*, XXII, 2/3.

Okonogi, M. 1988. 'The Ideology and Political Leadership of Kim Jong Il', in M. Okonogi (ed.), *North Korea at the Crossroads*. Tokyo.

Omid, H. 1994. *Islam and the Post-Revolutionary State in Iran*. Basingstoke.

Paltiel, J. T. 1995. September. 'PLA Allegiance on Parade: Civil-Military Relations in Transition', *The China Quarterly*, 143.

Park, H-S. 1979. 'The Ideology of North Korean Communism: A Critical Assessment', in J. K. Park and J. G. Kim (eds), *The Politics of North Korea*. Seoul.

Park, H. S. 1982. Winter. 'North Korea's *Juche*: Its Premises, Promises, and Problems', *Korea and World Affairs*, 6, 4.

Park, J. K. 1979. 'Power Structure in North Korea', in J. K. Park and J. G. Kim (eds), *The Politics of North Korea*. Seoul.

Pérez-López, J. F. 1991. 'Bringing the Cuban Economy into Focus: Conceptual and Empirical Challenges', *Latin American Research Review*, 26, 3.

Pérez-López, J. F. 1992. 'The Cuban Economy: Rectification in a Changing World', *Cambridge Journal of Economics*, 16.

Pérez-Stable, M. 1989. 'Castro Takes the Economy in Hand', in P. Brenner *et al.* (eds), *The Cuban Reader: The Making of a Revolutionary Society*. New York.

Pérez-Stable, M. 1993. '"We Are the Only Ones and There is No Alternative"': Vanguard Party Politics in Cuba, 1975–1991', in E. A. Baloyra and J. A. Morris (eds), *Conflict and Change in Cuba*. Albuquerque.

Perthes, V. 1994. 'Stages of Economic and Political Liberalization', in E. Kienle (ed.), *Contemporary Syria: Liberalization between Cold War and Cold Peace*. London.

Perthes, V. 1995. *The Political Economy of Syria under Asad*. London and New York.

Petras, J. F., and Morley, M. H. 1992. 'Cuban Socialism: Rectification and the New Model of Accumulation', in S. Halebsky and J. M. Kirk (eds), *Cuba in Transition: Crisis and Transformation*. Boulder, San Francisco and Oxford.

Pike, D. 1986. *PAVN: People's Army of Vietnam*. Novato, Cal.

Pike, D. 1991. January. 'Vietnam in 1990: The Last Picture Show', *Asian Survey*, XXXI, 1.

Pike, D. 1992. January. 'Vietnam in 1991: The Turning Point', *Asian Survey*, XXXII, 1.

Pike, D. 1994. January. 'Vietnam in 1993: Uncertainty Closes In', *Asian Survey*, XXXIV, 1.

Pipes, D. 1990. *Greater Syria:The History of an Ambition*. Oxford.

Pollack, J. D. 1992. 'Structure and Process in the Chinese Military System', in K. G. Lieberthal and D. M. Lampton (eds), *Bureaucracy, Politics, and Decision Making in Post-Mao China*. Berkeley, Los Angeles and Oxford.

Pölling, S. 1994. 'Which Future for the Private Sector?', in E. Kienle (ed.), *Contemporary Syria: Liberalization between Cold War and Cold Peace*. London.

Porter, G. 1993. *Vietnam: The Politics of Bureaucratic Socialism*. Ithaca and London.

Prime, P. B. 1993. September. 'The Economy in Overdrive: Will It Crash?', *Current History* 92, 575.

Qaddafi, M. A. 1987. *The Green Book*, 10th ed. Benghazi.

Rabinovich, I. 1972. *Syria Under the Ba'th 1963–66: The Army-Party Symbiosis*. Jerusalem and New York.

Rabinovich, I. 1993. 'Stability and Change in Syria', in R. B. Satloff (ed.), *The Politics of Change in the Middle East*. Boulder, San Francisco and Oxford.

Ramazani, R. K. 1986. *Revolutionary Iran: Challenge and Response in the Middle East*. Baltimore and London.

Ramazani, R. K. 1989. Spring. 'Iran's Foreign Policy: Contending Orientations', *The Middle East Journal*, 43, 2.

Rassam, A. 1982. 'Revolution within the Revolution? Women and the State in Iraq', in T. Niblock (ed.), *Iraq: The Contemporary State*. London.

Reinhardt, J. 1993. 'Industrial Restructuring and Industrial Policy in Vietnam', in M. Than and J. L. H. Tan (eds), *Vietnam's Dilemmas and Options: The Challenge of Economic Transition in the 1990s*. Singapore.

Rhee, K. S. 1987. August. 'North Korea's Pragmatism: A Turning Point?', *Asian Survey*, XXVII, 8.

Rhee, S-W. 1991. January. 'North Korea in 1990: Lonesome Struggle to Keep Chuch'e', *Asian Survey*, XXXI, 1.

Rhee, S-W. 1992. January. 'North Korea in 1991: Struggle to Save Chuch'e Amid Signs of Change', *Asian Survey*, XXXII, 1.

Roberts, D. 1987. *The Ba'th and the Creation of Modern Syria*. London and Sydney.

Rugman, J. 1994. 1 November. *The Guardian*.

Sadowski, Y. M. 1988. 'Ba'thist Ethics and the Spirit of State Capitalism: Patronage and the Party in Contemporary Syria', in P. J. Chelkowski and R. J. Pranger (eds), *Ideology and Power in the Middle East*. Durham and London.

Saich, T. 1992. December. 'The Fourteenth Party Congress: A Programme for Authoritarian Rule', *The China Quarterly*, 132.

Saich, T. 1995. 'China's Political Structure', in R. Benewick and P. Wingrove (eds), *China in the 1990s*. Basingstoke.

Salamé, G. 1994. 'Introduction: Where Are the Democrats?', in G. Salamé (ed.), *Democracy Without Democrats?: The Renewal of Politics in the Muslim World*. London and New York.

Sarabi, F. 1994. Winter. 'The Post-Khomeini Era in Iran: The Elections of the Fourth Islamic Majlis', *Middle East Journal*, 48, 1.

SarDesai, D. R. 1992. *Vietnam: The Struggle for National Identity*, 2nd ed. Boulder, San Francisco and Oxford.

Savory, R. 1988. 'Ex Oriente Nebula: An Inquiry into the Nature of Khomeini's Ideology', in P. J. Chelkowski and R. J. Pranger (eds), *Ideology and Power in the Middle East*. Durham and London.

Scalapino, R. A. 1992. *The Last Leninists: The Uncertain Future of Asia's Communist States*. Washington, DC.

Scalapino, R. A., and Lee, C-S. 1972. *Communism in Korea*. Berkeley, Los Angeles and London.

Schram, S. R. 1984. September. '"Economics in Command?" Ideology and Policy Since the Third Plenum, 1978–84', *The China Quarterly*, 99.

Schram, S. R. 1988. June. 'China After the 13th Congress', *The China Quarterly*, 114.

Sciolino, E. 1991. *The Outlaw State: Saddam Hussein's Quest for Power and the Gulf Crisis*. New York.

Seale, P. 1988. *Asad of Syria: The Struggle for the Middle East*. London.

Seale, P. 1994. 'Preface', in E. Kienle (ed.), *Contemporary Syria: Liberalization between Cold War and Cold Peace*. London.

Selden, M. 1993. 'Agrarian Development Strategies in China and Vietnam', in W. S. Turley and M. Selden (eds), *Reinventing Vietnamese Socialism: Doi Moi in Comparative Perspective*. Boulder, San Francisco and Oxford.

Shambaugh, D. 1991a. *Beautiful Imperialist: China Perceives America, 1972–1990*. Princeton.

Shambaugh, D. 1991b. September. 'The Soldier and the State in China: The Political Work System in the People's Liberation Army', *The China Quarterly*, 127.

Shirk, S. L. 1993. *The Political Logic of Economic Reform in China*. Berkeley and Los Angeles.
Silverman, B. 1971. 'Introduction', in B. Silverman (ed.), *Man and Socialism in Cuba: The Great Debate*. New York.
Simons, G. 1993. *Libya: The Struggle for Survival*. Basingstoke.
Smith, H. 1994. 'The Democratic People's Republic of Korea and its foreign policy in the 1990s: more realist than revolutionary?', in S. Chan and A. J. Williams (eds), *Renegade States: The Evolution of Revolutionary Foreign Policy*. Manchester and New York.
Solinger, D. J. 1992. 'Urban Entrepreneurs and the State: The Merger of State and Society', in A. L. Rosenbaum (ed.), *State and Society in China: The Consequences of Reform*. Boulder.
Springborg, R. 1986. Winter. 'Infitah, Agrarian Transformation, and Elite Consolidation in Contemporary Iraq', *The Middle East Journal*, 40, 1.
Starr, J. B. 1984. September. 'Redefining Chinese Socialism', *Current History*, 83, 494.
Stavis, B. 1989. Summer/Autumn. 'The Political Economy of Inflation in China', *Studies in Comparative Communism*, XXII, 2/3.
Stern, L. M. 1993. *Renovating the Vietnamese Communist Party: Nguyen Van Linh and the Programme for Organizational Reform, 1987–91*. Singapore.
Stork, J. 1982. 'State Power and Economic Structure: Class Determination and State Formation in Contemporary Iraq', in T. Niblock (ed.), *Iraq: The Contemporary State*. London.
Suh, D-S. 1988. *Kim Il Sung: The North Korean Leader*. New York.
Sukkar, N. 1994. 'The Crisis of 1986 and Syria's Plan for Reform', in E. Kienle (ed.), *Contemporary Syria: Liberalization between Cold War and Cold Peace*. London.
Sullivan, L. R. 1988. June. 'Assault on the Reforms: Conservative Criticism of Political and Economic Liberalization in China, 1985–86', *The China Quarterly*, 114.
Tamaki, M. 1988. 'Open Policies of North Korea: Prospects and Political Structure', in M. Okongi (ed.), *North Korea at the Crossroads*. Tokyo.
Thayer, C. A. 1994. June. 'Sino-Vietnamese Relations: The Interplay of Ideology and National Interest', *Asian Survey*, XXXIV, 6.
Thoburn, J., and Howell, J. 1995. 'Trade and Development: The Political Economy of China's Open Policy', in R. Benewick and P. Wingrove (eds), *China in the 1990s*. Basingstoke.
Tripp, C. 1989. 'The Consequences of the Iran–Iraq War for Iraqi Politics', in E. Karsh (ed.), *The Iran–Iraq War: Impact and Implications*. Basingstoke.
van Dam, N. 1979. *The Struggle for Power in Syria: Sectarianism, Regionalism and Tribalism in Politics, 1961–1978*. London.
Vandewalle, D. 1991. Spring. 'Qadhafi's "Perestroika": Economic and Political Liberalization in Libya', *The Middle East Journal*, 45, 2.
Vandewalle, D. 1995a. 'The Libyan Jamahiriyya since 1969', in D. Vandewalle (ed.), *Qadhafi's Libya, 1969–1994*. Basingstoke and London.
Vandewalle, D. 1995b. 'The Failure of Liberalization in the Jamahiriyya', in D. Vandewalle (ed.), *Qadhafi's Libya, 1969–1994*. Basingstoke and London.
Vo Dai Luoc. 1995. 'Monetary Stabilization: The Vietnamese Experience', in I. Nørlund *et al.*, *Vietnam in a Changing World*. Richmond, England.

Vo Nhan Tri. 1988. 'Vietnam in 1987: A Wind of "Renovation"', *Southeast Asian Affairs 1988*. Singapore.

Vo Nhan Tri. 1990. *Vietnam's Economic Policy Since 1975*. Singapore.

Vu Tuan Anh. 1995. 'Economic Policy Reforms: An Introductory Overview', in I. Nørlund *et al.*, *Vietnam in a Changing World*. Richmond, England.

Walker, P. G. 1993. 'Political-Military Relations Since 1959', in E. A. Baloyra and J. A. Morris (eds), *Conflict and Change in Cuba*. Albuquerque.

Wang, J. C. F. 1992. *Contemporary Chinese Politics: An Introduction*, 4th edn. Englewood Cliffs.

Wank, D. L. 1995. 'Bureaucratic Patronage and Private Business: Changing Networks of Power in Urban China', in A. G. Walder (ed.), *The Waning of the Communist State: Economic Origins of Political Decline in China and Hungary*. Berkeley, Los Angeles and London.

Waterbury, J. 1994. 'Democracy Without Democrats?: The Potential for Political Liberalization in the Middle East', in G. Salamé (ed.), *Democracy Without Democrats?: The Renewal of Politics in the Muslim World*. London and New York.

Watson, A. 1988. March. 'The Reform of Agricultural Marketing in China Since 1978', *The China Quarterly*, 113.

Whiting, A. S. 1995. June. 'Chinese Nationalism and Foreign Policy After Deng', *The China Quarterly*, 142.

Williams, M. 1987. December. 'Vietnam: The Slow Road to Reform', *The Journal of Communist Studies*, 3, 4.

Williams, M. C. 1992. *Vietnam at the Crossroads*. London.

Womack, B. 1992. Spring. 'Reform in Vietnam: Backwards Towards the Future', *Government and Opposition*, 27, 2.

Womack, B. 1993. 'Political Reform and Political Change in Communist Countries: Implications for Vietnam', in W. S. Turley and M. Selden (eds), *Reinventing Vietnamese Socialism: Doi Moi in Comparative Perspective*. Boulder, San Francisco and Oxford.

Wright, J. 1982. *Libya: A Modern History*. London and Canberra.

Wurfel, D. 1993. '*Doi Moi* in Comparative Perspective', in W. S. Turley and M. Selden (eds), *Reinventing Vietnamese Socialism: Doi Moi in Comparative Perspective*. Boulder, San Francisco and Oxford.

Yang, H-M. 1987. Fall. 'North Korean Concepts of the Nation and Its Practical Tasks', *Korea and World Affairs*, 11, 3.

Yang, S. C. 1980. Spring. 'The Kim Il-sung Cult in North Korea', *Korea and World Affairs*, 4, 1.

Yeung, G. K. 1995. 'The People's Liberation Army and the Market Economy', in R. Benewick and P. Wingrove (eds), *China in the 1990s*. Basingstoke.

Zhou, X. 1995. 'Industry and the Urban Economy', in R. Benewick and P. Wingrove (eds), *China in the 1990s*. Basingstoke.

Zimbalist, A. 1989. 'Incentives and Planning in Cuba', *Latin American Research Review*, 24, 1.

Zimbalist, A., and Eckstein, S. 1989. 'Patterns of Cuban Development: The First Twenty-Five Years', in P. Brenner *et al.* (eds), *The Cuban Reader: The Making of a Revolutionary Society*. New York.

Index

DATE DUE